BETRAYAL

OTHER BOOKS BY JON LAND

*Published by Forge Books

BETRAYAL

ROBERT FITZPATRICK

with JON LAND

A TOM DOHERTY ASSOCIATES BOOK / NEW YORK

A Forge Book
Published by Tom Doherty Associates, LLC
175 Fifth Avenue
New York, NY 10010

www.tor-forge.com

Forge® is a registered trademark of Tom Doherty Associates, LLC.

Library of Congress Cataloging-in-Publication Data

Land, Jon.
  Betrayal / Robert Fitzpatrick and Jon Land.—1st ed.
      p. cm.
  "A Tom Doherty Associates book."
  ISBN 978-0-7653-3551-7 (hardcover)
  ISBN 978-0-7653-3550-0 (trade paperback)
  ISBN 978-1-4299-6366-4 (e-book)
  1. United States. Federal Bureau of Investigation—Fiction. 2. Government
investigators—Fiction. 3. Fitzpatrick, Robert—Fiction. 4. Bulger, Whitey,
1929—Fiction. I. Fitzpatrick, Robert. II. Title.
  PS3562.A469B48 2012
  813'.54—dc23

                                                              2011033165

First Edition: January 2012

Printed in the United States of America

0 9 8 7 6 5 4 3 2 1

For my parents,
who tried

For Father Kenny, Sister Jean Marie, and Brother Elliot,
who made me strong

And, especially, for my wife, Jane, and my children,
Brian, Robert, Alicia, and Erin,
who keep me that way

BETRAYAL

PROLOGUE
SOUTH BOSTON, 1984

"You want a bullet in the head?"

A few hours before he was murdered on a raw November night in 1984, John McIntyre thought he'd been invited to a party. At least that's what drew him to a South Boston house owned by Pat Nee, a top associate of Boston's Irish crime boss James "Whitey" Bulger.

Two weeks earlier, McIntyre had been aboard a ship called the *Ramsland* when it sailed into Boston Harbor carrying thirty tons of marijuana that would have netted Whitey somewhere between one and three million dollars. But the cargo was seized, putting a sizable dent in Whitey's pocketbook. And it was seized because McIntyre had told federal authorities about the shipment to keep himself out of jail. Believing his informant status still to be safe and secure, McIntyre agreed to go to the party, figuring he'd be able to strengthen his hand with law enforcement even further. Only when he arrived at the house, Bulger stepped out of the shadows and stuck a machine gun in his gut.

McIntyre was thirty-two, of average height and weight, and bearded with dark blue eyes that belied the hardscrabble life of a man who made his living at sea. He had rough, callused hands from handling fishing nets with the texture of razor wire. But in addition to fish McIntyre was also known to carry marijuana, bringing most of his supplies into the Boston area by boat. Small time mostly and not on anyone's radar, until he caught the attention of the murderous Bulger and his Irish Winter Hill Gang, who were determined to muscle in on Boston's drug trade in the 1980s.

Whitey was also involved in smuggling large shipments of weapons to the Irish Republican Army in Northern Ireland, for which he commandeered McIntyre as an engineer on a boat called the *Valhalla*. A military veteran, McIntyre kept his wits about him and didn't view the criminal lifestyle as anything more than a means to supplement his fishing and boat-building jobs. The money was just too easy and plentiful to turn away from, and McIntyre rationalized his actions by the need to support the young family he was struggling to hold together.

In September of 1984, the *Valhalla* set sail into the Atlantic with its holds full of guns and ammunition instead of marijuana, or iced swordfish and halibut. The voyage was smooth and uneventful, ending when McIntyre supervised the transfer of arms at sea onto a trawler called the *Merita Ann*. A few days later, off the coast of Ireland, British authorities boarded the *Merita Ann*. The weapons were seized and the crew was arrested.

The ramifications of the seizure reverberated all the way back across the Atlantic. Once the *Valhalla* docked back in Boston, Customs officials took McIntyre and another crewmember into custody on suspicion of gunrunning charges. After routinely questioning McIntyre, they released him. But a few weeks later the Quincy, Massachusetts, police arrested McIntyre on a domestic assault beef. Facing a potential prison stretch, he agreed to become a government informant and cough up the information on the infamous Irish gang leader's criminal activities. The feds assured McIntyre he'd be safe, that his informant status would be revealed only to those officials associated with the case.

Now, though, on an autumn night that felt more like winter, John McIntyre found himself staring at the machine gun barrel propped over his belt. Stephen Flemmi and Kevin Weeks, two more of Whitey

Bulger's most trusted lieutenants, grabbed him and threw him on the floor. Then McIntyre watched in horror as Bulger opened his duffel bag of death. He took out a rope, chains, and an assortment of weapons that gleamed slightly beneath the naked lightbulbs with strings dangling from their outlets like spaghetti. Flemmi hand-cuffed McIntyre to a chair and then chained him to it as well for good measure.

"We're gonna have a talk, you and me," Whitey told him. "I think you're a rat. Are you a rat, Johnny?"

According to testimony given in court years later by both Nee and Flemmi, Bulger proceeded to break McIntyre's fingers one at a time until he finally confessed to his role as informant. Between shrieks of pain, McIntyre apologized for being "weak," claiming he'd panicked, had no choice. Give him another chance and he'd prove himself loyal. He'd tell Customs and the FBI he'd made it all up to keep himself out of jail on that domestic assault charge.

But Bulger, having been told otherwise by at least one of those McIntyre thought was protecting him, wasn't buying it.

"I think you're full of shit, Mac."

"No, no! I fucked up, but I'll make things right, I swear!"

"Swear to God?"

McIntyre just looked at him.

"'Cause God's not here. I'm here. You believe in God, Johnny?"

McIntyre nodded.

"You go to church?"

McIntyre didn't say anything.

"Yeah," Bulger picked up. "What's God done for you anyway, com-pared to all I've done? And this is how you pay me back. By fucking me"—Bulger backhanded McIntyre across the face—"in the ass."

He was grinning now, enjoying himself. Bulger knew that John McIntyre had already told him everything, but that didn't stop him from continuing the mental and physical torture for another five or six hours. When he finally tired of the process, Bulger placed a boat rope around McIntyre's neck and tried to strangle him. But McIntyre refused to die. Bulger then slammed him repeatedly in the skull with a chair leg. McIntyre still refused to die.

"You want a bullet in the head?" Whitey asked, leaning in close to his ear.

McIntyre nodded, rasping out "Yes" through the blood and spittle frothing from his mouth.

Whitey shot him as promised. The impact threw him over backwards, still strapped to the chair and, incredibly enough, still alive. Flemmi grabbed his hair and pulled his head up while Bulger shot him again, repeatedly.

"He's dead now," Whitey said, and then went upstairs to take a nap.

PART ONE
COMING TO BOSTON

"Kick ass and take names."

1

WASHINGTON, D.C., 1980

"Fitz," Assistant Director Roy McKinnon said the day he summoned me to his office at headquarters in Washington in late 1980, "we need an Irishman to go to Boston to kick ass and take names."

I laughed but he didn't.

"Any suggestions?" he asked instead, staring me in the eye.

McKinnon was the ultimate straight shooter. He had a square jaw and wore his salt-and-pepper hair cropped military close. I seem to remember he'd been a Marine; either way, there was a directness of purpose about him befitting a military mind-set, right down to the orderly nature of his office, in which nothing, not even a single scrap of paper, was ever out of place. He told me the assignment was important for a variety of reasons. He sounded grave about my new adventure and talked about difficult problems in Boston without specifically outlining what those problems were. Right out of the gate, loud and clear, he ordered me to put Boston on the "straight and narrow." My initial reaction was it sounded like déjà vu, having had an assignment in Miami in the mid-to-late 1970s where, in fact, I did kick ass and take names in the ABSCAM investigation that nabbed numerous public officials, including a sitting U.S. senator. ABSCAM was a sting operation that targeted corrupt politicians and possible law enforcement personnel. I supervised the sting undercover, getting targets, including Senator Harrison Williams (D-NJ), to implicate themselves on tape. It was, in all respects, the FBI at its best.

I was Miami's Economic Crimes (EC) supervisor at the time and also worked undercover on our yacht, the *Left Hand.* I had procured the sixty-foot yacht from U.S. Customs, which had acquired the boat as part of their seizure in a major drug sting. We needed a "come-on" for our undercover gig and the *Left Hand* fit the bill beautifully. Before we docked the boat in Boca Raton, my squad cleaned it and installed surveillance equipment around the large foredeck, which was perfect for entertaining, and inside a trio of well-appointed cabins for private meetings. Soon, the *Left Hand* became an attraction and developed a notorious reputation in South Florida, fostered in large part by our undercover persona.

ABSCAM became the biggest case ever on the EC squad, recovering millions of dollars in fraudulent securities and various white-collar crime scams. We decided to have a final party and invited all of the criminals we had evidence on to attend. We equipped the boat with additional surveillance equipment and captured our future arrestees on tape. The "Sheik," an undercover agent, was posing as the wealthiest person in Miami, a connected Arab. While I sat up in the control room with the Strike Force chief, we encountered a problem. Senator Williams had appeared and demanded that he be allowed to attend our party. We declined and he demanded to see the Sheik anyway.

Under orders from FBIHQ we were told in no way could the senator board the boat. The Strike Force chief insisted we finish the sting, but FBIHQ demanded we close the operation down. HQ's concern was that allowing the senator to come aboard a boat laden with druggers, prostitutes, and criminals might be seen as a form of entrapment.

Afer much deliberation with FBIHQ, the FBI special agent who was playing the sheik, told me, "Bob, I won't allow alcohol, drugs, or anything that could harm the senator aboard my boat!"

I laughed at him and said, "You're crazy. What kind of party are we supposed to throw?"

He looked at me and, in the dignified role and manner of a true sheik, said, "I am the sheik and I won't let it happen!"

The party went forward on the pretext its host, our undercover sheik, could not be in the presence of drugs or alcohol for Muslim religious reasons. The recorded conversation and surveillance tapes played at Harrison Williams's trial dispelled any notion that we had entrapped the senator, and he was found guilty and convicted in federal court by his own voice. I took no pleasure in taking down a sitting U.S. senator; to me, he was a criminal who was extorting agents of the federal government sworn to uphold the law.

In this unique experence, I became no stranger to corruption, learning how to dig it out and destroy it. And that's why I supposed I was being transferred to Boston.

Tom Kelly, my former boss in Miami and an FBIHQ deputy at the time, had filled McKinnon in on my experience in ABSCAM, making it plain that I had cleaned up Miami and could probably do the same in Boston. Contrary to what was apparently going wrong up there, a key factor in the decision to send me north was my ability to pursue investigations without anyone tipping off the press or the target. ABSCAM was successful because all FBI agents working for me diligently did their jobs of investigating high-ranking government officials in a major scam without a single leak. Not one.

I was on a career fast track, groomed, I anticipated, for even bigger things to come. Not bad for a kid who'd grown up in a church-run institution, an orphanage on Staten Island called Mount Loretto. But that's where my dream, this very FBI dream, was born.

2

ASTORIA, QUEENS, 1944

"I have to pee," I whined to the cop. Then I screamed, "I really have to pee!"

The cop, whose name was O'Rourke, looked at me indifferently. I thought he could care less until he knelt, picked me up, and carried me to the kitchen sink. After I relieved myself, he carried me back into the living room of my New York City apartment demanding clean underwear and clothes from my warring parents. Officer O'Rourke, who came from the 114th Precinct, had five kids of his own, so I guess I should consider myself fortunate he was the one who responded to yet another fight between my parents that was loud enough to rouse the neighbors.

"You guys better calm down in there," he called to my mother and father. "Your son's coming with me. Pack some clothes in a bag."

They'd been warned what the upshot of one more complaint would be, but that hadn't stopped their constant onslaught in the least. This time O'Rourke had responded after some neighbors complained that "the people next door were going to kill each other." O'Rourke knew if he couldn't stop my parents from doing that, he could at least stop them from doing it to me.

"If you guys don't stop with the bullshit I'll be taking you in!" he shouted when they still failed to heed his warning. "Right now I'm taking Robert over to the Fourteenth. You'll be hearing from the social worker in the morning."

O'Rourke bent over to pick me up again, this time heading for the door. I started to cry so O'Rourke soothed me by explaining that we were going for a short car ride to the police station. The elevator was broken again and he carried me down all eight flights of stairs, without the bag of clothes my parents had failed to produce.

"This is O'Rourke," he said to the police dispatcher. "I've got a four-year-old ready for a remand to social services. Get some clothes and food and I'll see you at the station in about fifteen minutes."

"What the hell are you doing, O'Rourke?" came the dispatcher's response.

"See you in fifteen" was all O'Rourke said in response.

So there I was, a scared four-year-old basically abandoned by my mother and father. At least that's the way the Family Court put it when the judge remanded me to the custody of the State. After shuffling through a series of child shelters, I wound up at Mount Loretto, better known as the "Mount," then the largest child-care home in the United States, with over a thousand charges living in "cottages" spread across 524 acres on Staten Island.

My initial stop at the Mount was the Quarantine House. First thing the sisters did when I arrived was to assign me a bed, check me for bugs and lice, and give me a physical exam. Everything was antiseptic and smelled like alcohol. And everything was like a portrait painted in stark white. The sisters wore white habits, white shoes. Their head coverings were white and even their rosary beads were white. The quarantine floor was lined with beds draped in white sheets set atop a white marble floor. The floor was cold all the time.

Once I was deemed "clean," I was taken to the residential side, consisting of six cottages housing sixty-six boys each. In Cottage 1, we were all new orphans, each with a box with a lid in which to store our possessions. Most of us had none. The boxes were arranged in a rectangular fashion around the perimeter of the cottage. Other boxes were attached to the cottage wall—these held our school clothes, shoes, and field clothes sometimes. All of our clothes were hand-me-downs, not at all fashionable or comfortable but better than nothing. In the lavatory we had stations that held toothbrushes, soap, and a towel on a hook. There were eight commodes and six urinals for sixty-six children. Half the cottage took showers at a time.

For sleeping, each of us had a cot on either the second or third floor. Bed wetters, all thirty of them, were crammed into the third floor, and the stench of urine wafted throughout the cottage, especially bad in the summer months when the heat putrefied the stench further and in the dead of winter when the windows were all closed. I would pass through all six cottages as I grew older, the stench evolving with the years too, though the routine and accommodations otherwise remained unchanged.

My two older brothers, Larry and Gerard, and older sister, Diane, had been moved to the Mount as well. But I hardly ever saw them. The older children almost never mixed with the younger under any circumstances, siblings or not. I'd often stare out the windows or across the fields, hoping I'd spot one of them. In my mind I saw myself lighting out toward Larry, Gerard, or Diane. But even if I'd glimpsed them, I'd never have done it. I was much too scared to dare challenge authority or break the rules. We were sometimes able to sit together in church on Sundays, but that was it. Regimentation and regulation were everything. Corporal punishment was the rule, not the exception.

There was brutality in this world where power was the only currency. I remember walking across the bridge that ran near a drainage ditch between the dormitory and dining hall. The bridge's structure was worn and it shook a bit when packed with young boys rushing to lunch to beat the February cold.

One wind-blown dreary day, as our counselors led us across the bridge, one of the ten-year-olds from my cottage yelled out, "Fuck you!"

"Who yelled that?" the counselor named Scarvelli demanded, stopping everyone in their tracks.

All of us remained silent.

"I'm gonna ask youse guys again: who yelled that?"

"Last chance," another especially sadistic counselor, Farber, chimed in. "Or you all pay."

But there were no rats in this group, so the counselors marched us straight back to our cottage where we were told to stand fast near our "boxes" directly beneath the hissing steam pipes that heated the buildings—or at least were supposed to.

"All right, you little assholes, grab the pipes," counselor Farber ordered. "Everybody holds on until somebody talks. Let go and we'll beat the shit out of you."

The pipes clanked and hissed as the hot steamed water coursed through them. I held tight, feeling my hands beginning to blister, and watched my first cottage mate drop to the floor to be beaten and interrogated, then the second, followed by a third and a fourth. When the bulk of us finally dropped, it was too much for the counselors to handle. They had us stand at our boxes and demanded each boy come into the wash-up area where one by one we were systematically berated and beaten again. Since I was the last to fall, they beat me only once but twice as hard. They had the power.

No supervisor interceded. Either they didn't know what was going on or they didn't care. Scarvelli and Farber beat some of the boys worse than others, including me since I was one of the youngest and smallest. But I didn't tell them what they wanted to know. No one did.

And neither did anyone rat out Scarvelli and Farber. We all knew that if we ratted out the counselors, we'd be beaten much worse and end up longing for the blisters the steam pipes left on our small hands. The message was clear and all of us got it: They were bullies and we were helpless against them.

My escape from times like these came in the form of the old-time radio programs playing over Sister Mary Assumpta's radio. She was kind enough to leave her door open after lights out so the sound filtered out into the dormitory. It was often garbled and not very loud, but I was entranced, whisked away to a world dominated by heroes where the good guys always won and the bad guys, the bullies, lost.

I'd lie in my second-floor dormitory bed listening to *The Lone Ranger, The Shadow,* and especially, *This Is Your FBI.* I say especially because I was already "old" and jaded enough by experience to know the difference between what was real and what wasn't. Neither the Lone Ranger nor the Shadow could swoop in and save me, because they weren't real, but the FBI was. I would lie there and imagine myself becoming a swashbuckling, crime-fighting hero someday, in large part because my life up to that point had been so bereft of them. In all of the "cops and robbers" games, I was always the FBI agent who got his man. I thought of O'Rourke and the others at the 114th and how kind they were.

It might sound corny, but in the Mount's big, Gothic church there was a huge stained-glass window. It showed Jesus with children around him and the inscription read, "Suffer the little children come unto me for their's is the Kingdom of Heaven." Jesus became my rescuer, to be replaced later, in my "cops and robbers" game, by the FBI.

In those minutes, as I lay with my eyes closed listening to the garbled tales of *This Is Your FBI*, I was spirited far away from the Mount to places where I was happy and secure, reliant on no one and fearing not a single soul. And maybe someday I was going to become for the world, and the country, what no one had ever been for me.

I'd found my dream, and through the years and pain that followed, I never let go of it.

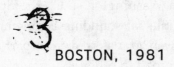

BOSTON, 1981

The FBI had lacked an authoritative face since the heyday of J. Edgar Hoover's reign as chief. His fall from grace had exposed plenty of what was thought wrong with the Bureau and unfairly dwarfed much of what was right. Certainly no one individual could restore the lost luster and repair a tarnished image. But appointing successful, high-profile agents in top-level positions seemed the next best thing. My wife and two young boys, unfortunately were less thrilled about the prospects of moving yet again. It seemed as if, in my fifteen years with the Bureau since my marriage, every time we'd just about get settled, I was transferred. Coming to a top-ten office like Boston to take over as ASAC (Assistant Special Agent in Charge) represented the pinnacle of my career, and I could see myself staying in the city for some time.

But my wife wasn't buying that, and my marriage dissolved. My wife was tired of sharing me with a dream that knew no end. I tried to convince her that Boston could be just that, the final stop. But she feared I'd end up returning first to Washington en route to yet another promotion and posting. She believed I loved the Bureau more than her.

She was both wrong and right, something I considered often on long, lonely nights in my small apartment, where it always seemed dark outside.

My entry into Boston had been through the proverbial back door. On the face of it I appeared to have a routine FBI transfer with no ulterior motive; there was no paperwork about my "official" mandate. Just an Irish guy going to an Irish city on another assignment.

I came to Boston straight from my post as head of the investigative nerve center of the FBI in Washington, D.C., the Special Agent Transfer Unit. SATU, an unusual sounding acronym, was the FBI unit from which agents were transferred from particular offices throughout the U.S. and abroad to other assignments, and from where investigative resources and funding were allocated to the FBI field offices worldwide. Not a single major case unfolded without my knowledge and involvement. As a bureau chief I had the responsibility to make recommendations after reviewing requests for manpower, investigative resource allocation assistance, and "specials." Major cases and specials were defined as the most important investigations, demanding supplemental manpower and sometimes extraordinary technical assistance in the form of surveillance equipment as advanced as any in the world at the time.

That's how I first became acquainted with the problems in Boston. Word was the agents there had taken their mandate to bring down the Italian mafia too far by allowing their informants, including one named James "Whitey" Bulger, free rein on the streets in return for providing intelligence that often produced nothing. Some in the Massachusetts State Police were livid that the FBI was letting a former street thug, like Whitey Bulger, currently running the vicious Winter Hill Gang out of South Boston, get away with murder— literally. Specifically, the execution of a major bookie and FBI informant named Richie Castucci. The Massachusetts State Police (MSP) didn't buy the Boston FBI office's conclusion that the Italian mob was responsible for Castucci's murder, not for one minute. More specifically, the MSP even accused a pair of FBI agents, John Morris and John Connolly, of feeding intelligence directly to Bulger, protecting him and aiding his ascent up the ladder of criminal power in the New England underworld.

The Bureau took its motto—Fidelity, Bravery, Integrity—seriously. But in Boston, if suspicions about Richie Castucci's murder were true, that motto had become more option than mandate.

My new job as Assistant Special Agent in Charge (ASAC) of one of the top ten Bureau offices in the country was to handle all organized crime for New England and command the Drug Task Force. Other duties that comingled with the organized crime investigations included White Collar Crime (WCC), Public Corruption (PC), and so-called nontraditional Organized Crime (OC) involving the Irish thugs who roamed free through the closeted, insular society of Charlestown, Somerville, and South Boston.

Larry Sarhatt, the Special Agent in Charge (SAC) of the Boston office, picked me up at the downtown hotel that served as my temporary residence on a damp chilly day in early 1981—the rain that had been forecast had yet to come. He drove me to the FBI office at Government Square, near the Italian North End in the heart of the former Irish bastion, Scolley Square, where we occupied the whole of the sixth floor. My office overlooked the front of the building, the infamous Boston traffic jams leading to snarled streets virtually all day long, the honking of horns and blowing of sirens providing a background din that became as familiar as the clanking of the corner radiator or the soft hum of the air conditioner. I could walk out my door and view the workings of most of the agents serving on any number of the squads I'd been placed in command of. Some of the more junior ones worked out of spaces that were little more than cubicles or shared cramped offices—well, smaller than mine. The office floor was always busy but never frantic, since so many of the agents spent their days in the field on active investigations, of which there were plenty. We had agents who lived for the blue lights and sirens, and those who did not. I'd met a number of them and knew others by reputation, enough to be sure they made for a good lot with plenty of solid casework and convictions to their credit.

Larry Sarhatt was eager to get on with business and welcomed any assistance, especially in the manpower area. He went through the prospective "priority one" La Cosa Nostra (LCN) cases on deck in Boston, specifically the investigation of Gennaro "Jerry" Angiulo, who reported directly to the head of the New England mob, Raymond Patriarca, out of Providence, Rhode Island.

Jerry Angiulo was the underboss of the New England LCN, presiding over sixteen ranking members who reported to him. Everything about these wiseguys was steeped in their own bloody traditions, such as the initiation ceremonies that offered a sense of code and moral backing to their actions, as loathsome and reprehensible as they were. *The Godfather* movies and "mafia" pulp fiction glamorized the culture, enticing wannabes to emulate the fictionalized images.

Not so the case for the members of the Winter Hill Gang. These Somerville wiseguys were decidedly Irish muffs tagged by the FBI as a nontraditional group of the organized crime element. We knew approximately twenty of these guys were in leadership positions, supervising three hundred soldiers and grunts, all under the auspices of Bulger and his right-hand man, Stephen "The Rifleman" Flemmi. It was abundantly evident that both groups had their preferred methods of violence and murder. The Irish wiseguys would "frag" a bunch of people to get their target, while the Italian wiseguys would just garrote the one target and stuff him in the trunk of some car. The Irish were definitely more homegrown, all in all, than the Italian mob, which led them to be even more insular.

I knew Bulger as a thug, a street enforcer who'd spent a quarter of his life behind bars, including a stretch at Alcatraz and another at Leavenworth in Kansas. I'd heard he prided himself on being a tough guy who inspired fear in allies and enemies alike. Ruthless and brutal, as his rise to the top of the Winter Hill Gang in the wake of Howie Winter's imprisonment attested. He wasn't a big guy physically, and word was he wasn't just street smart; he was smart, period, capable of playing chess while those around him opted for checkers. But he played for real, to which the forty-three murders he's allegedly responsible for more than demonstrate.

Sarhatt briefed me on the informant situation, explaining that a major informant against the Angiulo family, Bulger himself, was being videotaped and surveilled at a mob garage on Lancaster Street in downtown Boston by the Massachusetts State Police (MSP). MSP grew incensed when Bulger and his associates suddenly and inexplicably clammed up, claiming that FBI agents John Connolly and John Morris, Bulger's Bureau handlers, had leaked word of the investigation to their prized informant. Sarhatt informed me that Colonel John O'Donovan, the much decorated and current head of the MSP, suspected as much and was livid over the fact that nothing had been done about it. Worse, he was convinced this was an ongoing problem.

An old-fashioned cop to whom a bad guy was a bad guy, O'Donovan was a stout, rangy man with sinewy muscles born of boxing as a kid and old-fashioned weightlifting into his fifties. He had a shock of balding gray hair that shifted with every toss of his head, and a single piercing blue eye that looked tired whenever I saw him. He had been shot in the eye by a gangster early in his career, earning him a much-deserved reputation. The real deal when it came to tough. In O'Donovan's mind, Bulger and Flemmi were nothing short of stone killers and the last people the FBI should be doing business with. He followed protocol by informing the Boston FBI office of his intentions to find incriminating evidence against Bulger and Flemmi in any number of crimes, specifically murder. Sarhatt's and the FBI office's dilemma was that they could not officially tell the MSP that their targets were informants for the FBI. Politics and internecine conflicts never entered the picture for O'Donovan or, if they did, were superseded by the bad blood Bulger was tracking through the city.

Larry Sarhatt was caught in the middle of this dilemma between loyalty to his own agents and his greater responsibility to the Bureau. The only way he could reconcile things was to determine whether to keep Bulger on the FBI books as an informant or "close" him. In his heart, I knew he wanted Bulger cut loose. He'd come to that conclusion after interviewing Bulger himself barely a year before, only to be overruled by Jeremiah O'Sullivan, the prosecutor running the federal Organized Crime Strike Force. O'Sullivan, along with FBIHQ in Washington, wanted Bulger to remain open as a top echelon criminal informant as long as he continued to provide information about the mob families out of Boston and Providence. He was, in their minds, too valuable to close. But the real question was just how valuable was Whitey Bulger, and answering it became my first mandate.

I wasn't a fan of O'Sullivan from the get-go. He seemed too much the button-down bureaucrat who wore his ambition on his sleeve. He was thin and pale, fond of flashing a narrow condescending smile to create a sense of false camaraderie. I remember his hair looked to be glued into place, every word and gesture made as if the cameras weren't too far away. I saw him in federal court several times, his spine straight, every move looking rehearsed—from the moment he first stepped into the building to the time he climbed back into his car parked outside Government Center.

Sarhatt, on the other hand, was a traditionalist whose nonflashy, by-the-book, pragmatic style had him running afoul of agents beholden to the more popular criminal agent SAC he'd replaced over a year before. So he told me he was relying on my background to make sense of the muddle. For manpower and resource management, he looked to my previous major case and experience at HQ; for assessment, he looked to my training in the Behavioral Science Unit at the FBI Academy, where I gained expert knowledge in profiling and polygraph as well as expertise in the area of abnormal criminal psychology. He knew operationally I had conducted major investigations all over the country—from New Orleans to Mississippi to Memphis to Miami—both undercover and not, and had handled complex cases, always achieving favorable resolutions. In other words, I was a "closer," and that's exactly what he needed on his side now.

More to the point, in retrospect, I was sent to Boston to offer all parties political cover. The thinking on the part of McKinnon and others was that the success I'd achieved in the ABSCAM investigation would trump the dueling viewpoints that had all but obscured any rational assessment of how much Bulger was actually contributing to the cause. And since I was an outsider, my objectivity could not be called into question.

Larry Sarhatt and I ended our first meeting with a simple mandate: If everything suggested by the Richie Castucci murder was true, we would tackle the problems in Boston once and for all.

4
BOSTON, 1980

Prior to my transfer to Boston, I was an instructor and supervisor at the FBI Academy, where Massachusetts State Police chief Colonel John O'Donovan attended one of my death investigations courses. Each attendee had to bring an unsolved case that was presented to the other forty-nine death investigators from across the country. These were cold cases, and tackling them with seasoned investigators was as informative as it was rewarding.

O'Donovan's contribution, his unsolved case, was the 1976 Richie Castucci murder in Boston. The colonel was pretty outspoken and criticized the Boston FBI office for "hanging" with criminals and "fixing" cases for the wiseguys. His presentation included the fact that Castucci was a sometime informant for the MSP, so he'd taken a personal interest in Castucci's murder. Upon arriving in Boston, then, one of my first orders of business was to discuss the case with both a former Boston SAC, Dick Bates, and the man I was replacing, Joe Yablonski, who served as co-ASAC with Weldon Kennedy. They filled in most of the blanks that O'Donovan had left out in the sordid tale, both having been intimately acquainted with different aspects of the case.

Castucci, they told me, had enjoyed a long association with Whitey Bulger's Winter Hill Gang. A bookie who reveled in their protection and profited richly off the positioning and posturing they allotted him, Richie also fancied himself an entrepreneur. He owned a nightclub on Boston's north shore in Revere. With the stench of stale beer and cigarettes imbedded in its plank flooring and walls, the Ebb Tide was hardly about to attract patrons based on its décor. But luckily for Richie he didn't have to rely on normal clientele for business. Instead, the club boasted a customer base drawn almost entirely from local criminals with whom Richie felt most comfortable.

The Ebb Tide had overcome a bad refrigeration system, outdated wiring, and windows that did little to keep the cold out in the winter to become a prime place for wiseguys and wannabes to hang out. A place to be seen, a place to congregate, to figure out where money was ripe for the taking. Castucci, for his part, loved the crowd and the attention, but hated the building that had fallen into a perpetual state of disrepair. Accordingly, for some time he'd been planning to sell his interest in the Ebb Tide in favor of a classy strip joint he called the Squire Club, which promised to be an even better hangout for his mob contacts and, thus, better for his business.

There weren't many patrons of the Ebb Tide who didn't enjoy a first-name familiarity with Richie. He was polite, affable, and pretty much liked by everyone on both sides of the tracks. He dressed in the style of *Saturday Night Fever,* an extremely popular film at the time. Richie fancied himself a poor man's version of the Tony Manero character played by John Travolta, adopting a disco seventies theme highlighted by his pointed shoes, perfectly coiffed hair, and manicured nails. He carried himself flamboyantly, as if he didn't have a care in the world, and for a time, he didn't.

Richie's real business was taking bets from his Boston clientele as well as most of the Winter Hill Gang in Somerville and South Boston. Always looking to branch out and expand his interests, he also purchased horses and raced them at a track outside Boston called Suffolk Downs. His dealings in this arena were usually made under pseudonyms so he could avoid tax and revenue problems and keep his profit margin on an even keel. Richie might not have been nearly as big as he made himself out to be, but he knew how to talk the talk and walk the walk.

He also distinguished himself from the average muffs by driving "big" in his Cadillac, a symbol that he was a comer. He had a rep for being generous enough to let late payers slide and for trying to please everybody, the go-to guy whenever anyone on either side of the street needed a favor.

But no one was more important to Richie Castucci than Whitey Bulger. Bulger was the boss to whom Richie paid "tribute," allowing him to work the Somerville, Southie, and Boston crowds. But Richie was also important to Bulger. Being somewhat of a made guy with his Italian friends positioned Richie as a conduit between them and Whitey's Irish gang out of South Boston. He served as a kind of early warning system, there to keep Bulger apprised of potential trouble, for the truce between the Irish gang and Italian mob seemed ready to collapse at any moment. The canary in this particlar coal mine, so to speak.

Outside of Boston, most of Richie's closest friends came from New York City. In an emergency situation, Bulger summoned Richie with news about a couple of Boston muffs who got caught up with the feds over a strong-arm robbery and instructed Richie to get them a place in Manhattan to hide out. Eager to make his bones with the Winter Hill crew, especially Whitey and his chief hench-man Stevie "The Rifleman" Flemmi, Richie was more than willing to oblige.

Aware of his easy reach into the Winter Hill Gang, the FBI paid Richie a routine visit around this same time. A baby-faced agent, nick-named "Opie" because of his resemblance to Andy Griffith's son in the popular television show, claimed in droll fashion that Richie's wife was seeing Sal Caruana, a known drug dealer and cartel im-porter of marijuana.

"We don't want anything from you," Opie insisted, smiling as if they were old friends. "We're just giving you the heads-up so you don't look like an asshole to your associates."

"I appreciate that," Richie told him.

"You're a stand-up guy," said Opie. "And we *appreciate* that."

Richie knew Caruana was handsome, a real lady's man with a reputation for cavorting about town. Sal was also Richie's pal and was over the house a lot, more than he'd known, apparently. It pained Richie to imagine his wife in this compromising way, especially since Opie supposedly had photos and "tin ear" chatter to go along for sound from the wire the Bureau had planted. What he saw and heard changed Richie's priorities in an instant. Suddenly, getting even with Sal Caruana was all that mattered. More than his book-making business, more than his nightclub, more even than his relationship with Whitey Bulger. (For the record, Richie's wife would later deny the affair in a 2009 lawsuit she filed against the U.S. government.)

"We can take care of Caruana for you," Opie assured Richie. "Get him out of your life for good."

"What's it gonna cost me?" Richie replied.

"Look, we need a favor, there are a couple of guys we're interested in and we thought you could help us out. We know about your 'book' and the action you take from the wiseguys. That's not our interest. We're interested in something heavier, and if you're game, we'll set some contacts up to make sure you are protected and this whole thing stays confidential."

"You want me to become a rat."

"And in return Sal Caruana goes down."

Richie grimaced, clearly conflicted. "I need some time."

"How much?"

"I'll give you a call."

Opie, hardly put off by Richie's loose hold on cooperation, once more flashed the photo that supposedly showed Sal with Richie's wife. Richie grimaced again, lips pursed tightly and his face showing a pained expression.

"You got a deal," Richie told him.

Opie grinned, counted out five one-hundred-dollar bills, and pressed them into Richie's palm as a show of good faith. Richie, however, remained unimpressed until the agent peeled off ten more Franklins—that finally got him smiling.

Opie returned the grin, and then took advantage of this moment to tell Richie he wanted him to stay in the bookmaking business and remain as close to the New York mob as he had in the past. The agent opened Richie as a criminal informant whose job would be to report on the criminal activities of his associates and also to divulge information on impending crimes. Richie learned that "subjects" were intended for prosecution while "suspects" were more "persons of interest." And he took to his new role with the same enthusiasm he brought to his dealings with the criminal targets his handlers were trying to bust. Opie figured it was more about Sal Caruana than the money, and he was always able to stall when Richie started pushing on when the Bureau intended to put Caruana away. In the end, they never did, leaving Caruana out there so Richie would have no choice but to continue cooperating.

In future meetings, Richie was informed by Opie and other agents of the rules and regulations governing the whole FBI informant program as outlined in manuals of administrative operations and procedure and in investigative guidelines. Opie debriefed Richie about his background with the criminals and any arrests or incidents he may have had along the way. Subsequently, Richie furnished personal information so the Bureau could check to make sure he was really cooperating.

Opie and his alternate agent handler, who would serve as Richie's eyes and ears inside the FBI to alert him of possible danger, began to build a bond that transcended the usual relationships developed with criminals on the street. Hip-pocket informants, who were never officially opened as informants, never got this kind of scrutiny. Others, just cooperating witnesses, fared the same. Richie was given special treatment, quickly becoming a "TE," a Top Echelon informant who'd report on organized crime and individuals of interest to the FBI.

Richie's status as a bookie served him well here because it made him innocuous, just a real friendly guy who took bets and lay-offs on gambling and never harmed anyone. Richie didn't know it, but he was also given a number symbol that protected his identity inside the FBI as well as outside, when his information was furnished to the court or other law enforcement agencies. He could feel sure that his identity would never be revealed to anyone outside the Bureau—not to the federal attorneys, the court, or anyone.

Richie heard numerical labels like "137," "209," "302" and other classifications that agents discussed among themselves. The 137 was the generic classification for informants; 209 was the report that is filed about the information the informants provide to their handlers; and 302 was the evidentiary report submitted for prosecutorial efforts.

Richie gave his handlers a great deal of information about gambling and scams involving bribery and race fixes. For instance, he explained to Opie that horse talk for fixing a race is called a "boatrace." The jockeys or their associates get together once in a while to make some money for themselves by pooling their dough and fixing the race in full awareness of which jockey will win. The wiseguys have their own informants who relay the information so that they, too, can turn a profit on a deal. Rumor had it that Richie was the best boatrace guy in the business, information dutifully recorded in his 137 file.

Richie wasn't worried because he was told that he'd never have to testify. Not once did it dawn on him that his handlers might be lying to him about this, about Sal, about everything. Richie had been all about being liked for so long that he'd bought into his own act. And he'd formed such a tight bond with the agents, especially Opie, that it was inconceivable to him that they were anything but on the up and up. Richie started looking at his handlers the same way he looked at the crowds he entertained at the Ebb Tide. He even came clean about how he got to be where he was, how strong-armed heists had scared him and turned him to the track and gambling, the whole ambiance of which was a better fit for his makeup.

Their bond cemented, Opie would come to Richie with a "shopping list" from time to time, gleaning from him more about past events, new events, and "what are you going to give us now" events. And Richie, ever guilty of wanting to please, was always on the lookout for anything that might help his new FBI pals. He found himself feeling respectable, liking the sense of being on the side of the good guys for a change.

In 1976, on a whim, Opie asked Richie about two murderous muffs from Irish Southie who were on the lam and had made it onto the FBI's Most Wanted list of top ten fugitives. Castucci knew immediately who he was talking about because they were associates of his: Joe McDonald and James Sims, the very thugs Whitey Bulger asked Richie to stash for him in New York.

Being on the Most Wanted list meant that every agent throughout the United States wanted to capture these guys. But Richie didn't make his handlers even work hard, stunning the agents when he simply told them where McDonald and Sims could be found. He insisted that Bulger had come to him "out of the blue" to get his assistance in hiding the two killers. Richie told Whitey that a pal of his, formerly in the can at the ACI in Walpole, was a "caretaker" in New York who ran a kind of boardinghouse for on-the-lam criminals. Whitey gave Richie the go-ahead to set up the hideaway for McDonald and Sims, the location of which he nonchalantly furnished to Opie.

McDonald and Sims represented a huge score, a double bubble—two for the price of one. Back at the FBI office, Opie was ecstatic. All of his research and background on Richie was paying off. Many of the agents had scoffed at Richie's selection as a target for informant development, especially a TE, but Opie's decision had now been vindicated.

"A happy informant is a productive informant and everyone is then happy!" Opie announced to the agents in his squad bay.

Ironically, Richie even then didn't push too hard about when the FBI was going to move on Sal Caruana. And, in point of fact, no one from the FBI had any intention to.

"Cheers!" the agents, including John Connolly and John Morris, bellowed in return.

That meant drinks were on Opie and he was more than happy to foot the bill. Thanks to his latest informant, after all, Opie was going to be instrumental in the nabbing of two Top Tens for the Bureau, a potential career-changing accomplishment.

Opie called the New York office of the FBI explaining that he had the inside skinny that would net the fugitives on their turf. The New

York agents were thrilled when informed that the Top Tens were holed up in the city. And they were positively ecstatic when they learned that the caretaker in the boardinghouse where the fugitives were hiding was an informant for the New York office.

What a field office's dream! Opie and the New York agents were glowing over the fact that a couple of Boston muffs, dangerous muffs, had walked into their lion's den. The FBI in New York had plenty of time to devise a plan to capture these stone killers from Boston. Precautions would be taken to assure that the operation was conducted in absolute secrecy, preventing anyone on either side from screwing it up.

Back in Boston, Richie continued to play both sides of the fence with his usual aplomb. Bulger and Flemmi were treating him like gold and Richie responded in kind by organizing a lucrative boat-race for the Winter Hill Gang. He put together the mother of all horse race scams at Suffolk Downs, calling in his chits from those who owed him. Bulger and Flemmi took part, and word of their participation brought others in as well. Richie even offered his new FBI pals a piece of the action. They refused.

At Boston FBI headquarters, Opie regaled agent John Connolly and his supervisor, John Morris, with his coup. Connolly was a "cock of the walk" agent who had a swarthy complexion and imitated the ethnic dress of the Italians he was committed to jailing; some even quipped that he looked like Richie. Morris dressed more simply and somberly, like a conservative businessman in dark suits, simple ties, and white shirts—in keeping with a silver-haired agent always looking straight ahead. Connolly and Morris were veteran TE developers and had had their share of glory. Like Opie, the other agents didn't really know which informants Connolly and Morris handled. Unlike Opie, they fumed over the success of others on turf they considered theirs and theirs alone.

Later, over beers, Opie bragged a little too much about his recent success, especially to Connolly, and revealed that his snitch had put the "nose" on Joe McDonald and James Sims in New York.

"No way!" Connolly exclaimed.

Opie embellished the details, savoring Connolly's unabashed

jealousy at his score. He could see Connolly chomping at the bit over the whole story, suddenly second-guessing himself for outing his own informant. But alcohol drowned out his concerns, and Opie finished the evening on a high note. Connolly, meanwhile, soaked up every word instead of booze. He had other things on his mind.

The Organized Crime (OC) squad was supervised by a senior agent at the time who had about thirteen agents under him. Connolly charged into his office a few days later with John Morris in tow.

"This better be good," the supervisor said, mincing no words.

"It's better than good," Connolly told him, after Morris had taken a seat. "We got people about to get dimed."

Connolly proceeded to carve out the details of the secret New York operation Opie had shared with him, and the supervisor listened pensively through the whole tale.

"McDonald and Sims are supposed to give us key intelligence about Angiulo's group in the North End," he finally said. "Seems to me the mission of the Three Squad's larger than a couple of muffs."

"Yes," Morris agreed.

Even though McDonald and Sims had been declared Top Ten fugitives, the OC squad's mission was to get the probable cause needed for the wire to penetrate the Boston Italian mob. Arresting McDonald and Sims at this juncture would "queer" the whole priority objective for the squad. "Management by Objectives" had been the hallmark for the organized crime priority and all of them knew it.

"Fuck Opie," the supervisor said. "His shit is penny-ante against ours."

Although successful in gaining the supervisor's support, Connolly and Morris blanched. They knew that Opie would now know they'd ratted him out and busted his operation to save their own. And they had an even bigger problem to contend with: Bulger and Flemmi.

Since harboring fugitives is a felony, and Bulger and Flemmi were hiding McDonald and Sims, they could lose their protected status as confidential informants. All it would take was for McDonald and Sims to fink them out to the New York office, leaving Connolly and Morris gnashing their teeth over the potential loss of their meal tickets.

But maybe there was a way they could come out of this okay and with the OC squad's operation intact.

According to Colonel O'Donovan, Connolly went to Bulger and Flemmi and told them the news about Richie and the New York caper. As the news sank in, Bulger stared Connolly down, his dagger-sharp eyes loosening the agent's bowels.

"So you want me to clean up your mess," Bulger said.

"It's your mess, too, now," Connolly shot back, listening to his own voice as if it was somebody else's.

For all Connolly knew, Bulger and Flemmi were going to whack him then and there. Instead, they simply turned their attention to the problem at hand.

Bulger called McDonald and Sims first. He told them they'd been ratted and needed to fly, and fast.

Next, Bulger summoned Richie himself and asked to see him about his boatrace. Richie boasted about the big bucks coming in, and Bulger responded by hitting him up for a loan for nearly all of the $800,000 take. Richie was happy to help his boss out. He was convinced the money would keep flowing his way, and that the loan only served to cement his relationship with Bulger.

After the meeting was done, Bulger was feeling especially good about how things had worked out. He had solved the problem Connolly had dumped in his lap and was now eight hundred grand richer for the effort. No doubt satisfied with a productive day's work, Bulger had just one more call to make: to his most trusted assassin, John Martorano.

At their next meeting, held on the pretext of expanding Richie's gambling concerns, Bulger and Flemmi sat down with the now doomed informant. Martorano stood back a bit from the table, a fact that strangely mirrored his life inside and out of Whitey's immediate circle. He dressed with style and class, seldom seen in anything but designer clothes that made him look more like a politician or even a celebrity. He spoke in complex, compound sentences and his deep-set eyes told you his thinking was always a step ahead of everyone else's. He was a college graduate and had gone to a swanky prep school where he played football. Never the best on the team but always the hardest working and probably the toughest. Howie Carr has captured and chonicled the contradiction that is John Martorano in his very well done *Hitman*.

Bulger had a macabre sense of humor, dark like his soul. He joked with Richie, coming up just short of revealing the truth.

"You gotta be careful all this new work doesn't kill you," Bulger grinned. "Can't enjoy much when you're dead."

If Richie was suspicious, he didn't show it. After all, he'd just lent Bulger nearly $800,000, easily enough to keep him in the boss's good graces for some time. Wearing blinders like the horses he took bets on, Richie had no reason to suspect he'd been made as an informant. Smiles and laughs were exchanged, and as soon as Richie stood up to leave, Martorano shot him in the head.

When the news broke at the FBI office that Richie had been hit, Opie simply distanced himself from Connolly, Morris, and the whole Organized Crime squad. He couldn't blame them entirely for what had happened since it had been his own indiscretion, in a bar no less, that had set the wheels in motion. Subsequently, he requested a transfer to a Resident Agency, one of the Boston FBI's off-site offices. That left the investigation of Richie's death in the hands of none other than John Connolly himself. Connolly filed a report that Richie had been killed by La Cosa Nostra (LCN) over a horse race debt. Not a single agent or supervisor at the Bureau disputed his conclusions, and Richie was laid to rest unceremoniously with that perpetual smile on his face. No one involved had any reason to suspect the story wouldn't hold.

No one except Colonel John O'Donovan, head of the Massachusetts State Police.

5
BOSTON, 1981

Of course, at this point I wasn't privy to all the untold details leading to Castucci's murder, most notably the fact that Connolly himself had done the leaking. But I did know that O'Donovan's own findings in the investigation just didn't jive with Connolly's at all. The Massachusetts State Police had key informants in Somerville, Southie, and Charlestown who disputed the FBI's conclusion that La Cosa Nostra was responsible for killing Richie. The MSP had developed their own criminal targets, namely Bulger and Flemmi, who had replaced the jailed Howie Winter as heads of the Winter Hill Gang. The MSP didn't trust certain FBI agents, and as time went on O'Donovan himself actually made complaints to FBIHQ. In August of 1980 he went so far as to insist on a meeting with my predecessor as ASAC, Weldon Kennedy, at a Ramada Inn in Brighton.

There, O'Donovan aired a litany of grievances for an audience that included Jeremiah O'Sullivan and Joe Jordan, commissioner of the Boston Police Department. Those grievances encapsulated the undercurrent of animosity brewing among competing law enforcement organizations throughout Boston. Along with O'Donovan's official complaint, the gripes grew more caustic as some Staties began accusing Connolly and Morris of actually covering up crimes committed by Bulger and Flemmi.

Sarhatt had taken over the Boston office in 1979 and was immediately thrust into the contentious and long-simmering battle between the FBI and the Massachusetts State Police that I was ostensibly sent in to settle. The Organized Crime squad celebrated their accomplishments with dinners that sat Bulger and Flemmi at the same table as their handlers and others. These contacts were never officially recorded, of course, since they were strictly off the books. The same year, to shore up control and gain prosecutorial support and protection, FBI agents Morris and Connolly (a fact Morris would testify to once granted immunity years later) informed Strike Force chief Jeremiah O'Sullivan that Bulger and Flemmi were, in fact, informants—another faux pas strictly against all Bureau regulations and protocol since Hoover first enacted the informant program. They had essentially ratted out their own rats, and for good reason, since O'Sullivan, in my view, was as petulant and self-serving as they were, and only too happy not to prosecute informants who might ultimately be helpful to his own OC cause.

But Morris and Connolly had another reason for breaking this hard-and-fast rule regarding informants. Indictments were to be handed down soon in the Tony Ciulla racehorse fix case, and the agents could not risk their prized informants getting pinched—something Strike Force head O'Sullivan backed them on one hundred percent.

Bulger and Flemmi paid their handlers back by tipping them off to a series of thefts from a trucking company called Interstate Shipping, along with a string of burglaries. John Morris put his imagination to work by using the RICO statutes to craft a case against a slew of co-conspirators served up for him on a platter. Morris claimed his case to be the "most successful law enforcement endeavor in the history of the Boston area." Conveniently, these arrests also helped Bulger and Flemmi eliminate a large portion of their criminal competition, further consolidating their deadly hold on the city.

I sought Colonel John O'Donovan out again as the newly assigned Assistant Special Agent in Charge of the Boston office. His mince-no-words allegations about the Richie Castucci murder and much more marked the first time I'd ever heard an entire FBI office criticized by someone of the highest authority in the state police. O'Donovan hadn't changed his attitude one bit and, in fact, he was more vehement than ever, because, in his mind, the murder of Richie Castucci remained unsolved in large part because of Connolly's falsified conclusions. O'Donovan was both befuddled and enraged by the FBI turning a blind eye and deaf ear to Connolly's actions, which seemed so clear to him as to be irrefutable. What the colonel, an old-fashioned honest cop, could not comprehend was the Bureau's arrogant, insular nature and overwhelming penchant to look after its own. *Never embarrass the Bureau* was the mantra, not to be violated under any circumstance. Of course, since agents were generally considered to be beyond reproach, the circumstances O'Donovan kept alluding to seemed inconceivable. Fidelity, Bravery, and Integrity, after all, was the FBI's motto.

The colonel used our former relationship to renew a unique trust and confidence, mostly on the phone since the Massachusetts State Police headquarters was located in Framingham, often a messy drive from Boston. But I did see him quite frequently at the 1010 State Police building, since I lived right around the corner. We, of course, threw a few beers down as we had at the FBI Academy beer hall in the past. Our other meetings normally took place in his office instead of mine, adorned with certificates, awards, and citations recognizing his many years of stellar service. I never recall seeing O'Donovan out of uniform, even when we met at a coffee shop halfway between Boston and Framingham. O'Donovan liked it here because he was a frequent enough customer to be left alone, especially when he took one of the back booths as his de facto office.

The colonel told me that the FBI in Boston had a history of complaints over a long period of time, at least from the MSP. He also confided that he was aware other law enforcement departments were complaining that some FBI agents were involved with wiseguys within their own jurisdictions. The colonel claimed he had proof that certain agents still in the FBI's Boston office couldn't be trusted either. His criticism was echoed by many law enforcement agencies in Boston and reached the ears of those at the FBI in Washington,

D.C., especially the higher-ups. But the colonel believed his complaints had either been covered up or simply ignored.

"I'm telling you, Fitz, these guys are dirty," he told me, referring to Morris and Connolly.

"But you can't prove that."

"We're running the Lancaster Garage wire and everybody goes quiet once the FBI finds out."

"That's not proof, Colonel."

"They're protecting their informants. They're letting them get away with anything, and that includes murder."

"We're talking about Bulger and Flemmi here."

"That's who we're talking about, yes."

O'Donovan didn't know I had already met with the assistant director of the Administrative Services Division at SOG, the "seat of government" for the FBI in Washington, D.C., and the operational and administrative nerve center of the Bureau. It was the ADIC, Assistant Director in Charge, Roy McKinnon, who had sent me north and ordered me to "clean up that mess in Boston" because the office "was in trouble!" In addition to the colonel's telling me about LE (law enforcement) issues, a pair of fellow agents contacted me about perceived "informant problems." Matt Cronin and Jim Crawford, better known as the "C and C Duo," tipped me off to the general atmosphere of mistrust inside the office. They had the best informants in the Boston Division and were instrumental in raising the red flags about Bulger and Flemmi. Because of the FBI's quasi-military structure and strict chain of command, I was limited in naming them for fear of reprisal and retaliation, but their help in deciphering the enigma that was Boston proved invaluable to me.

Even Larry Sarhatt confided that there was a turf war within the office over informants and territory that emanated from the Organized Crime squad. The OC squad was one of thirteen separate and distinct squads that handled various criminal classifications. Among these were the squads I was going to be responsible for as ASAC, including public corruption, financial crimes, cartel drugs, and labor racketeering. Sarhatt identified the conflict over informants as the root cause of all the office's troubles. One Boston agent, Jim Knotts, even insisted that John Connolly was fictionalizing information he received from Bulger and Flemmi, actually "stealing" the information from Knotts's 209 informant reports and ascribing it to his own informants to make up for the fact they were giving him nothing of value.

Knotts went one step further by directing my attention to an infamous bank robbery that had looted the Depositors Trust in Medford, Massachusetts, around Memorial Day of 1980. Connolly gave Whitey the credit for naming the crooks, information that led to their eventual arrest. But Knotts told me that was a lie. He knew Medford police chief Jake Keating, and Keating had told him Bulger hadn't provided the information at all. It had come from other sources, enabling Medford to build a successful prosecution.

According to Knotts, if Connolly wasn't stealing or embellishing reports, he was downright making them up. A combination of that also came into play when Connolly gave Bulger credit for giving up Jimmy Chalmas in the murder of ex-FBI informant Joseph Barboza in 1976. Trouble was, Knotts told me, San Francisco homicide detectives had interviewed Chalmas the very night of the murder as a prime suspect three months before Connolly got the news from Bulger. So, too, Knotts utterly debunked the myth that Bulger's intervention had saved the lives of two undercover FBI agents in the late 1970s, a story, he told me, that was blown way out of proportion. The agents in question were never in any real danger and, in fact, the operations in question had been shut down by the time of Bulger's warning. Knotts suspected the entire episode had been concocted by Connolly to further build the efficacy of his prized informant and keep him active on the daily reporting "rotors."

These rotors contained all of the Organized Crime 3 Squad's informant files, making those files vulnerable for cherry picking or enhancing information. Although I would change this process during my tenure, plenty of damage had apparently already been done. To further complicate the situation, Connolly and Morris confided to the Boston SAC that the Massachusetts State Police was interfering with *their* informants. Of course, O'Donovan and the MSP had a different view. They were certain Connolly and Morris were thwarting their investigation and believed that leaks of information to Bulger and Flemmi were coming straight from the FBI, thereby preventing MSP from making a case against them for any number of violent crimes, including multiple murders.

I was told that Bulger and Flemmi were accused of violence, in many cases demanding tribute from the Italian mob and anyone else doing business in the territory their gang had carved out—the cost of doing business. Yet I was also told that they were central to the FBI getting probable cause against the Angiulo gang, promulgating more wires and deeper penetration of the mafia stronghold. But Matt Cronin and Jim Crawford, lead agents on the case, never trusted the Bulger and Flemmi "assistance." They'd never seen evidence of any such thing and firmly believed it didn't exist.

Bringing down La Cosa Nostra, though, presented the highest priority set by Department of Justice in conformance with the FBI Director's official mandate. And powerful forces in both Boston and Washington continued to deem Bulger and Flemmi crucial to that goal no matter the indications to the contrary. At the same time, the Massachusetts State Police set an equally high priority on putting Bulger and Flemmi, in their estimation the two most dangerous gangsters in Boston, in jail as well.

Did the FBI lose a sense of perspective in letting the LCN investigation override all other concerns, even though the strategy left Bulger and Flemmi running loose in the streets? Was it an "Irish" thing that the mafia remained priority number one in Boston, even though the Irish mob was deemed far more threatening according to other law enforcement agencies?

Everywhere I turned and everywhere I looked for answers, everything kept coming back to Whitey Bulger. So, to do the job I'd been sent to Boston to do, it was time for a face-to-face meeting.

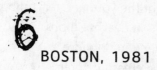

BOSTON, 1981

        In preparation for my meeting Bulger, and making my decision as to his fate as an informant, I set out to research as much as I could, assimilating the facts from file reviews and relying on previous experience and knowledge of the players involved. I drew off my Miami supervisory experience in ABSCAM, which taught me that file reports were important, but they don't tell the complete story, especially when trying to determine what's really going on in a man's head.

        They say a man is the sum of his deeds. Well, I started out by trying to learn everything I could about James "Whitey" Bulger's deeds. I already knew he grew up in Southie, an Irish enclave just outside of Boston proper. Bulger's home of Southie had been a hotbed for criminal activity long before he was born, making it an easy road to take. His brother Billy took a theoretically more civil road known as politics, following in the footsteps of congressmen like John William McCormack and Joe Moakley, to become president of the Mass-chusetts State Senate at the statehouse in Boston.

        Whitey followed the gangster route and in 1956 was convicted of bank robbery. By 1975, when he was reopened as an informant by

John Connolly shortly after Connolly's transfer from the New York office, he had served nine years in various penitentiaries, including Alcatraz and Leavenworth. He had a reputation in Southie for being a nice kid, a kid who helped the elderly, the kind of kid who worked with the church in handing out turkeys on Thanksgiving and Christmas holy days.

Connolly liked to tell the "ice cream" story about how Whitey befriended him at the time the future FBI agent was being taunted by bullies in Southie. Whitey bought the younger, fearful boy an ice cream cone and sat down with him on nearby stoop.

"Those punks ain't gonna bother you no more."

Connolly looked up from the ice cream dribbling down the side of the cone.

"I'm gonna have a talk with them," Whitey continued. "You got nothing to be scared of."

From that point on, Connolly could hardly be objective in his dealings with Bulger. I suppose he viewed the expensive diamond ring Bulger would give him years later as no different from the ice cream cone.

What's missing from Connolly's heartwarming ice cream story is that Whitey was in reality the biggest bully in Southie, actually in all of Boston for that matter. Over the years, and despite Connolly's sentimental view of him, Whitey had built a well-earned reputation as a stone-cold killer. He'd proven himself a brutally effective enforcer against the muffs who welched on their bets, as well as a part-time hit man for Raymond Patriarca, the head of the New England mob. Far from the saintly protector Connolly idealized, there was no arguing that Bulger was more comfortable with a gun in his hand than an ice cream cone. For years, the Massachusetts State Police, Boston Police Department, and Drug Enforcement Agency had Bulger lined up in their investigative crosshairs, only to have their efforts rebuked by Bureau interests committed to Whitey's protection at all costs.

In preparation for assessing Bulger firsthand, I reviewed his FBI in-house files and materials. Morris and Connolly talked him up as a "great guy" who, more important, had provided a great deal of evidence about the mafia and drugs. Yet the "evidence" they boasted about was nowhere to be found in any of the files, just as Agents Knotts, Cronin, and Crawford had told me.

Morris emphasized the fact that Bulger did not drink, he did not do dope, and, in fact, had it in for the dopers in his territory around Boston, especially Southie. They painted a picture of Bulger as a veritable Robin Hood who distributed turkeys over the holidays to the poor and elderly just like he gave an ice cream cone to a bullied young boy years before.

"You'll like Jim," Morris and Connolly kept telling me, never referring to him by his more accepted nickname.

Connolly boasted that Bulger was a "great friend" of the FBI who never accepted money for his informant work, providing his services for the love of his country instead. Morris seconded Connolly's benevolent description of Bulger as a guy I would not only like, but "love." Morris, it seemed, had the unenviable job of cleaning up Connolly's crap on paper. And both looked at the string of accolades coming their way from FBIHQ as a license to handle Bulger and Flemmi any way they chose, even if that entailed letting them "get away with petty crimes and such."

Connolly understood that his informants had the right to continue their gambling operation and loan-sharking business and even to collect rent from bookmakers as long as there was no violence. His attitude was one of "don't ask, don't tell." If the FBI had no direct corroboration from its own independent sources, then the office effectively knew nothing because Connolly didn't want them to know anything.

The great paradox here was that Connolly was a self-proclaimed loyal agent who idolized and idealized the FBI in every way. In ironic counterpoint, he had that diamond ring Bulger had given him engraved with the motto of the Bureau: Fidelity, Bravery, and Integrity. I would later learn that the ring was stolen property. If the suspicions of Colonel O'Donovan and others were correct, Connolly had already provided Bulger plenty in return, in clear violation of the FBI's *Manual of Investigative Operations and Guidelines*. That manual clearly states that agents are "to insure that [informants] are not provided any information other than that necessary to carry out their assignment." The manual might have been vague about what crimes were permissible for informants, but made very clear the informant could not be a murderer or the head of a criminal enterprise. The head of a gang, like the Winter Hill organization, then, should have expressly been off limits.

Early one evening in late March of 1981, Morris drove me to Whitey's condo in Quincy; it stood amidst a neat row of others just like it, plain vanilla and innocuous. Along the way he regaled me with story after story of his own experiences with the gangster, finishing each story with, "You're gonna like this guy."

I asked Morris about Whitey being described as the head of the Winter Hill Gang.

"Howie Winter is in jail," he told me. "So it's just a temporary appointment."

"For how long?"

"Don't know."

"As long as Winter is in?"

"Could be."

"That's a long time."

Morris seemed to have no problem with the fact that Bulger, as an FBI informant, was the acting head of an organized crime gang. After all, Morris was the "pencil" who could write up the reports in a way that convinced his superiors that Whitey was at the time the best informant to get the Bureau what it wanted. Everything else he covered was vague, noncommittal, and even muddled. I knew about informants; I had run enough of them myself in high-profile cases to know when the tail was wagging the dog.

In 1967, I was on special assignment in Mississipi from Memphis, where I'd been assigned after beginning my Bureau career in New Orleans two years earlier. I was charged with infiltrating the Ku Klux Klan and trying to develop informants. There had been a rash of murders down there, including hanging and shooting blacks and bombing synagogues.

My job was to get probable cause and evidence on Sam Bowers, the head of the White Knights of the Ku Klux Klan of Mississippi

(WKKKKOM) and the perpetrator behind all the violence. There were klaverns, the Klan clubs, in my area around Hattiesburg and Laurel where I played the undercover role of a New Yorker going to school in Jackson. I would act naïve around people, especially those I suspected of being Klan sympathizers, in no small part because these "kluckers," as we called them, were fundamentally proselytizers.

I'd always choose a propitious moment to reveal my true identity and attempt to develop an individual as an informant who could penetrate the klavern in question. The key was knowing how to identify kluckers or members of the WKKKKOM. Distinguishing the wannabes or would-bes from the true players being the trick.

The first person I tried to turn was anything but a wannabe. Joe Danny Hawkins turned out to be the head of the klavern in Jackson, as well as an avowed hater of law enforcement. Nothing I could say or do was going to change his mind. And the mere fact he was head of the klavern rendered him off limits to me as a potential Klan informant, anyway; opening him, in the Bureau's eyes, would be an endorsement that the FBI approved some actions taken by him in the klavern. That made him a target as opposed to a potential RI, or Racial Informant.

Instead, I stepped down from Hawkins to go after lower-ranking members as informants, kluckers who weren't in a position to make us complicit in their actions while they snitched on the Klan. Otherwise, we were no better than they, condoning any number of heinous acts that may or may not pay off in the end. That's called professionalism, the polar opposite of what I found was transpiring when I got to Boston.

In one instance, I worked diligently on a female klucker named Kathy Ainsworth who was an elementary school teacher in the Jackson school system. She hailed from Brooklyn, New York, and I used our common roots to get friendly. Kathy was also the girlfriend of Thomas Tarrants, a hit man for the WKKKKOM and a member of the Silver Dollar Club, the secret group responsible for most of the killings and bombings throughout Mississippi.

Kathy rejected my overtures initially; she was a racist but against killing, and knew full well what was going on. I appealed to her humanitarian side, challenged her with the question of what kind of role model she was for her students? By condoning Tarrants's actions, I made her see she was also effectively complicit in them. As a former social worker, I was able to appeal to her moral side. She'd gone into teaching "to do the right thing," and I was offering her the opportunity to do another right thing.

Through "fisur," or physical surveillance, and other techniques, we found the hideout and factory where the Silver Dollar Club made bombs and planned attacks on the black and Jewish communities. After accumulating probable cause and evidence, we followed Tarrants and Ainsworth to Meridian, Mississippi, for their planned attack on the Meyer Davidson Synagogue.

Tarrants arrived at the synagogue, whereupon he got out with a satchel of explosives to be placed at the back of the building, leaving Kathy in the car. At the time, the FBI did not have exclusive jurisdiction, so we turned the takedown over to the locals, including the Mississippi State Police. The targets were bull-horned by these law enforcement officials and told to drop the satchel.

Outside, Tarrants opened fire with a 9mm machine gun, drawing return fire from law enforcement immediately. Kathy was shot and killed at the wheel of the car. Tarrants threw her out of the car and began a wild chase through town. He was captured and taken into custody after taking several shots to his legs and chest.

The information ultimately provided by him and others we drew into our net was instrumental in stopping the bombings and murders. Director Hoover gave us all commendations. My "attaboy" recognized my informant development and contribution to the arrest of none other than Sam Bowers himself, the mastermind behind all the Klan's activities. Our real FBI investigative code name, Bombings in Mississippi, came to an end soon thereafter in what remains a crucial, game-changing moment for the civil rights movement that would be immortalized in the Gene Hackman film *Mississippi Burning*.

To this day I feel ambivalent about what happened to Kathy. She had helped us nail Tarrants and ultimately Bowers, and she had given her life in the effort. On the other hand, she knew who these people were and supported them every way imaginable. While she may not have condoned killing, she was apparently a self-avowed racist who'd enabled the actions of Tarrants and others in causing pain and heartache for countless victims while terrorizing an entire region. I was sorry she'd been killed but I couldn't let myself be way-laid by her death. No one forced her to take the wheel of the car that day, any more than the other times she'd been along for the ride on Tarrants's murderous escapades.

I told the story of my experience with Bombings in Mississippi and ABSCAM to Morris and others to make them understand that the FBI cannot have the leader of an organization as an informant. Morris listened attentively but showed no sign that my message was getting through. Maybe he had learned to lie so well, he was suc-cessfully doing it to himself.

I wanted both him and Connolly to know going into the meeting with Bulger that they were operating under my rules and standards now. At that point I thought I had FBIHQ backing me up. I thought this play was mine to make alone.

Maybe Morris and Connolly's smug attitudes should have told me something then and there. In retrospect, it was clear that they knew something I didn't.

What I did know was that I was about to meet the gangster guilty of presiding over an unprecedented reign of terror throughout the city of Boston, much of it condoned and supported by two FBI agents who knew I was about to interrogate him.

"Here we are," John Morris said, pulling up to Bulger's condo-minium in Quincy.

7

I directed Morris to stay in the car and "lay chickie," a euphemism for watching someone's back from my days at Mount Loretto. Morris responded with a look of bemusement. The truth was I didn't want Morris present because I wanted to get an independent, objective assessment of Bulger. Morris, it was becoming more and more evident, was too enamored with Whitey to be anything but counterproductive to my task.

"You're gonna like this guy," he said one more time as I climbed out of the car in front of Bulger's condo, reaffirming my decision.

Prior experience with informants conditioned me to know that Morris might actually be right. The informants I had developed and met through other agents have led me to believe that they were mostly decent people doing whatever they could to please for whatever motive: money, ego, revenge, or simply to avoid incarceration. I've learned over the years that there are good informants and bad informants. Good informants are all alike, while the bad ones are all different.

Bulger opened the door, his face hardened and expressionless, looking like a guy who clearly thought he had something better to do. He was wearing a Boston Red Sox cap angled low over his forehead to cast his face in shadows, gnawing at a toothpick wedged into the side of his mouth. In the foyer, I greeted him with an extended palm. He ignored it and just walked away, placing himself behind an island in the kitchen area.

I felt his eyes on me the whole time, something we called the "long eye" at the Academy. Always the tough guy, Bulger must have been figuring he could intimidate me as easily as he'd intimidated so many others. Well, Morris and Connolly might have read of my previous exploits, but Bulger clearly hadn't. It was doubtful they would've shared the information with him for fear of making him think he was doing business with someone more powerful than they were.

As I returned his stare, more of a snarl really, I noticed John Connolly lurking to the right of Bulger in a darkened corner. I was surprised to see him there, since I was supposed to be conducting the interview alone and had not been forewarned of his presence. I would later ream out Morris, Connolly's supervisor, for allowing this. But it was clear to me now that he wasn't the one calling the shots, nor had he ever been. Neither was Connolly. Indeed, the way Connolly positioned himself had left little doubt as to who the alpha dog here was. Everything about his body language suggested utter subservience to Bulger, a "suck-up" in the truest sense of the word. But I determined that if Connolly had so much as opened his mouth, I'd have his ass right then and there.

The light in the kitchen was dimmed, casting shadows around the room. I could picture Bulger doing that on purpose as a means of increasing his own ability to intimidate. It could also have been that the relative darkness masked his relatively small stature. Age had robbed him of the physical attributes he'd once relied on, leaving him with only his brutal reputation and glare. He was no more than five-eight, maybe five-nine, with a lean, sinewy build. Hardly imposing, but a testament to his violent reputation.

To Bulger's left stood a woman later described as his girlfriend to whom I was not introduced. I recall that Connolly faintly said hello and then disappeared back into his shadowed alcove. Bulger's girlfriend pressed out one cigarette and lit up another, blowing the smoke from her mouth and nose in plumes that wafted upward to hang heavy in the air. Her presence here was also clearly designed to unsettle me, Bulger's witness if he needed one.

Everything about Bulger, every quirk and gesture, was about control. He hadn't greeted me cordially in order to better control the situation. He had me follow him into the kitchen and left us to speak across the island, controlling our discussion by putting a physical barrier between us, his dark side against a brighter one.

One of the psychological concepts I taught at the FBI Academy was "Body Space," scientifically called "proxemics." By working the distance between us to his liking, Bulger projected that he was running the situation instead of me. He made a show of letting Connolly walk right up to him to demonstrate who he needed to pay deference to and it wasn't me. Again, the alpha dog! He never once took off his sunglasses, which, with the soft, diffused light, prevented me from seeing his eyes. "No eyes," I thought, recalling a movie where the prisoner on a chain gang tested the guard who always wore dark sunglasses. The prisoner couldn't see the guard's eyes and had to calculate whether or not he'd be shot if he tried to escape. As it turned out, he was.

Based on the game Whitey was playing, maybe he had read up on me after all.

My psychological training taught me to understand eyes as elements of "pupilimetrics" or "chromatics." And if the eyes were in fact the window to the soul, then Bulger had shut the blinds over them. He wore a T-shirt over his surprisingly lithe frame, wore it out over his shiny slacks as if to make me think he had a gun wedged in the waistband. More intimidation, as if I was going to turn tail and run before the questioning even began.

I knew I was looking at a stone killer, a psychopath, and it was hardly the first time. There'd been others, lots of them, but the one that came to mind the most as I faced Whitey Bulger for the first time was James Earl Ray, the man who assassinated Martin Luther King, Jr.

Soon after returning to Memphis from the Sam Bowers investigation in Mississippi, I was thrust into yet another, and tragic, high-profile case. I'd been serving mostly as relief supervisor for the Memphis Special Agent in Charge, Bob Jensen, and dealing with any number of civil rights investigations. In Memphis, a lot of these issues focused on an ongoing strike by sanitation workers. Almost all the workers were black and the city mayor refused to negotiate a new contract. So they went on strike and I was put on "special" again at the exclusive direction of the Department of Justice in Washington to investigate the considerable, escalating violence that remained an upshot of the strike.

My new schedule entailed coming into the office at four in the afternoon, either staying through the night or at my post at a local fire station across the street from the Lorraine Hotel in downtown Memphis, where Martin Luther King was staying. The interesting, and unfortunate, thing here was that King had actually come to Memphis at the behest of the striking sanitation workers who wanted him to rally them and solidify their commitment to a labor action that by then had stretched into months. Since I was still supervising the case, I had voluntary informants inside the church where King gave what they described as a "rousing" speech in which he stated, ironically, that he didn't care if his commitment to the workers' cause got him killed.

The next afternoon I was at the fire station, eyeballing the Lorraine Hotel where King and his entourage were staying, when our dispatcher, Leah Bramlett, called on the radio.

"Bob, we've got reports that Martin Luther King's been shot!"

I had been watching the hotel with binoculars on an intermittent basis and hadn't seen anything threatening or suggesting anything had happened. Nor had I heard any shots.

"Look," I told Leah, "I'm gonna check this out right away and get back to you."

I ran outside into the flood of responding Memphis police, including the Tactical Squad, arriving at the scene and finding a man named Charlie Stephens, a resident of the boardinghouse with the odd address of 422½ South Main Street. He told me he'd heard a "loud noise" coming from a bathroom containing a window that looked right across at the Lorraine Hotel balcony where King had been standing when he was shot. Stephens, who was clearly drunk but nonetheless lucid, reported seeing a man running from Room 5B down the stairs carrying a "wrapped" object in his hands.

"Bobby, Bobby!" called Captain Zachary, in charge of the Memphis PD. "Over here!"

I followed him into the rooming house, and, guns drawn, we stormed up the stairs. We had called for additional backup, but there was no time to wait for it. So while the rest of his "Tac" team secured the building, we went in.

I realized right away this was a flophouse, used by bums and transients in a part of the city that was in transition. The stench of booze, urine, and body odor filled the stairwell and the decaying steps creaked under our pounding. The building's panicked occupants had seen all the activity and were rushing about everywhere. Zachary and I tensed, aware that any of these men could have been the shooter. I scrutinized their movements as they surged past us, knowing body clues would give the perpetrator away. None did.

The landlady looked too old and withered to be running such a place. She directed us to Room 5B, which she said she'd rented earlier that day. Inside that room we found a box of rifle shells and a pair of Bushnell binoculars. Then back downstairs, wrapped up inside a rooming house bedspread tucked in an alcove, I spotted a rifle. The 30.06 Game Master with a Redfield scope, it turned out, was the one that had just been used to assassinate Martin Luther King, Jr. Later, we found a transistor radio bearing the number "00416," later shown to be James Earl Ray's prison ID at the Missouri Penitentiary, along with a pair of men's underwear hand sewn by Ray while he was imprisoned there.

Deliberately false information and constant chatter was flying wildly over the radios. Everything was chaos. We had dozens of separate sightings. Racial aspects of the shooting were evident in these false reports. I assigned agents to gather more intelligence and to identify what kind of car the suspect had driven off in. I sent agents to interview everyone in view of both the flophouse and the Lorraine Hotel, while I rushed to the airport with the rifle and bedspread tucked in an evidence bag for delivery to the FBI lab in Washington. The last plane out of Memphis for Washington that night had already taxied onto the tarmac, so my agent driver and friend Andy Sloan chased the 727 down the runway as the Memphis FBI office frantically ordered the Memphis tower to hold the flight.

"This better be good," the pilot said, eyeing the bundle I was carrying as I ran up the manual gangplank and came on board.

"It is," I told him.

He saw the evidence bag in my hand, his eyes begging for more information.

"This is the rifle that killed Martin Luther King," I told him.

The pilot nodded and, in complete stunned silence, turned back to the controls. Minutes later, we were airborn, and the evidence bag lay across my lap for the entire trip.

Only we couldn't land in Washington; radioed reports described gunmen shooting at our plane and the whole downtown D.C. area on fire from rioting. Word of King's assassination had reached the streets and the FBI had to act fast to stop the violence from spreading across the country.

The plane landed in nearby Baltimore, where agents were waiting to drive me—and the rifle—to the lab at headquarters. Meanwhile, Memphis Special Agent Bob Boyle asked the FBI Indentification Unit to check the Bureau's files on prison escapees. And a hand search of those 36,000 files managed to pinpoint James Earl Ray's from fingerprints taken off the rifle I'd given to a special agent named Frazier in the Firearms Unit.

This was the FBI at its best. At the time it was the biggest investigation and manhunt in the FBI's storied history, all the better when it came to a successful conclusion. Ray, our investigation revealed, had driven to Atlanta from Memphis, making his way to Canada and then England. Forensics gathered from our investigation at the scene, including marks on a window ledge on which a rifle had been steadied, left no doubt Ray was the shooter and that the rifle we recovered from the scene had killed Dr. King. To preserve the chain of evidence, I later returned to Memphis to personally secure the bullet as soon as it was removed during the autopsy. Before long FBI Most

Wanted flyers featuring Ray's face and aliases were distributed everywhere.

Thanks in large part to the speed and thoroughness of our response, Ray was apprehended at London's Heathrow Airport by British authorities on June 8, two months after the assassination. After Ray emerged from a flight originating in Lisbon, an alert Immigration official recognized his face from our FBI Wanted poster and immediately summoned the Special Branch of Scotland Yard. Although I didn't participate in his actual apprehension, Director Hoover ordered Bob Jensen and me, as lead investigators, to perform the first interviews with James Earl Ray at Brushy Mountain Prison. I remember how unimpressed I was when I first laid eyes on him. He looked squirrelly, his gaze shifting and constantly furtive. An utterly common guy who had taken on the stench of the flophouse where he'd been holed up waiting to take his shot at Dr. King.

Back in Boston, facing Whitey Bulger from across that kitchen island in 1981 made me think of facing James Earl Ray from the other side of a steel interrogation table. It was extremely uncommon among FBI informants to display such hostile behavior; we were on the same side, after all, at least that's what they were supposed to think. Normally informants went out of their way to be cordial and make an impression, knowing the wrong word from one of us could land them back in the jam they were in at the start.

"Nice place you got here, Whitey," I said, enjoying myself.

"I never got your name."

"That's 'cause you didn't shake my hand. It's Fitzpatrick."

"You don't understand," he boasted. "I was in Alcatraz; I was in the toughest penitentiaries. I'm a bad guy, not somebody you wanna come out here and mess with."

"Is that what I'm doing, Whitey? Messing with you?"

"You tell me."

"I just asked you."

"You got any idea of the stuff I've done?"

"That's why I'm here, to find out what you've done and what you're doing for us. See, you wanna tell me about all the stuff you've done when I want to hear what you're doing for me. Because you're the informant." My last remark, a caustic taunt.

Bulger bristled when I said "informant." I recognized that the word was explosive. Especially for an Irish guy who grew up loathing informants, and still did to this day. His reaction told me Whitey didn't really consider himself an informant at all. In this case there was very little to be gained from a man who hated the very creature his handlers made him out to be, further explaining why Morris and Connolly had handled Bulger with kid gloves.

I measured his stance. Psychologically, the way he carried himself evoked a "tough guy" and an "in your face" attitude, coupled with a sinister bravado gained from his murderous deeds, aimed at further intimidating me. This man was every bit a tried-and-true, hardboiled thug who'd long ago grown weary of any sense of moral obligation, and had no need for the simple courtesies that might make him appear weak or, just as bad, ordinary. He relished his toughness. Wore it as a talisman.

"Whitey, what are you doing for the FBI?" I finally asked when he lapsed into silence, even though the answer was already written on the parts of his face I could see through the dim lighting. "What are you doing for *me*?"

I put the stress on the word "me" to let him know who he was dealing with now, to whom he needed to pay deference. I thought I caught Connolly wince in the shadows. I deliberately avoided looking at him and kept my focus on Bulger. I could smell the smoke from Whitey's girlfriend's cigarette.

I'd known lots of guys like Bulger, part and parcel of growing up in New York City's Hell's Kitchen and the Mount, and plenty of them were tougher than he was. Even if he did have a gun stashed under his T-shirt, I was hardly intimidated by this guy and he sensed that. I recalled the Puerto Rican kid I'd fought for the Golden Gloves title at Madison Square Garden while I was a kid at Mount Loretto. No matter how hard I hit him, he wouldn't go down. Impervious to pain, not even seeming to know my punches were landing. I hit the guy with everything I had and still lost on points. A guy like that would make mince meat out of Bulger.

"You gonna answer my question, Whitey?"

"What question is that?"

"The one I just asked you."

"I forgot."

"What are you doing for me?"

"I don't do shit for you," he said, casting a sidelong glance at Connolly, perhaps expecting him to intervene.

"Talk to me about drugs."

"I got nothing to do with drugs."

"Tell me who's moving the shit through Boston, then. Tell me what you know."

"I already did," he said, coming up just short of a grin.

"How about some names?"

No response at all this time, and my instincts told me no answers would be forthcoming.

"How many people have you hurt, Whitey?" I asked, hoping to get a rise out of him.

His spine seemed to arch proudly. "I don't have to tell you that."

"How about since you've been an informant?"

He bristled again at the term.

"You kill anyone since you've been an informant, Whitey?"

"Know what?"

I didn't answer him.

"I took on plenty of guys like you," he continued anyway. "Turned out they weren't so tough either."

8
BOSTON, 1981

I had to make a decision. My questions were getting blown off and redirected. How he had kept the wool over Connolly's and Morris's eyes for so long I didn't know, nor did I particularly care at that point. My intention going in had been to get into areas of investigation, mostly drug investigations and cartel intelligence that he was supposedly supplying. Bulger, though, didn't answer a single question in either regard and it was obvious to me why.

My research in the office indicated that Whitey was not being truthful about street drugs and how they got there. He evaded anything to do with drug cartel connections, cartel distribution, entry points, and when braced on these issues, he grew angry. My judgment was that he was not being honest and truthful, and that negated his purpose as a TE informant. Since trust was and is the prime ingredient of informant relationships, how could the FBI continue to rely on Bulger when clearly he was a man not to be trusted?

I'm going to close this son of a bitch, I muttered to myself.

Bulger thought he was gaming me, pulling the tough guy act to show that whatever he had to say he'd say to Connolly or Morris, not the new guy on the block who hadn't earned his respect. I didn't have to earn anything from Bulger, though; he had to earn it from me. I showed no frustration over his continued refusal to answer any of my questions over our thirty-minute interview. Instead I grew more and more relaxed, casual, letting him think he had beaten me down and the dark night belonged to him.

In college, part of the curriculum to fulfill my dual major in psychology and sociology involved on-site study at Rockland State Hospital in New York where I observed countless subjects who'd been adjudged psychopaths by psychiatrists and mental health experts. I knew I was looking at a psychopath now, and realized that the whole time I was assessing him, Bulger was assessing me, too. And since I didn't have sunglasses on, as he did, he had a much better shot of reading me than I did of reading him.

When I left the Quincy condominium, I didn't extend my hand and Bulger, again, didn't extend his. I could feel his eyes burning into me all the way through the door.

"So," John Morris said, as I slid back into the passenger seat, "did you like him?"

"No, John, I didn't."

Morris seemed shocked and surprised, perhaps having been assured by Bulger that he intended to put on a good show for me. "You didn't?" was all he could manage.

"We're going to close this guy."

Without missing a beat, and suppressing his surprise, Morris responded, "No, you're not."

"What do you mean?" I challenged, holding back my anger.

"You'll never close Bulger," Morris said defiantly.

I felt my blood course at his impertinence and, seething with anger, did not want to discuss this any further with him at that point. I had just assessed Bulger and watched as his handler Connolly lurked by his side at the scene. Now I had to listen to Morris, Connolly's direct superior, tell me what I could and couldn't do. Morris's response had caught me equally by surprise, and I tried to calm myself as he drove me back to my office. I made some mental notes to speak with the SAC as soon as possible, though not in the presence of Morris.

After Morris dropped me off, I spent all night working on a detailed report that I presented to Larry Sarhatt the following morning. My unequivocable recommendation was to close Bulger as an FBI informant, not just for his propensity for violence, but because he definitely could not be trusted. Telling the complete truth was paramount to me, and in my usual idealistic manner, I thought this was the best and most professional thing to do. I dictated my report to my secretary, outlining the criticism and points I needed to make about Bulger's lack of cooperation and lack of performance, particularly in the drug area. I also knew that because of Bulger's status as a Top Echelon informant, my assessment was going to ruffle more than a few feathers at headquarters. Heads might even roll, though not mine.

My two-page report had Sarhatt's complete attention, and when he finished reading, I braced myself. But his response caught me off guard.

"Well," he said. "What are we going to do?"

"We keep it simple and just tell Washington that we are closing Bulger."

I don't remember Larry responding at all to my statement, which I took as him affirming my plan. As Special Agent in Charge, Larry was the one dealing with FBIHQ and I wasn't privy to any specific immediate outcome or resolution. There were other cases in progress in the Boston office that took me away from Bulger, who was far from my only pressing concern. At that time, we were doing undercover operations to expose organized crime penetration of the Boston stock market, as well as a corruption case against a Boston politician. Ironically, that politician, and a main target in the corruption case, was none other than Whitey Bulger's brother Billy, president of the Masschusetts State Senate.

A month later, during one of our annual FBI inspections, Connolly made overtures about bringing me to see Billy Bulger in his sumptuously reconditioned State House office. Connolly made a show of introducing me to "the power," as he described it. I found it strange that Connolly, as an FBI special agent, even knew these people. He nonchalantly reminded me that he was a Southie boy, born and raised around the Bulger family, and that he was a good friend of theirs. He may have even told me his ice cream story again. As part of this annual inspection of investigative procedures from top to bottom, it was common practice to introduce the inspectors and brass to "important" people in Boston, whose input would likely be included in the assessment.

Connolly's story didn't hold. I knew he was bringing me to see Billy Bulger as the guy who posed a threat to his brother and, perhaps, to him by connection. Or, maybe, I thought, Billy had requested the meeting so that he could get a look at his nemesis. If I'd had any questions about where Connolly's loyalties lay before, I didn't now. His taking me to Billy Bulger carried with it an implicit threat in the form of the political connections I'd be up against if I continued to press my case against Whitey. There was no doubt in my mind that Billy had already been briefed on the fact that I was the guy who wanted to close his brother as an informant, subjecting Whitey to arrest by O'Donovan's State Police and Billy to endless public embarrassment. Sure, I was an Irishman, but I was also an outsider sent up from Washington with no clear picture of the lay of the land and no allegiance to Connolly's ilk.

Billy couldn't have been warmer or more gregarious. His new office smelled of the leather furniture and freshly stained floor. He sat behind a gargantuan desk and his small stature made it look even bigger. He made it a point to tell his assistant he was in an important meeting and to hold all his calls. He said that looking at me, not Connolly. Again, body language was everything.

He didn't look like his brother, didn't sound like his brother. But when I shook his hand I had the same feeling as when I'd first met Whitey. They were just different sides of the same coin and I caged the rest of the meeting in a framework that Billy, too, was a con man used to getting what he wanted and taking whatever action was necessary when he didn't. He wasn't accustomed to being told no either, and was even less accustomed to anyone standing up to him. Shaking hands was just part of his con.

The specter of that arrogance never once rose in our carefully worded, yet cautious exchange. Connolly and I sat down in matching leather armchairs set before Billy Bulger's large desk, so new I found a sales tag taped to the arm's underside. We could have used the office's sitting area, but, from a body language perspective, Billy wanted me to know who was running the show here. I was a guest, that was all, and he was granting me an audience like a power broker might.

The sun shined in over Billy, making his features seem even paler as he leaned back comfortably in his chair. "So what are your plans after the Bureau?" he asked me.

"Haven't given it much thought really."

"You should," he said. "Plenty of your predecessors have gone on to bigger things." His eyes twinkled, coming up just short of a wink above his cherubic cheeks. I knew he was talking about Dennis Condon, now with the Massachusetts Department of Public Safety, and Paul Rico, with World Jai Alai based at my old stomping ground of Miami. "We like to take care of our own here."

"I appreciate that, Mr. Bulger," I replied, still unsure where this was going.

"Billy," he corrected. "Everybody calls me Billy."

We exchanged more small talk, but nothing of substance. The subject of his brother never came up, and I didn't expect it would. Twenty minutes into the conversation Billy started checking his watch, a clear indication to Connolly that it was time to leave. And, like a dog on a leash, Connolly rose on cue. I followed, extending my hand across the desk to take Billy's palm again.

"Anything I can do for you while you're in town, just call," he said, the sun bouncing off his pearly white teeth.

Connolly and I didn't speak on the way back to the office. He had a smug look on his face the whole time, as if his point had been made: Whitey Bulger was not a man to be messed with and, thus, neither was he. I knew what it was like to be bullied, pushed around, and that's the feeling that grabbed hold of my gut. Billy Bulger was a bully using power in place of his fists. And he wanted me to know I was alone, helpless against powerful forces I could neither control nor fully comprehend.

Sitting in that office that one and only time brought back many memories, but mostly it made me feel like I was back in the Mount, a little boy trying to learn enough to survive in unfamiliar territory. Not knowing whom to trust. I remembered it so vividly that my meeting with Billy Bulger brought back all the pain and heartache.

I had made the trek through city shelters to court for appropriate remands or petitions for neglect and destitute labels that had made me a ward of the State. At the Mount I was bunched with over sixty-six other kids in a cramped cottage, freezing in the winter and steaming in the summer. Privacy became a thing of the past. Affection vanished from my young life. No hugs and no familial intimacy. In other words, be and let be. There was plenty of pity to go around, but no love.

Fear was everywhere—fear of the unknown, fear of failure. We had a word for failure: Nabut. This was the cop-out for "You know, I didn't want it anyway." Nabut meant you could promise yourself anything because the mental reservation you held meant you really didn't have to do it. This was born of the many promises made to all of us and never kept. Lying and deception were part and parcel of the concept of Nabut. Many, if not all, of the children were promised things—food, security, and safety, among others—but they were never delivered. Promises became meaningless. Trust ceased to exist.

Above everything else, I remember the constant loneliness and the sinking feeling in the pit of my stomach that was there with every step and stray thought. In spite of all the abuse I witnessed on my mother's part and the sadness left unresolved in me, I still wanted to be with her. At the Mount I let out my emotion; I kicked and screamed and cried but no one heard me. The realization that I would never return to my mother set in. The look on her face as she walked away, half-turned with her shoulders hunched and her eyes filled with tears, will stay with me forever. She had signed me over to the State.

I've come to know that anger is the flip side of fear. And I dealt with that anger and fear the only way I knew how: by promising myself I would never ever feel this way again. Not in this or any lifetime.

And I hadn't, not once, until that meeting with Billy Bulger brought it all back. In that moment I felt strangely like I was back at the Mount again, hanging by the steam pipes of Cottage 3, my flesh blistering as the sadistic counselors Scarvelli and Farber waited for me to drop. Something was happening in Boston that left me feeling helpless in a way I hadn't since that day someone had yelled "Fuck you!" on our march across the bridge to the dining hall. Now it seemed someone was saying "Fuck you" to me instead.

Only this time I was no longer that frightened, lonely child. This time I would fight back. I would do what was right, just like the brave heroes recalled from *This Is Your FBI* playing over the radio down the hall from Sister Mary Assumpta's bedroom.

"We're going to close this guy."

"No, you're not."

"What do you mean?"

"You'll never close Bulger."

As I drove back with John Connolly to Boston's Federal Building, I knew exactly what I needed to do: close Whitey Bulger and put the Boston office back on track, no matter how many names I had to take or asses I had to kick.

9
BOSTON, 1951

To understand exactly how and where order and discipline had come apart in the Boston office of the Bureau, you'd need to go all the way back to 1951 when Special Agents Paul Rico and Dennis Condon joined the FBI. They came to duty in the wake of World War II, before the onset of Korea, at a time when the country remained hungry for heroes and the FBI under J. Edgar Hoover was more than happy to oblige. The agency was, after all, the glorious domestic protector and enforcer that had kept the country safe from foreign and homegrown spies alike. While America was helping to rebuild Germany and Japan from the ravages of war, the Bureau needed a new enemy with new G-men heroes to sustain its image and prove its usefulness to society. Slick and ambitious, Rico and Condon were more than happy to step into the spotlight.

At the same time, a juvenile thug named Joseph Barboza was lining his pockets with cash from petty thefts and beginning to make his presence known around Boston with a string of strong-arm burglaries. At seventeen years of age, he was already on his way to prison for the first time. By 1954, within weeks of his escape from Walpole State Prison, Barboza reached the criminal big time with a string of local armed robberies, kidnappings, and extortion. Many who knew Barboza described him as a smart kid, but his harsh features belied that. Those features included a massive, jutting jaw; a ridged, Simian-like forehead; and protruding cheekbones that cast shadows over the lower half of his face. People were known to cross to the other side of the street when they saw him coming; Barboza was that intimidating and that repulsive.

James "Whitey" Bulger's ascent through the ranks pretty much mirrored Barboza's during this period. Like Barboza, he was involved in armed robbery and numerous assaults, according to the local police blotters. And, like Barboza, he was described as a bright but extremely dangerous kid: unstable, vicious, and utterly without conscience. Unlike Barboza, though, people didn't cross the street to avoid him. Early descriptions, in fact, depict Whitey as "cute with a wry smile" that belied his true intentions, and a "capacious appetite" for violence that knew no bounds.

During his stretch inside Leavenworth, the prison psychiatrists tagged Bulger with a "sociopathic" personality—the same label they would give Barboza in the years to come. But even the simplest of local residents in and around Boston recognized both Barboza and Bulger for what they were: stone killers.

When I lectured at the FBI Academy and at law enforcement agencies around the country, one of my specialties was abnormal psychology, allowing me to profile the masks of sanity that men like Barboza and Bulger wore. Whether they were deemed psychopaths or sociopaths, criminals like Bulger and Barboza represented an entirely different species that we were just beginning to understand. These men, whose vicious behavior propelled them through the gang ranks in the fifties and sixties, exemplified the type with whom the FBI, inexplicably, decided to do business.

Well, maybe not so inexplicably.

In 1961, Attorney General Robert Kennedy listed New England's mafia chief, Raymond Patriarca, as "one of the thirty-nine top echelon racketeers in the country," set to be targeted for FBI investigation and prosecution by Kennedy's office. Director Hoover took Kennedy's baton and ordered each field office to infiltrate "top echelon organized crime groups" with FBI informants. Thus, on June 21, 1961, the Top Echelon Criminal Informant Program (TECIP) was formed to ensure the success of the FBI attack against organized crime racketeers. In addition to these informants, the Bureau was beginning to employ early electronic microphone surveillance ("misur"), which Organized Crime units later dubbed the "black bag" bug.

The Bureau had found the new enemy it needed and new means, along with new heroes, to fight it. By 1963, Rico and Condon were having moderate success in Boston with the microphone surveillance information, anonymously encoded in Patriarca's case as BS-856C (Boston 856 Confidential). BS-856C was actually an illegal, non-court-ordered microphone surveillance that surreptitiously and electronically captured information from the mafia gangsters. This "tin ear" morphed into a "live ear" through its use by informants wearing what is now referred to as a "wire."

Whatever you call it, this new tool was very effective in gaining unique and raw insight into the mafia's organizational structure and operations, so that the Bureau's response could be appropriately mapped out. The technology was so cutting edge at the time that there were some questions as to whether these wires were legal or not, but back then they were seen as the only means to combat an organized crime entity whose power was growing unchecked.

Jerry Angiulo, the underboss of Boston underworld rackets, as well as his chief lieutenants and his boss Raymond Patriarca himself, were the initial targets when the new surveillance system went into operation. And the effectiveness of the misur and informant program was proven early on. In 1964, a hood by the name of Frank Benjamin was murdered, and Vincent Flemmi, aka The Butcher, was the prime suspect.

"All I want to do is kill people," Flemmi explained to an associate over Condon's tin ear surveillance tape. "You can leave hitting banks to somebody else, 'less I get to go in blasting."

A shocking revelation in all respects. By this time, Condon and Rico had managed to turn Joseph Barboza into an informant, allowing him to avoid a life sentence on yet another murder rap. Whether they actually had the evidence to make the case stick became a moot point, since the new surveillance techniques had been enough to turn Barboza. Barboza claimed that "Flemmi had killed Benjamin and cut off his head." His assertion was independently verified through a wire intercept, as the relentless capacity for bragging by thugs everywhere found a counterbalance in electronic surveillance. Wiseguys loved to talk, and such constant boasting of their own brutal conquests often led to their ultimate undoing. They could no longer kill with impunity. Thanks to the FBI's new surveillance techniques and technology, the rules of investigation were changing.

The tin ear in question revealed particularly grisly stuff: Vincent Flemmi wanted to be the "contract man" in Boston; he talked about a number of killings, admitting that he murdered Benjamin and boasting about cutting off his head. Procedure, and protocol, inside the FBI was changed forever as both the electronic surveillance and TECIP programs, engineered in Boston in large part by Rico and Condon, were expanded nationwide.

Rico notified FBIHQ that Vincent Flemmi wanted to be the best hit man in Boston, which, Rico believed, could eventually make Flemmi the best informant. In 1964, Rico told the FBIHQ that Flemmi wanted to kill Teddy Deegan, a small-time hood, because he "owes us money, about $300, and is welching on the deal." The threat by Vinnie Flemmi got back to Deegan, who vehemently denied Flemmi's allegation, telling his Irish mob friends that Flemmi was just out to kill him. Even with that threat on the books, along with everything else on the wire, Flemmi was targeted as an informant by Boston FBI, just as Joseph Barboza had been before him.

But even their Boston mob associates recognized that Flemmi and Barboza were taking things too far.

"People are afraid of Flemmi and Barboza," New England crime boss Raymond Patriarca was told one day in Providence. "You gotta shut them down."

The word Patriarca put out must never have reached Barboza and Flemmi, because their killing spree continued. Either that or they simply didn't care and disregarded the order from their boss. Besides, they had their next target already picked out.

Teddy Deegan was described by the Irish guys as a "pain in the ass." He was a wannabe whose reputation as a lowlife upset his friends. Always hustling for dough, Teddy frequented a number of bars including the Ebb Tide (informant Richie Castucci's place in later years), where one night Barboza and Flemmi lay in wait for him outside. When Deegan emerged through a side exit into an alley, they gunned him down.

The tin ear told Rico and Condon that a notorious hit man called the "Animal" had gotten permission from mafia boss Patriarca to whack Deegan. They made Barboza out as the Animal and they were right. Barboza confessed but refused to name Flemmi. Without any other way of nailing him, the agents were left with an informant they didn't want to put away and a stone-ass killer they couldn't. Believing they had no other choice, Rico and Condon sat passively by while four other suspects were arrested for the Deegan murder. Those same suspects were later convicted in large part due to Barboza's sworn, and perjured, testimony. Rico and Condon neither said nor did anything to prevent the wrongful convictions. The two agents had inarguably crossed an ethical line and, while they might have been the first, they were far from the last.

For his part, Barboza had played the agents perfectly. He had implicated the subjects due to a grudge he'd held against one of them, Joseph Salvati. The FBI had offered the Animal a perfect means to get even over a perceived debt, enabling him to settle his score. He'd gotten away with Teddy Deegan's murder and then helped get Salvati and his gang put away for it. It was a saavy and effective move by Barboza, leaving a pair of top-flight FBI agents totally beholden to him.

Agents Rico and Condon had occasion to visit another wiseguy, Frank "Cadillac" Salemme, in an attempt to develop him as an informant as well. They'd meet regularly in his garage for doughnuts and coffee and do little more than "shoot the shit." Salemme was an aspiring mob boss who loved busting Condon's balls about backing Joseph "the Animal" Barboza's perjured testimony on the Deegan killing. The inside mob joke was that the FBI was protecting Barboza for no other reason than they could. No one on the street really believed that Barboza was a reliable FBI informant, except for the FBI.

After all, Barboza was little more than a brutal killer who viewed his own informant status as a license to murder without fear of repercussion. He'd mastered the game of keeping his handlers, Rico and Condon, dependent on him for information that he invariably hinted at but never delivered, at least not in full. Like many future informants, he was the one calling the shots when it should have been quite the opposite. He was the figurative fox in the FBI henhouse, which didn't stop Rico and Condon from trying to turn the equally brutal Salemme into an informant as well.

"You're a fucking Catholic, right?" Salemme taunted.

"Sure," said Condon.

"Fucking Catholic and royal fucking Knight of Columbus, and that doesn't stop you from putting four muffs on death row for crimes they didn't do."

Salemme seemed to find the whole thing sadistically amusing and was clearly busting Condon's balls. Salemme, of course, had no idea at the time that Barboza and Vincent Flemmi were FBI snitches, and that Flemmi had become a Top Echelon informant, a kind of dark knight for Condon and Rico.

In the bullpen back in the FBI office, agents Rico and Condon had become the "big cheese" in the Organized Crime squad bay, the inside joke being that you need "big cheese" to take care of "salami" and his pals. They'd become new heroes for a new age. Their handling of TEs and other informants gained them stature at FBIHQ and assured the manpower and resources necessary for continuing the agents' fight against the mafia. Their work received compliments from the Strike Force, the U.S. Attorney's Office, and even the Department of Justice. Using their high-powered informants they were able to turn a whole chain of wannabes into "squeals," furthering the FBI effort to penetrate the myriad factions of organized crime mobs throughout New England in keeping with the stated goals of headquarters.

The problem that would come back to haunt the Bureau again and again was that few people inside and outside the FBI actually knew who these informants were. Only symbols and numbers were used to identify them, and the refusal to name informants, under any circumstances, became sacrosanct. The worst sin in the church of the FBI was to reveal an informant's identity, even in a court of law. They were to be protected at all costs, even if that meant ignoring actions totally out of step with existing law.

Information gleaned from squeals trumped everything else, regardless of how much it actually yielded. There was always tomorrow went the thinking, and after investing so much time and resources into the effort of building them up, no agent was going to close down his own informants. Everything seemed upside down. In Boston, for example, Top Echelon informants like Barboza and Flemmi were targeted against major players in the Angiulo and Patriarca crime families throughout New England. That was enough to let anything and everything else go. Having serious, self-serving bad guys working directly with the FBI, though, represented a remarkable sea change and an exceedingly dangerous one.

These mob informants, especially the TEs, gained efficacy with each successful prosecution produced by the intelligence they provided. As a result, their value to the FBI provided them with a safety net, and as it became apparent that they could conduct their business without fear of prosecution, they became increasingly violent. The FBI understandably did not want altar boys. But neither could they have wanted the violent, irredeemable criminal element that could not be trusted. In fact, agents were finding that it became easy to turn the worst of the worst precisely because it facilitated their ability to do business unencumbered by fear of arrest or prosecution. This also spawned the "getting on the bus" syndrome that insidiously encouraged many informants to lie and fabricate their tales based on secret, inside information wittingly or unwittingly furnished to them by their enforcement handlers.

While Boston's Special Agent in Charge at the time saw the reports describing the crimes committed by the infamous Barboza and Flemmi, he still wrote Director Hoover that "Special Agents Paul Rico and Dennis Condon should receive a salary increase for their fine work in handling TEs." Hoover's return memo applauded Rico and Condon's handling and development of TEs in the Boston office. Emboldened by accolades from the pinnacle of FBIHQ, Rico and

Condon continued their efforts to expand their stable of informants, adding Stephen Flemmi (Vincent's brother) to the fold designated with symbol number BS (Boston) 955–C-TE (Criminal–Top Echelon) informant.

Flemmi, who was destined to become Whitey Bulger's right-hand man, might have been reared in a family steeped in crime, but he also served as an army paratrooper, passing the rigorous training to become a sniper. Instead of endearing him to a different kind of lifestyle, the army served only to strengthen his bonds to crime. His tour added to his toughness and mystique. Like Bulger, he was only of average size. Unlike Bulger though, Flemmi quickly tired of an exhaustive physical regimen to keep himself in shape. He ended up growing a paunch and wearing his hair so long that stubborn patches would drop down over his forehead. Also like Whitey, he showcased a sexually flirtatious fondness for women, some say to hide the rumors of homosexuality that had surfaced while he was in the army. The same rumors abounded about Bulger, making some think his whole tough-guy act was a façade meant to disguise his true nature.

Praise for their efforts knew no bounds and neither did their ambitions. The TEs were giving the agents what they wanted, and the agents were giving their TEs what they needed in return. Both had clear paths to attaining power and neither could get there without the help of the other, forming an inexorable bond between cop and criminal.

People, in other words, were quite literally getting away with murder, and nobody seemed to care.

10

BOSTON, 1968

By 1968, Joseph Barboza had become the most dangerous individual known to Boston law enforcement. Obviously, he would make a great witness against La Cosa Nostra, and he was encouraged by Paul Rico and Dennis Condon to testify against Patriarca, deemed the "LCN boss and possible Commission member."

Barboza did in fact testify, resulting in the conviction of Patriarca and his crew in federal court at Boston in 1968. Rico and Condon were crowned golden boys in the Boston office of the FBI, no longer able to do any wrong in spite of the wrongs they'd already done. They had used Barboza to work his black magic in the takedown of the Italian mafia in New England. And Barboza, in turn, had used them to absolve himself of the Teddy Deegan murder and send four innocent men to prison in his stead. Throughout that trial, Rico and Condon continually checked on Barboza's well-being while he was in protective custody. Actually, the gangster would later claim that the feds were telling him what to say to make sure his story stuck.

Rico and Condon were in court the day the verdicts against the four men were handed down. The Boston Strike Force commented to

FBIHQ that "as a result of FBI investigation in state court in Boston, four more [gangsters] are convicted in the 1965 slaying of Teddy Deegan." Two of these were sentenced to death while Salvati and another defendant identified by Barboza got life sentences. Shortly after the convictions, commendations direct from Hoover himself at FBIHQ kept arriving, praising Rico and Condon's work on the case. Hoover wrote the agents personally that "The successful prosecution of these subjects was a direct result of your noteworthy development of pertinent witnesses."

But the seeds of the nefarious doings and ultimate unraveling were firmly in place. In early 1970, Condon reached out to Barboza, now living in San Francisco, to let him know his life might be in danger, something the agent had learned through another informant. The Boston office of the FBI denied that Barboza was still cooperating as an informant and refused to offer him any further help. The temperamental Barboza decided to get even by recanting his testimony that convicted the four innocent men of the murder of Teddy Deegan. He also tried to give evidence that mob boss Patriarca should be exonerated due to additional perjured testimony he provided to FBI agents and the court.

"I got enough that will convince any court that I was lying," he said at the time, determined to make Rico and Condon pay for abandoning him.

None other than F. Lee Bailey, acting as Barboza's attorney, reiterated that Deegan's slayers were convicted on false testimony by Barboza and that they were innocent. By October 1970, FBIHQ was advised that witnesses in affidavits "will allege that Barboza told them he lied about Deegan, about Patriarca and others," naming the Strike Force and the FBI itself as being responsible for his perjured testimony. F. Lee Bailey went public insisting that Barboza had similarly committed perjury against Patriarca, Angiulo, and the Deegan suspects on the prodding of his corrupt handlers, Rico and Condon. Ultimately, Bailey's strategy accomplished nothing from a legal standpoint, while casting even more aspersions on the FBI. But Barboza was then paid at least $9,000 by the FBI on the pretext of cosmetic surgery to alter his appearance. He first disavowed his new story, the truth, only to go back to telling it to anyone who'd listen until he was shotgunned to death on a San Franciso street in 1976.

Still, the blowback resulting from their protection of Joseph Barboza as an informant at all costs would haunt both Rico and Condon for years after they retired. During the House Committee on Government Reform's hearings in 2003, Representative Dan Burton asked Rico about his complicity in sending an innocent man to jail for over thirty years. Rico replied curtly: "What do you want from me? Tears?"

Desperate to redeem himself with the Bureau decades before then, Condon had opened another informant, James "Whitey" Bulger, whom he knew through Whitey's brother Billy, an aspiring Boston politician. Whitey had been arrested by Condon's partner Rico on a bank robbery charge, so all the pieces seemed to be in place. Except in his first go-round as an FBI informant, Whitey Bulger proved utterly unproductive and was closed three months later and jailed soon after that.

But Bulger's relationship with the FBI's Boston office was far from over. In 1973, just when the careers of Rico and Condon were winding down and they were about to leave Boston, an upstart agent named John Connolly arrived.

11

Connolly had never forgotten how Whitey had bought him an ice cream cone as a boy. And he quickly saw an opportunity for the two Southie natives to serve each other, never grasping how one-sided that relationship would become.

John Connolly had enjoyed a successful, though hardly distinguished, career in the Bureau up until that point. He'd spent his formative years as a grunt with the New York office, his tenure fairly unremarkable save for his apprehension of Frank "Cadillac" Salemme in Manhattan in 1975. To hear Connolly tell it, the tale evoked images of the Wild West, two men coming face-to-face in a desperate confrontation only one of them could survive. In reality, Connolly caught Salemme because he happened to recognize him crossing the street. The inside FBI story was that Connolly was given the information as a "setup" to get Connolly back to his home turf in Boston. And, in fact, the routine arrest won him his prized transfer to the FBI office just a few miles from where he'd been born and raised.

Coming home represented the attainment of a career goal Connolly had long pursued and he took full advantage of it. He dressed in flashy suits, had his hair professionally styled, and carried himself with a swagger and cockiness not at all in keeping with limited achievements that hardly made him the epitome of the modern-day FBI agent. Ironically, he reminded some veterans in the Boston office of a more polished version of Richie Castucci, acting "big" with not a lot to back it up.

But Connolly had a plan to change that.

Intimately acquainted with the exploits of Whitey Bulger from their common roots in Southie, the thirty-five-year-old Connolly set his sights on opening him as an informant, believing he could succeed where Paul Rico and Dennis Condon had failed. Indeed, because of his Southie ties, the young agent had legitimate street credentials—something the Bureau lacked in Boston at the time.

Bulger, though, resisted Connolly's initial overture, held in the agent's Plymouth overlooking Wallaston Beach, and that may have proven fortuitous for the ambitious Connolly, since there had been a change in tenor and tolerance expressed by FBIHQ. In a warning about informants, U.S. attorneys at a national conference in 1974 expressed a "belief" that the FBI had become "overly protective" of informants and made "efforts so that informants are not prosecuted so that they continue to provide intelligence information." With both Rico and Condon taking that as their cue to leave the Bureau, the Boston office escaped recrimination and business pretty much returned to normal, only with new players, led by John Connolly, in place. History was about to repeat itself, with Whitey effectively becoming a new incarnation of Joseph Barboza, the lessons of the past not being heeded whatsoever.

Connolly's subsequent meetings with Bulger proved much more productive precisely because Bulger saw in the ambitious agent a new means to help him achieve his own nefarious ends. Among other things, he was facing a major rift with the Angiulos, the local Italian mob family, over the lucrative placement of vending machines in various area establishments. Since Connolly's only reason for wanting his help was to bring down those very Angiulos, Bulger saw a way to enlist the agent as an unwitting accomplice in solving his current dilemma. Bulger brought along his right-hand man Stephen "the Rifleman" Flemmi, and Connolly saw his opportunity to find the same glory achieved by Rico and Condon while avoiding the excesses that led to their ultimate downfalls at the hands of Barboza.

At the outset anyway, he was not disappointed. In 1976, Stephen Flemmi and Bulger provided information that allowed Connolly to turn a co-conspirator into a cooperating witness, identifying Joe Russo as the killer of none other than Joseph Barboza, who was gunned down in San Francisco just days after his release from prison. In a typical execution-style murder, Barboza was clipped by Russo and his gang from inside a Ford Econoline van that pulled up next to Barboza's car and pumped him full of bullets. The van was abandoned alongside Barboza, who was left lying in a pool of blood, eerily reminiscent of victims he had left behind.

Having proven himself to his handlers, Bulger wasted no time in taking over the Winter Hill Gang in the wake of gang leader Howie Winter's incarceration. The fact that the Italian mob remained the Bureau's number one priority gave Bulger carte blanche to run the Irish mob however he saw fit. In fact, the more powerful he could become, the more power he could exert on the Bureau's behalf. At least that was the thinking at the time. Connolly and his supervisor, John Morris, and Bulger and Flemmi shared one thing in common: ambition. But that was enough to drive their relationship forward and sustain it so long as each was helping to promote the success of the other.

Boston watched as the Winter Hill Gang under Bulger and Flemmi consolidated its vicious hold on the city's rackets, thanks in large part to the federal arrests and subsequent incarceration of the competition they served up neatly on a plate. They fed names to Connolly and Morris, and the agents would take things from there. The relationship flourished, as the parties continued feeding off each other's greed and opportunity.

But they did so at the expense of the residents of Boston, who found their lives adversely affected, even endangered, by a pair of sociopaths who had free rein to wreak havoc on the city. Whitey Bulger and Stephen Flemmi had effectively replaced Barboza and Vincent Flemmi, among others; their actions now fully facilitated by their status as FBI informants. And they also replaced Barboza as informants with the same goal in mind: receive as many free passes as needed, so long as they appeared to be furnishing good intelligence— the operative word being *appeared.*

Some of that intelligence from Bulger, code named BS 1544–C-TE, helped net Joe Russo, which, in turn, netted Jimmy Charlmas, aka Ted Sharliss, for masterminding the hit on Barboza for "the Office." When Connolly reported, though, he changed "Office" to "Outfit," a euphemism for the New England mafia that the Boston office was still desperate to bring down. The subtle alteration was clearly designed to muddle a picture already blurred by false information. Something Connolly did quite well in his 209s, the internal vehicle for reporting informant information, whether true or not.

Connolly hit the street running on the same track as Rico and Condon, not only making the same mistakes they made, but even worse ones. Having grown up with Bulger in Boston's Southie neighborhood, Connolly had no problem accepting a gift from the informant he also saw as his pal: that diamond ring he had emblazoned with the FBI motto: Fidelity Bravery Integrity. The ultimate irony and sadly so.

Connolly had betrayed the Bureau by going "native," essentially choosing his Irish Boston roots over his loyalty to the organization he purported to love. There was no going back for Connolly at this point. In his determination to avoid the inglorious fates of Rico and Condon, he had assured himself a much worse one. He would later declare in court testimony, "We knew what these guys were. . . . All of them, top echelon informants, are murderers. The government put me in business with murderers."

And he found a willing and able partner in fellow agent John Morris, who was promoted to supervisor and immediately got Connolly assigned to his squad. Internally, Morris was described as "imaginative, innovative and extremely industrious" with no hesitation to tackle "major projects." They seemed perfectly matched, although Morris was as humdrum as Connolly was flashy. A family man with a receding hairline and a crumbling marriage, Morris was cut from the cloth, initially anyway, of more staid Bureau agents of the past, conservative and, you would think from appearances, by the book.

But his looks belied his cunning. And he plunged into his job as much as anything as a way to counterbalance his troubled personal life. The arrows were moving in opposite directions and the more the separation grew, the more Morris threw himself all-out into a career being propelled by none other than Whitey Bulger. He and Connolly were free to do whatever they wanted so long as they produced. Similarly, Bulger and Flemmi were free to do pretty much whatever they wanted, so long as they produced as well. "Quid pro quo," as one agent put it.

It was a clear recipe for an impending disaster.

Indeed, Morris and Connolly would and did do anything necessary to protect their Top Echelon informants, whom they saw as fast-track tickets to fame and glory. They aspired to be viewed as crime-fighting heroes of the FBI, even though the means to those ends made them anything but. Bulger and Flemmi had to be kept out of jail and out of harm's way. Priority one. Simple as that.

None of this was happening under the radar either. The Massachusetts State Police and Boston Police Department were hearing things from their own informants—rumors of feds who were enabling felons—and complaints were flowing into the Boston FBI office as a harbinger of the firestorm ignited by MSP head Colonel O'Donovan after the Lancaster Garage incident.

The FBI attempted to walk a fine line by ensuring that these clandestine Top Echelon relationships resulted in more good than harm. Summing up that ultimately impossible challenge, John Connolly would later tell me in reference to Bulger and Flemmi, "Sure, they're bad guys, but they're *our* bad guys."

PART TWO
BLOWBACK

"You got me."

12
MOUNT LORETTO, 1958

When I left the Mount in 1958 it was to enter still another institution—the U.S. Army. Without telling anyone, I enlisted as a young private and did my infantry training at Fort Dix in New Jersey. I had no money and needed a job, and for most of us kids in the Mount, the military was the way to go. I felt at home with a cot, three squares, and some pocket money to boot. My training took me to a succession of military instruction schools in Texas and New Mexico, the most exciting being a nuclear warhead school in Los Alamos—until, that is, I learned that we might have been guinea pigs for nuclear testing the whole time! Looking back, that became a strangely appropriate metaphor for what I'd later face in Boston, since the office was truly toxic.

Once my training was complete, I was shipped to Germany, just outside Mainz and Wiesbaden. The culture shock I experienced was disorienting at first. Here I was, a kid fresh from the Mount, finding myself in postwar Germany, where the ruins and spoils of war were still evident. Yet it was also mysterious and exciting, and I was being paid to do this. I was fortunate enough to take over the company supply unit, and within a year I had my sergeant stripes and more opportunity. Being overseas was a great adventure for me, and later, I'd reflect that I grew up in this new culture, which expanded my horizons beyond my wildest dreams.

It was wonderful. I went to schools at Wiesbaden and Mainz and Heidelberg, grabbing college credits for future enrollment. The barracks I stayed in was an old SS casern with a fair amount of history. As a basic infantry soldier with a "supply military occupational specialty," I traveled throughout Europe increasing and enhancing my desire to know more. My boss, a Ranger captain, signed me up for OCS (Officer Candidates School) and even got me a nod to West Point, after which my Seventh Army commanding general put me in for a slot. I was achieving beyond my wildest expectations.

At the same time, Father Kenny, who'd long taken an interest in me at Mount Loretto, suggested a scholarship to St. Peter's College in New Jersey in lieu of West Point. Father Kenny saw the priesthood in my future, believing my compassion made me ideal for the job. There had not been many successs stories like that from the Mount, and to the good Father I looked like a legitimate candidate.

"You know *people*, Fitz," he told me once.

"What do you mean, Father?"

He just smiled in response, but I gathered that he recognized that I was an effective listener and that I had a way of understanding and interpreting information beyond the words people used when talking to me. Perhaps Father Kenny was sensing in me the traits that would later make me one of the FBI's new profilers. I had used those skills in my one and only meeting with Whitey Bulger, learning from his body language more than he had thought he'd told me. I had a visceral sense that matched his. Bulger's persona was pure selfish stuff to enhance his own perceived legend. But Father Kenny was also talking about my compassion, a compassion born of feeling for the weak, needy, and indisposed; I had been all of these things myself as a boy and had learned to recognize them in those I was drawn to help. A coping mechanism, I guess, but it helped me become the man I was and led ultimately to my rise through the ranks of the FBI, assisting other agents when necessary.

I finally decided to go back across the pond to New Jersey's St.

Peter's College in 1961. Had I gone to the Point instead, I would've inevitably ended up in Vietnam, which I wanted no part of. It wasn't that I was shirking my duty or wasn't patriotic; I just felt I'd already spent too much of my life fighting a war. Leading a charge up a proverbial hill was a metaphor for so much of my youth that the notion of doing it for real was just too much to bear. St. Peter's was definitely the saner, safer choice.

College offered yet another structured environment in my life and development, and one in which I thrived. I'd always been scholastically minded, and even took my share of taunts from the Mount kids for being "too smart." Back then, being selected to go to New York's St. Peter's Boys School on a scholarship from Mount Loretto allowed me to be "outside," to see the world beyond the Mount's shuttered walls. All I ever wanted to do was get my college education so I could join the FBI, and my years at St. Peter's offered me that and more. A passport to a better life and a chance to be able to change my family history.

Having spent the better part of my life living communally, at both the Mount and in the military, freedom had been limited and decisions were pretty much made for me. College provided me with the freedom I needed to grow and learn. I had far more real-life experiences than my college classmates and pals, but this didn't stop me from forming friendships that remain to this day. I also used the opportunity to get my fellow students engaged in projects to benefit the boys back at Mount Loretto. I went to college originally as little more than a precursor to joining the Bureau, but it became a wonderful experience on its own.

I never lost sight of the Mount and, in fact, worked full-time there through my college years. The classes I'd taken over in Germany enabled me to work as a social worker for the Catholic charities that administered Mount Loretto, a role that was sorely needed at the Mount and one I was prepared to embrace. Not only did that help me fund my studies in a small way, it also allowed me to give back to the place that had, for all intents and purposes, saved me and then raised me. I saw so many kids in those years who weren't much different from me. They had the same scowl, the same fear and hatred of life, and I endeavored to help each and every one of them in any way that I could.

The world of the Mount was full of unpredictable problems, sometimes fraught with aggression that could turn violent. You always had to watch your back, and I think part of why I lay awake those long nights listening to *This Is Your FBI* was that I was afraid to fall asleep. There were always enemies, varying by the day, week, or even hour. One of the reasons I joined the boxing team was for survival. Now I was back "home," no longer needing an outlet for survival and with a hopeful desire that the current Mounties wouldn't either.

I can remember Father Kenny sitting in on my sessions, smiling and nodding as he watched, and I couldn't help but recall his pronouncement that "You know *people*, Fitz." As a kid from the Mount myself, I understood the plight of these boys and could guide them through their problems from an experienced point of view. I figured Father Kenny still harbored hopes I'd join him in the priesthood and, perhaps, even return to the Mount on a full-time basis.

The formative college years, combined with full-time "social work" at the Mount, gave me a keen practical sense of fulfillment. I was able to advance from child-care counselor to child-care supervisor to full field social worker. I drew the worst cases involving the most troubled youth from Harlem, Spanish Harlem, Bedford Stuyvesant, the Bronx, and Corona, Queens. I worked some family cases where a child was killed, and others where children had to deal with the killing of a parent. I also worked gang-related cases, becoming an amicus curiae for the kids in State court.

My life had come full circle, with the wealth of my experiences being utilized in the very last way I'd ever imagined. There were so many nights when I'd lay awake fretting, hating this place and wishing I was anywhere else. Now I was back and determined to help other children shedding late-night tears just as I did. These years were crucial not only for the sense of fulfillment they provided me, but also for the "people experience" they allowed, something I am convinced to this day was paramount in my success in the Bureau. Later on I used to tell the good Father that you really get to know people when you live among twelve hundred children each day; that's a lot of different stories coming at you all at once.

I remember when my college days and my work at the Mount were coming to an end. Father Kenny had yet to give up his hope I would enter the priesthood and asked one last time what my plans were.

"Father, I'm going to join the FBI."

I thought he'd try to talk me out of it, make a case for all the good I had done and could continue to do. Instead he just smiled that warm, reassuring smile I knew so well. He'd aged badly over the years, wracked by a bad heart condition that he hid well, but the smile made him seem young again.

"Fitz," he said, "there's not a more honorable thing in this world you could do."

13
BOSTON, SPRING 1981

Listening to *This Is Your FBI* while growing up at the Mount, one thing was certain: The FBI always got their man, always did the right thing. That's the way my career had played out so far and I had no reason to believe Boston would prove to be any different. I had done my due diligence, interviewed Whitey Bulger himself, and came to the only conclusion I could draw: He should be closed as an informant there and then.

I filed my report with Special Agent in Charge Larry Sarhatt, recommending we close Bulger as an informant, and pretty much figured that would be the end of it since my mandate in coming to Boston was clear, and Sarhatt gave me no reason to believe anything to the contrary. In fact, my discussions with him right up until my fateful interview with Bulger more than confirmed this. He seemed to have one burning desire, which was to find out whether Bulger should remain an informant or not. And since Morris and Connolly's handling of him had become a mess for Sarhatt administratively, I believe to this day that he wanted Bulger off the books once and for all. I was the cover he needed to get that done, especially since the Boston office was about to undergo a vigorous inspection.

The Inspection Division sends agents on a regular basis to audit all offices for compliance and attention to rules and regulations. My memo advising that Bulger be closed as an informant would come under review and give Sarhatt just the ammunition he needed when he sat down with the inspectors to justify his position.

Before and after I'd filed my memo to close Bulger, this evaluation of the agents' priorities and prowess (or lack thereof) was echoed by others with no axe to grind at all. Dick Bates, a former SAC at Boston who used to be my boss in Washington, D.C., when I was a supervisor in the Criminal Division, was one of them. We met periodically for coffee after he called me upon my reporting to Boston, sometimes at a Dunkin Donuts in Dorchester not far from where informant John McIntyre's body would be found twenty years later. Bates was also a Deputy Assistant Director in Division 6, the Criminal Division at HQ when I was assigned to the Name Check section. We handled the most secret files in the Bureau, which were available to only selected agents. We had access to J. Edgar Hoover's most sensitive documents, which were needed to answer inquiries from foreign governments and super-sensitive intelligence agencies in the U.S. government and governments worldwide.

In effect, our liaison duties were extremely complex in view of the myriad of rules and regulations governing the release of this info. Hoover's documents were the most interesting since they shed light on the Director's thoughts and dealings with the internal workings of the FBI and other agencies.

Once, a memo from Hoover came across my desk in relation to an FBI investigation nationally. Hoover was responding to a field office about a particularly sensitive matter. The memo to Hoover had requested permission from HQ to conduct this investigation. The memo's writer had taken the entire page in his request and left no room for pagination or handwritten comments. Hoover squeezed into a space at the very bottom of the memo: "Watch the borders!" The file was replete with actions to be taken upon Hoover's instructions. So virtually every field office across the country was instructed to "watch the borders." Of course, no one knew exactly what they were "watching" for, but dutifully did so anyway, not daring to ask Hoover for an explanation.

Hoover, though, had simply meant that he had no place to put his remarks and pithily noted that the writer should watch the borders, or pagination, so he could remark uninhibited by such a lack of space. Hoover, either in person or on paper, was never disputed. No one ever asked him for an explanation nor would anyone dare to. Dick and I would recall these amusing moments and get a chuckle here and there, even with the ever-escalating situation I was facing during the first months in my new job.

When I first got together with Bates for coffee in Boston, he was fighting to quit smoking. We met at a diner where it was still permitted and Bates wore his displeasure in the lengthening of the spider veins that crisscrossed his cheeks. He'd always been a suit-and-tie guy, and the casual dress just didn't fit him well. His discomfort increased when he imparted to me that the Bureau office was "in a mess." While not directing criticism at Sarhatt, he did clue me in on the office rivalries and "turf" battles that had been brewing for a long time and now seemed on the verge of erupting into an all-out war. He cautioned me about certain agents "backdooring" decisions made in the field only to be countered by HQ later on. He found that the office had become "too political," especially with regard to the Organized Crime 3 Squad, now under the leadership of John Morris, John Connolly's supervisor.

Bates's opinion was that some of the decisions regarding sensitive investigations were discussed privately by agents with HQ instead of following the established chain of command. He found this particularly offensive and disconcerting. He spoke of "cabals" in the office and noted a situation involving one Organized Crime squad supervisor being too "close" with Strike Force head Jeremiah O'Sullivan, a U.S. attorney, and of ex-agents Dennis Condon's and Paul Rico's "closeness" with people outside the FBI.

He'd also heard all the rumors about Morris and Connolly and did not like them one bit. Like Colonel O'Donovan, Bates was old school, believing there was a right way and a wrong way to do things, a line never to be crossed. Yet by all indications, by the time I got to

Boston, that line had already been crossed. Bates became my go-to guy. He was tight-lipped and not given to rumor, focused instead on factual situations in which he explained the history of the hornet's nest I had walked into in Boston. I called him Merlin for his wizard-like proclamations about incidents and his knowledge of the territory and turf battles by agents and others. Dick expected anonymity and he got it. This is the first time I've ever mentioned his name in any writings, filings, or discussions stemming from my years in Boston.

We chatted about the Massachusetts State Police complaints. While there were some FBI agents Bates did not trust, he did not entirely trust the MSP either. Bates was a very loyal spokesperson for the Bureau and would never embarrass it. He defended the informant program as a necessary evil, yet had reservations about certain informants and the agents handling them. He cited Condon and Rico as being "too big for their britches" when they ignored FBI rules and regulations in their handling of Top Echelon informants like Joseph Barboza. He thought Connolly was "brassy" and too "immature" for his position. Morris he described as "bright" but "fawning," meaning he could be influenced by others and was too dependent on Condon as a mentor.

He warned about the politics, especially the Strike Force under the leadership of Jerry O'Sullivan. He saw O'Sullivan as a "climber" who was extremely ambitious and obsessive over his war on the mafia. And Bates brought me up to date on the infamous Race Fix case of 1979 that had taken down a number of muffs while letting Whitey Bulger and Stephen Flemmi off scot-free. To Bates this was all the proof he needed that O'Sullivan, as head of the Strike Force, knew they were FBI informants, another sharp deviation from established protocol. An unethical, if not illegal, breech of policy that O'Sullivan himself would later admit to.

Bates was further of the school that the FBI should plan investigations and present facts to the U.S. Attorney's Office for a prosecutorial opinion. It's here that he saw the politicking of O'Sullivan around the La Cosa Nostra investigations, and the handling of informants like Bulger and Flemmi, as having twisted everything around. The internecine struggle for power, especially in the Organized Crime area, had regrettably become a prime component in the fight against LCN that clouded the issue and made it increasingly difficult to tell the good guys from the bad guys.

Still, the handling of Bulger and Flemmi remained an anomaly in Bates's mind and mine, too. We had reliable informants that provided the key evidence to support affidavits by agents required for Title III applications for wiretaps against LCN. Boston agent Jim Knotts's informants, for example, furnished great info and that became a sore point with Connolly. There was no room for two in Connolly's ego-driven vision of the limelight, and Knotts evolved into a spoiler for him by providing truthful evidentiary info that revealed LCN activities in Boston and throughout New England. Knotts got that done without pandering to the likes of Bulger and Flemmi, much less facilitating their criminal activities. With him there was never a doubt as to who was controlling the situation—quite the opposite of Connolly.

Knotts also provided info about nontraditional organized crime like the Winter Hill Gang out of Somerville, now run by Bulger. These were the Irish guys commonly referred to as the "Irish Mafia." By the time I reached Boston, they had about three hundred gang members reporting directly to Bulger and Flemmi. By contrast, there were about seventeen confirmed LCN members with about one hundred and thirty associates. Add to that the fact that plenty in law enforcement, especially Colonel O'Donovan's State Police, rightfully viewed Irish gangs as more violent than their Italian counterparts, and you had the recipe for continued and expanded strife between the various law enforcement bodies.

One of the Strike Force prosecutors confided to me one day that there was suspicion around the 209 submissions Connolly was making. These were the forms filed by handlers detailing the intelligence provided by their informants, composing a critical part of the investigative, evidentiary, and prosecutorial processes. This same prosecutor was assigned to the Organized Crime squad to guide the agents in the legal application of affidavits and provide general legal counsel around probable cause issues and similar legal issues. The prosecutor was aware, unofficially anyway, that Connolly was running Bulger and Flemmi, and I detected a certain amount of trepidation in the chats focusing on them. This prosecutor also felt that O'Sullivan, the chief of the Strike Force, was a major concern. All this left him to conclude that the probable cause furnished by Connolly in his 209s was not accurate, that it was at best in doubt and at worst fabricated to justify him keeping Bulger open as an informant to serve his own career-based needs.

O'Sullivan was also seen as being too close to the Bulger and Flemmi crew, especially since he had been the recipient of their info for an inordinately long period of time as such things go. The prosecutor felt that O'Sullivan was far from "impartial" and, in fact, may have come to hate the "Italians" in the same way that the Irish mob hated them, forming a twisted alliance that was a prime recipe for the corruption I'd been sent to clean up. The last thing Boston wanted or needed was what this prosecutor described to me as a "racial" war, but by all indications that's where all this was heading.

Not long after my arrival in Boston, Agent Knotts came to see me in my office so anxious and upset he couldn't sit down.

"You're not going to believe this, Fitz."

"Try me."

"I think John Connolly's stealing my 209 files. He's giving Bulger credit for info actually being provided by my TEs."

I leaned forward in my chair. "You tell this to Sarhatt?"

"Yup, and nothing happened, so now I'm telling you."

Sarhatt hadn't acted on Knotts's suspicions clearly to prevent the closing of Bulger and Flemmi. His hands, I'd later learn, were tied by higher-ups in Washington who were buying Bulger's act hook, line, and sinker. I do not think for one minute that Sarhatt was party to the corruption already running rampant in Boston when I arrived; he was, instead, the victim of circumstances that had spiraled out of his and everyone else's control. Still, assimilating Knotts's claims left me in a quandary. I couldn't tell anyone since I received them in the strictest confidence. And yet his report convinced me still more that the problems in Boston ran much deeper than I'd been led to expect.

In spite of the inspection by HQ and special meetings at Quantico, the squabbles between the FBI and the Massachusetts State Police continued. MSP's Colonel O'Donovan made it plain that he disliked Connolly and Morris for their actions at Lancaster Garage. Inside the FBI, Connolly and Morris took the stance that O'Donovan was a "good guy" but misguided in this area and well past his prime. They went to the Strike Force and enlisted O'Sullivan's support to back up their contention that Bulger and Flemmi were solid informants crucial to the takedown of LCN in Boston. Not surprisingly, O'Sullivan agreed.

Another bomb was tossed when Agent Jim Knotts reported Bulger again, this time for drug running and exacting "tribute" from other gangsters to allow drugs in Boston. Connolly's mantra was always that Bulger did not work the drug trade, and that he was obsessively devoted to keeping them out of his native Southie. Yet another fabrication, as it turned out. It was Knotts's info that first divulged the relationship between Bulger and the drug cartel leadership diametrically opposed to Connolly's insistence that Whitey was clean in this regard. Knotts also named others, including Sal Caruana, the drug distributor who once supposedly had an affair with the wife of Richie Castucci, for their association with a "friendly" Strike Force attorney named Dave Twomey.

An investiation conducted by agents Matt Cronin and Jim Crawford, in fact, revealed that Twomey was a snitch for the cartels. Cronin and Crawford went to O'Sullivan who dismissed their findings by claiming their informant lacked credibility. So Twomey was allowed to remain with the Strike Force even though agents on my squad were convinced he was leaking. When Morris and Connolly learned Knotts had evidence of this unholy alliance, in the form of a body recording made in a North End mob restaurant, they warned Bulger off, even as Twomey did the same for the cartels. I personally warned O'Sullivan that he had a leak, but he disparaged the info by again claiming the informant was a known "drunk" and thus unreliable. His strategy became one of disregarding and discrediting Knotts, as well as Cronin and Crawford, instead of acting on the intelligence they provided. Anything to protect his cherished infor-

mants, Bulger and Flemmi, who in reality were giving him no ac-
tionable intelligence at all.

And it would get worse.

Connolly kept his daily liaison with his mentor, former agent
Dennis Condon, then with the Department of Public Safety, and
became a constant conduit of information that would subsequently
be funneled to others. Connolly would learn of O'Donovan's strategy from Condon while Condon would become aware of the FBI
tactics in stopping the MSP wiretaps. It was Condon who primed
Connolly to take over Bulger as an informant, and now the vicious
circle was closing with me caught squarely in the middle.

I found myself part of a culture of corruption that had enveloped
not only the Boston office of the FBI, but seemingly all of those
whose mission was to prevent the very thing they had become party
to. I became convinced U.S. Attorney Jeremiah O'Sullivan played a
central role by his power of prosecution and protection of Bulger
through immunity. Billy Bulger, Whitey's politico brother who'd
made his intentions plain enough to me, was a beneficiary as well.
After all, the FBI's protection of Whitey would keep him from ever
embarrassing his brother, while continuing to let Billy's adversaries
think Whitey could "hurt" them if they bothered him. Whitey and
Stevie Flemmi used their referred power to build an enterprise that
competed against the LCN enterprise currently under intense investigation by the FBI.

On that subject, the House Government Reform Committee, in
their report entitled "Everything Secret Degenerates: The FBI's Use
of Murderers as Informants," issued in 2003, chastised the Bureau
for adopting an "ends justifes the means" approach. The report concluded that "No one disputes the proposition that destroying organized crime in the United States was an important law enforcement
objective. However, the steps that were taken may have been more
injurious than the results obtained."

But the FBI rationalized that the number one priority was to
destroy the mafia, and if the Irish guys could help so much the better, even if they were just as bad, if not worse. The MSP and DEA
became more and more frustrated as they lost battle after battle to

develop their own informants to counter Bulger's and Flemmi's erroneous and worthless intelligence. It couldn't have gone any other way, since they were playing by the rules and everyone else wasn't.

"The FBI," Stephen Flemmi would admit years later in his plea bargain deal, "made Mr. Bulger and I aware of a number of drug investigations."

Inside the Strike Force another power play was in motion. The cartel druggers were co-opting O'Sullivan's office at the same time Bulger was co-opting the FBI. Twomey continued his leaking and informants reported the possibility of another former member of the Strike Force, a lawyer named Martin Boudreau who represented many of the druggers he once put away, being involved in the leaks that penetrated virtually every major case being investigated by the FBI and possibly DEA. Some agents, myself included, had come to believe O'Sullivan was trying to deflect evidence presented to him by FBI agents, especially in Bulger and Flemmi's case, and blocked info from agents that would have exposed attorney leaks from his office.

Incredibly, it seemed to me that O'Sullivan would defame the same FBI reports he made sure were leaked to drug cartel attorneys containing top-secret prosecutorial info. The end result: the drug cartel was able to flourish and inundate Southie with dangerous drugs that ruined the lives of teens and young adults on the very streets where Bulger and Flemmi had grown up.

Bulger's hypocritical claim of staying out of the drug trade was undermined as he sought tribute from the drug lords and provided them protection from law enforcement and prosecution. The inside information he obtained from the FBI made him the most powerful gangster in Boston's history. Without John Connolly, John Morris, Jeremiah O'Sullivan, and all his other enablers, he would've been just another Irish thug from South Boston, always one bust away from prison.

O'Sullivan had allowed Bulger and Flemmi to escape prosecution in the Race Fix case involving sports bribery and game fixing, the first, I believe, in a long string of cover-ups the then U.S. attorney had a hand in. Years later, in 2002 while testifying before the

Government Reform Committee, O'Sullivan pretty much admitted to this and more. The following exchange with Connecticut Representative Chris Shays, with regards to the Race Fix case in 1979, was typical.

"I said did anyone from the FBI ask you not to indict Bulger and Flemmi. I thought you said no and now you are saying yes?"

"In my opening statement," O'Sullivan answered, "I said that when I made up my mind not to indict them, that Morris and Connolly came over after the fact and asked me not to indict them."

"So when I asked you the question did anyone from the FBI ask you not to indict them, you said no to me. Really what you should have said is yes, but—"

"That's correct, Congressman."

"Did anyone from the Justice Department tell you not to indict them?"

"No, Congressman. Absolutely not."

"Did anyone from the state police at anytime ask you—"

"Absolutely not," O'Sullivan interrupted.

"So the only people, according to your testimony, that asked you not to indict, are the FBI."

"Yes," O'Sullivan admitted.

"Now," Shays continued, "did you respond with some degree of . . . somewhat incredulously like, 'What do you mean these are FBI informants? They are known murderers?'"

"No, I did not, Congressman."

"Why not?"

"I assume that when you have informants at that level they are involved in crimes."

"Let me understand something. If you are an informant and giving testimony against someone else, are you allowed to be killing people?"

O'Sullivan, of course, never really answered the question, and later, when confronted with a memorandum refuting his recollection of the events, all he could say was "You got me." And he said it with a wry but fearful smirk, the same smirk I recalled when I warned him there was a leak in his office.

Later, the committee's final report would state, among other scathing findings, that the FBI's relationship with Bulger and company "must be considered one of the greatest failures in the history of federal law enforcement."

14
BOSTON, SPRING 1981

Prior to reporting to Boston in late 1980, I had several assignments that proved prescient when it came to what I'd be facing in Boston. Most notable among these was one detailing gangsters who were frequenting the Miami Jai Alai fronton, gangsters directly connected to Whitey Bulger. Although I was vaguely aware that former agent Paul Rico had been hired as head of security down there, I didn't think much of it at the time, and the whole incident might have passed from my memory if not for the murder of Roger Wheeler, the new owner of World Jai Alai, at a country club in Tulsa, Oklahoma, in 1981.

As both *The Brothers Bulger* and *Black Mass* have expertly reported, John Callahan, a glorified Jai Alai accountant who washed money for Bulger's Winter Hill Gang, informed Whitey that Wheeler had gotten wise to the fact that more than a million dollars a year was being skimmed off the top of his Miami fronton's take. This represented clean profits for Bulger based on a strong-arm agreement he had with Wheeler's predecessors, an agreement that Wheeler clearly had no intention of honoring. He'd already grudgingly agreed to a partner he didn't need in the Bulger-backed jai alai rep Richard Donovan, and to a head of security he didn't want in Paul Rico.

Wheeler's response to the Winter Hill Gang's pressure was to commission an internal audit almost sure to reveal the cagey Callahan's complicity in the skim, perhaps incriminating Bulger and Flemmi as well and possibly revealing Rico to be a facilitator for the whole enterprise. Wheeler was a very good businessman, not easily intimidated and comfortable in a world where numbers could be as effective a weapon as bullets. But Wheeler also believed that living across the country in the middle of nowhere offered a degree of insulation from the murderous gangsters he was confronting back East.

He was wrong.

Accepting counsel from Callahan, Bulger and Flemmi decided to cut out the middleman; they'd take over World Jai Alai altogether by whacking Wheeler. And they had an ally firmly in place to help them in the form of Paul Rico, the agent who, along with Dennis Condon, had blazed a trail to glory in the Boston office and had been Whitey's guy at the Miami fronton all along. Apparently sitting in the sun while collecting a pension and hefty salary to boot wasn't enough for him. Rico saw an opportunity for advancement by helping the gangster muscle Wheeler out of the action once and for all by supplying whatever intelligence Whitey demanded. Of course, muscling Wheeler out could mean only one thing in Whitey's world, and the question became would he risk his empire on the pretext of expanding it?

The answer was a resounding yes, especially since Bulger was convinced Connolly and the FBI could protect him as easily for a murder he was behind in Oklahoma as they'd been protecting him in Boston. In fact, there is some evidence to suggest that Connolly had uncovered some shady business dealings in Wheeler's past and passed them on to Bulger. It wasn't much, but it may have been enough to point the finger at several other possible suspects who made more sense than trying to pin the rap on gangsters out of Boston, which seemed like a world away. I had come to know that a Connolly MO (modus operandi) was to blame everything on the other guys. Admit nothing, deny everything, and make counter accusations.

John Callahan thought Brian Halloran, a Winter Hill Gang member, would be perfect to send to Tulsa to do the deed. But Whitey didn't like or trust Halloran and had grown tired of his ever-growing cocaine habit. He suggested John Martorano for the job instead. Martorano was his most trusted button man, his "go-to guy," implicated at that point in no less than eighteen murders on Whitey's orders. But Martorano was no psychopath and was actually more a partner than simple button man or thuggish enforcer. To him, it was all about business. When someone needed to go, they needed to go. Still, Martorano's reputation and prowess made for a great counterbalance against any of Bulger's gangster foes, even considering doing him harm out of fear of what Martorano would do to them if they failed or, even, succeeded. For those familiar with *The Godfather*, book and movie, Martorano to a great extent was for Whitey what Luca Brasi was for Vito Corleone. The difference being in Martorano's classy case his gun was concealed by Armani, Brioni, or Zegna. I heard somewhere that Martin Scorcese has snapped up his life story for a million dollars, and I can see why.

In May 1981, Wheeler was leaving the prestigious Southern Hills Country Club in Tulsa when a man wearing a fake beard closed in from behind. He followed Wheeler to his car, and when the businessman took a seat behind the wheel, the stranger raised a paper bag and a single shot rang out. Witnesses at the club's swimming pool, including a police officer, were startled to see the stranger calmly walk across the parking lot and slide into a car that drove him away.

John Martorano had once again come through for Whitey Bulger, the slaying taking place at a country club where he could just as easily have been confused as a member. All that was missing was a fish wrapped in newspaper to signify Wheeler's ultimate fate.

True to Connolly's assertion that nobody would look eastward for the killer and motive, Wheeler's murder might have gone unsolved if not for a few Oklahoma informants who dimed "Boston gangsters" for the hit. Tulsa authorities, led by a dedicated, no-bullshit homicide detective named Michael Huff, contacted our Boston office and was referred to me. Remembering my earlier fleeting experiences with

Boston gangsters seen frequenting Miami Jai Alai during ABSCAM, the pieces of the puzzle were suddenly all on the table. It would take months to put them all together, but I was convinced of Bulger's complicity in Wheeler's murder, giving me what I needed to close Whitey once and for all and put an end to the leaks.

SAC Sarhatt clearly hadn't acted on my earlier recommendations, acting instead on Morris's countermemo suggesting that Bulger be allowed to remain open "until such time that incontrovertible proof of his participation in a criminal act became clear." To change things, I would need to prove that Whitey was indeed involved in the murder of Roger Wheeler. So I set my other squads to work on the Tulsa-based murder case.

But I had other problems to contend with as well. Even as I began assembling the facts of the Winter Hill Gang's part in the Wheeler killing, the two men directly responsible for my assignment to Boston moved on. Assistant Director Roy McKinnon, who'd told me to "kick ass and take names," retired due to health issues. And Tom Kelly, who championed me after supervising my work in ABSCAM, was promoted to SAC of the FBI office in Dallas. Kelly had pushed for me to clean up the mess in Boston after I'd done similar work in Miami.

While their HQ replacements were certainly briefed on the particulars of my assignment, they could in no way understand the depths to which the Boston office had fallen. Worse, they were Organized Crime guys who lived by the mantra of "get the mafia at all costs." It was much simpler to tacitly accept the words of agents there over those of locals like Colonel John O'Donovan of the Massachusetts State Police, especially when Strike Force attorney Jeremiah O'Sullivan backed up everything those agents said. And Larry Sarhatt acquiesced, because to do otherwise would be to cast aspersions on his own office and leadership. He wasn't about to throw himself under the bus, which meant leaving me squarely in front of it. Of course, Roger Wheeler never would've been murdered in the first place had my original memo recommending that Bulger be closed as an informant been acted upon.

I could read the writing on the wall, but I had been sent to Boston to do a job and I still had every intention of doing it. My meeting with Billy Bulger had made things squarely personal. Going it alone was nothing new for me. I'd gotten used to it in my youth at Mount Loretto as well as in my time as an FBI agent and supervisor, the feeling personified in this case by the fact that my family had not accompanied me to Boston and my marriage had crumbled, leaving me estranged from my two boys. My apartment was small and dark, inconsequential since I never expected to be there for as long as I was.

Being alone brought back more painful memories from my days at the Mount, the most painful of all. My mother visited me there several times, but never for long enough to renew the bond that had been severed. I eventually dealt with my fear and anxiety by turning off any feelings of attachment and longing. I became the classic "stone child" of literature and profile typing. I surrendered to detachment in what could be called passive-aggressive emotions, and I began the task of coping and persevering for myself and for my mother. I now recognize that her reluctance to visit me at the home was because of her own pain and shame, and the knowledge that she was dying. In fear of exposing any weakness, I internalized every painful emotion, but since no one heard me crying out it became my own personal grief. It was the same with all the other children at the Mount. We shared the same misery, the same deep and dark despair, but on the surface we shared only the same regimented routine.

The church was the heart and soul of Mount Loretto. The sprawling cathedral had Gothic architecture, flying buttresses, stained-glass windows exotically reflecting scenes of saints and sinners. There was a huge altar and in the rear a choir loft for singing Latin hymns and reciting ancient prayers. The elegantly carved hardwood pews were darkly stained to match the medieval church décor and blended with the community of Mount people: priests, nuns, brothers, and over seven hundred homeless boys. At Sunday mass or at a holy day feast celebration in this elegiac theater I would sing in the choir as well as serve as acolyte and altar boy.

One night I couldn't sleep, haunted by a premonition of death—not mine, my mother's. In the dream, I couldn't do anything about it or call for help because I was alone in my dormitory bed. My mother appeared to me smiling sweetly, assuring me that no matter what happened, she'd always be at my side. She told me many things and we talked the better part of the seemingly sleepless night. When she rose from my bedside, I pleaded with her, *"Don't leave me, never leave me!"* and she shushed me to sleep. Then, all of a sudden, she was gone despite my fearful pleas.

During mass on the next Sunday, restless and uneasy, I sat in the Gothic church and vaguely heard the priest's words, "We now pray for the repose of the soul of Alice, wife of John," who had died that Sunday morning. Blood rushed to my face and the familiar flutter of loneliness and abandonment returned to my stomach in an instant of panic and denial. It couldn't be *my mother* Alice; hadn't she promised she'd never leave me? Wasn't my eventual return to her what had kept me going through the years?

It was with those numbing words, spoken by a priest during a Sunday-morning mass, that I learned of the death of my mother. I left the church, light-headed and on unsteady legs, with the unmistakable feeling of everyone's eyes upon me. There were expressions of pity and sorrow, but there was no love, no reassurance, and now, no hope of a return to my mother.

The reality of my mother being gone forever overwhelmed me and deadened my senses. I resisted anyone touching me or getting close. Just a firmer reiteration of the "no-hug" policy. I wanted to escape, but to where? The nuns saw a hurt child, with all the agony and pain, and no doubt wanted to help. I wouldn't let them. Soon, I began to embrace the heartbreak and the longing because feeling something was better than feeling nothing, even if it meant torturing myself. My recollection of the funeral and its immediate aftermath remains vague. My oldest brother Larry had already left the Mount for the Marine Corps. I was allowed to spend time with my other brother Gerard and sister Diane, but it did little to ease the numbing pain that consumed me.

I found solace in hating my mother and then hating God, and became immune to the special conciliatory expressions of kindness by the nuns and priests. I was an altar boy, a choirboy, an honor student, but what good had that been in the eyes of God? He hadn't just stolen my mother, he had stolen my hope and my dreams. The message at the Mount was that suffering makes you strong so that when you fall you always get up, often to suffer all over again.

When I instructed at law enforcement classes across the nation, I met an untold number of police officers who were divorced. I passed it off to the overwhelming stress they were under and the long anxious hours they worked, all the time taking comfort in the fact that it would never happen to me. My wife understood me and my passions; that was the man with whom she fell in love, after all. Then I got a phone call and it was over. Just like that. She decided not to join me in Boston. An annulment followed, then divorce.

Had I lost sight of my personal life, the fact that I was a father and a husband? In retrospect, I suppose I had.

But the FBI was my home too, as it had been, I guess, since I fell in love with the Bureau listening to those old radio shows drifting down the hall from Sister Mary Assumpta's room. And I wasn't about to let anything change that now.

15

BOSTON, 1982

I knew Brian Halloran was the weakest and most easily exploited link to Bulger. His drug habit was pretty well known by that time, and he'd confided to more than one lower-level associate that he was being phased out of the Winter Hill Gang and was afraid of what Whitey might do to him. How much this had to do with Whitey's not using him for the Wheeler hit was moot. The seeds of their detachment had been bred of the cocaine Halloran shoved up his nose. That fact rendered him unreliable and no longer fit for Bulger's inner circle.

But it made Halloran very fit to pursue for what I was after: incontrovertible evidence of Whitey's complicity in the gunning down of Roger Wheeler. Bulger may not have pulled the trigger, but I knew that he effectively put the gun in the shooter's hand. We suspected Martorano had been involved and were convinced we'd never be able to turn him. But Brian Halloran was another case altogether because he feared for his life.

By early 1982, more and more circumstantial evidence continued to surface in Tulsa linking the Winter Hill Gang to Roger Wheeler's murder. By then I had already assigned two agents on my nontraditional Organized Crime squad to test the waters with Halloran. The nontraditional label didn't mean they could break any rules, but it did allow them to circumvent some procedures in "turning" an informant, such as not filling out reports. No paper trail, in other words, nothing for John Connolly to get his hands on this time.

Halloran began to talk; slowly at first, knowing he had to make himself valuable enough to us so we'd protect him and ultimately offer him a chance in the Witness Protection Program. I assigned two more agents to handle Halloran in what was now a full-fledged informant "fight" against Bulger and Flemmi, using daily intelligence reports and contacts with Halloran to get info about the Wheeler murder in Tulsa. The investigation was conducted in secret, under the office radar, because of the kind of leaks that had already cost informants like Richie Castucci their lives.

At the same time, my job was to stay in secret contact with HQ in Washington in an attempt to finally put a stop to the myriad leaks that had riddled criminal investigations in Boston for too long. In essence, I had gone undercover in my own office, taking on a Serpico-like role in Boston, which was something unprecedented. But then nothing in the Boston office seemed to have any historical precedent. More accurately, the tradition here seemed to be about rewriting local FBI history instead.

To further my efforts, I requested a secret wire and authored documents to FBIHQ spelling out the purpose and the expected results it would bear. I wanted Halloran to wear the wire against Callahan and others to verify the informant information and corroborate the specific allegations implicating Callahan's collusion with Bulger and Flemmi in the Jai Alai's business dealings in Florida. There was also a chance I could get incriminating evidence on tape about the Wheeler murder. This was complex, confusing stuff, and I would need every bit of intelligence at my disposal to convince HQ powers-that-be of just how deep the problems were as I went about this by the book.

I was also working to develop Callahan as an informant, trying to get him to wear a wire as well in an effort to bolster Halloran's anticipated testimony later on. If I could accomplish this, I'd be able to place Halloran and Callahan in a conspiracy with Bulger and Flemmi involving a massive racketeering-influenced corruption matter. We'd be working a full-blown RICO case instead of just a murder rap.

Since Morris at the time was in charge of the Organized Crime 3 Squad responsible for going after La Cosa Nostra, and this remained in large part an LCN matter, I had no choice but to use his resources for surveillance support. His Organized Crime agents knew the territory and the players, and I had no reason to believe that Morris would go to the extremes he ultimately did to protect Whitey Bulger. Still, Morris would be used only to cover my meets with Halloran and Callahan, which were fraught with danger because of what Bulger would do to them if he found out they were talking.

Also unpredictable was how Morris would react. From my initial entry into the Boston quagmire, I had viewed Morris and John Connolly as an unholy alliance and had viewed the manipulative Connolly as capable of twisting Morris around his finger. I questioned whether it was worth it to inform and involve him at all, but much of the FBI's long-tenured success could be attributed to its militarylike, hierarchal chain of command. Playing things by the book meant never going over another head or trying to pull an end run. Just because Connolly had made a career out of this didn't mean I was going to. There was no way I was going to become the kind of agent I hated most to get the goods on Bulger. I would do my job the way it was supposed to be done, and even though I was officially undercover at this point, that meant bringing Morris's squad into the case I was building against Bulger and Flemmi. Following procedure, I kept HQ at Washington in the loop explaining my strategy in confidential teletypes and other communiqués.

Morris knew what my overall mission was but not my undercover mission, namely to nail Bulger and Flemmi and other conspirators in what amounted to a RICO sting similar to the one I ran in Miami with ABSCAM. The sting, using Halloran and hopefully Callahan eventually, would be to get Bulger to admit to sending Martorano to Tulsa to kill Roger Wheeler. Morris was well aware of what I had accomplished in Miami, and things had already progressed too far for him to stand in my way in Boston when it came to this case.

ABSCAM had started as a huge effort to expose scams and corruption in Florida and beyond, but quickly morphed into something even greater as more and more politicos were implicated. The investigation culminated in the arrest of Senator Harrison Williams, who was receiving money for furnishing identity cards to foreign illegals to evade Immigration and Naturalization laws.

The difference, of course, was that Bulger had something the senator did not: corrupt FBI agents willing and able to inform him of the FBI's intentions and plans. I chatted with Morris and he agreed that his squad would lend support for logistical and surveillance purposes. As his boss, I instructed him to keep things close to the vest and made it plain that Connolly should be kept out of the loop altogether. I stressed that careers, his included, were at stake here, since at that point I could see no way the higher-ups in the Bureau would hesitate to back me up now that we had an opportunity to bring down a massive criminal enterprise.

Colonel O'Donovan of the Massachusetts State Police wasn't so sure. To him this was the Lancaster Garage all over again and it was only a matter of time before it blew up in my face. But that never happened in the radio broadcasts of *This Is Your FBI.* And I was still idealistic enough to think that once squarely in my sights, even Whitey Bulger wouldn't be able to escape justice.

So I prepared to interview Halloran and Callahan on the sting angle. I tried to build a Chinese wall of silence and secrecy separating the agents involved in my undercover operation from those handling Bulger and Flemmi as informants, a tricky situation to say the least. Sure, Morris was a pal of Connolly's, but he was also his supervisor along with at least eighteen other agents assigned to various Organized Crime duties. In effect, Morris oversaw Connolly's handling of Bulger and Flemmi, but this case was actually about the murder of Wheeler in Tulsa and the graft uncovered at Miami Jai Alai. Morris would have to straddle a very fine line and it was hard to imagine him risking his career to back Bulger, and thus Connolly.

I actually believe both Morris and Connolly were deathly afraid of Bulger and what he would do if they threw him to the proverbial wolves. He'd already had people killed with the FBI supposedly watching; imagine what would happen if he had nothing to lose!

To make matters administratively worse, Strike Force chief Jeremiah O'Sullivan was still convinced that Bulger could give him what he wanted most: the Italian Angiulo mob in the RICO case *he* was trying to build totally separate from my squad's. Closing Bulger, pinning the Wheeler murder on him along with a separate RICO case, would eliminate Whitey as a cooperating informant and witness and threaten to undermine so much of the evidence O'Sullivan had accumulated. He'd have nothing to show for years of work.

The problem, of course, was that Bulger had really given O'Sullivan nothing of substance. Whitey was playing an elaborate shell game of information never delivered and promises never kept. But O'Sullivan was so single-mindedly focused on the FBI's obsessive mandate to nail the mafia at all costs that he couldn't see how little Bulger was actually providing. That fact put his interests diametrically opposed to mine, and promised to be difficult to reconcile.

What most people in later years found difficult to comprehend, as we did, was that Morris at the time of the Bulger sting was considered to be a highly reputable agent, a trusted supervisor, and a superior strategist in taking down LCN in Boston. There was little if any indication on our part that he was actually a turncoat who was already dirty, having gone along with John Connolly's tactics for so long that there was no going back. The mystery had always been the origin of the leaks of sensitive info in our cases that put our agents in harm's way and destroyed countless investigations. Who was warning Bulger and his crew about our operations? Who was warning Bulger about the other informants?

Labeling Morris as a snitch for the Irish gang at that point seemed preposterous, so I honestly believed our sting operation was safe from Connolly's corrupted clutches. And it better have been, since Morris was privy to all of the details of what Brian Halloran was telling us, as well as of our plan of how to make use of the information to turn John Callahan, too.

Complicating matters further was SAC Larry Sarhatt's increasing withdrawal from a leadership role as his retirement loomed. He acted like a soldier in a war zone with his tour coming to an end, afraid of doing anything that might upset the brass at HQ and throw an administrative monkey wrench into the works. Besides, he'd already taken his stand by accepting Morris and Connolly's memo countering mine, which had recommended that Bulger be closed as an informant. How could he fully support my efforts now?

I should have suspected that whatever was going on reached much deeper. This wasn't, and never had been, about a single agent handling a single Top Echelon informant, even if that informant was Whitey Bulger. Competing agendas were in play, the common denominator between them being everyone involved wanted to take down the Boston mafia using whatever means necessary. I also underestimated the culture of corruption that had become so pervasive during the Rico-Condon era that it was now pretty much business as usual.

The point is that agents like Connolly and supervisors like Morris had no fear that Sarhatt would intervene against them, and that left me as the only thing standing in their way. Still, Morris disclosing my intentions to Bulger, either through Connolly or not, could make him an accessory to murder since there was no doubt Whitey would kill anyone ready to dime him. At this point Bulger rightfully believed that he had the FBI, as well as O'Sullivan's Strike Force, in his pocket. My next move was to relay to HQ that I was worried about additional leaks cropping up that could destroy my planned sting operation and put the life of my snitch, Brian Halloran (along with John Callahan in the not-too-distant future), in jeopardy.

I recall expediting my secrecy coverage and cloaking all info by instituting a secure communications system to cap all leaks. The top echelon HQ people—including Sean McWeeney all the way up to the Bureau's number two man John Otto and the assistant to the director, Oliver Revel—I was dealing with were aware that all info was secret, that no one from Boston should see any of the reports. I was filing coded TELEX reports directly with them and communicating with FBIHQ TEs in person. This was for my protection, since

I faced the very real possibility that I could just as easily become the target of the bad guys I was after, both inside and outside of the Bureau.

What I did not know, *could* not know, was that something even more insidious was taking place in this shadow world I had entered. Powerful forces in the federal Organized Crime squad at HQ under McWeeney, concerned that the entire basis for their high-profile case against the Angiulo mob was about to go up in smoke, "back-doored" some of the secret info I was relaying to them in my under-cover status *back to Morris and Connolly*! The Chinese wall I'd constructed came crashing down as, among others, a major vending machine operation we'd launched against forces of Whitey's Winter Hill Gang crashed and burned thanks, I'd later learn, to John Morris. I cannot say that McWeeney himself was responsible for the flow of information back to Boston. Nor do I believe McWeeney, Otto, Revel or anyone else at HQ was actually party to the ongoing corruption in Boston; instead they were enablers, complicit in their unwitting facilitation of that corruption.

So all the precautions I had taken to keep the information safe from the foxes guarding the henhouse turned out to be for naught and quite threatening. Without Roy McKinnon and Tom Kelly to back me up in Washington, Whitey Bulger's crucial status as an in-formant rendered him untouchable as the subject of a criminal in-vestigation, lest the house of cards O'Sullivan and others had built got blown down. I started to wonder if my transfer to Boston, and its stated purpose, weren't so I would get Bulger, but to provide the illu-sion that the effort had been made. Provide cover, in other words, for those at HQ who were afraid of the blowback when and if things turned. It was the ultimate setup and seemed too paranoid and over-the-top to believe at the time.

In the end, though, it turned out to be true.

My first suspicion that things, incredibly, were turning in this di-rection came when former agent Paul Rico's name surfaced in a major way in our investigation. His being hired originally, and then retained by the doomed Roger Wheeler, at Miami Jai Alai had little to do with his solid credentials and résumé, and *everything* to do with Whitey wanting his guy inside the massive cash-generating operation. Rico was Flemmi's and Bulger's original handler in the sixties and seventies, and all the information we were getting indicated he had a pipeline to at least some of the agents involved in my investigation, though not necessarily part of my squad.

In my mind, it boiled down to a simple issue: Richie Castucci wasn't the first FBI informant to be killed by Whitey and he wouldn't be the last. Unless something was done and fast, Brian Halloran and John Callahan were going to become Bulger's next victims.

16

BOSTON, 1982

I thought it was imperative to get both Brian Halloran and John Callahan into the Witness Protection Program. Once they felt safe from Bulger's long, murderous reach, I felt confident they'd sing like canaries.

It should have been fairly straightforward, but it wasn't. HQ management trusted Morris and Connolly, and the Boston Strike Force under O'Sullivan needed their prize informants to remain credible. Otherwise O'Sullivan feared the weight of the entire case he was building against the Angiulo family would collapse in the resulting scandal. This was shaping up to be the biggest case in Boston organized crime history. But here's the kicker: If O'Sullivan was aware of Bulger's informant status, which he unquestionably was, it would be a grievous breach of security. This gangster, as head of a mob enterprise every bit as bad as Angiulo's, defined the very kind of target the FBI and any prosecutor would have wanted a chance at in federal court.

But O'Sullivan wasn't just any prosecutor. He'd already gone to bat for Bulger and Flemmi in the Race Fix case, letting them off prosecution on the advice of Connolly and Morris and promises of future intelligence Whitey would provide. And now he and the Organized Crime people at HQ were convinced, obsessed even, that Bulger was the only one who could give them Angiulo even though he'd given them nothing of value in all his years as an informant. It was all smoke and mirrors, a tragic con that HQ bought into in their obsession to bring down the Boston mob even if it meant letting a murderer go on killing. Just as Rico and Condon had let Joseph "the Animal" Barboza kill with impunity, framing innocent men for a murder he committed, it appeared that Connolly, Morris, and O'Sullivan were willing to do the same for Whitey Bulger.

My job, though, was to take Bulger down and now I finally had the means to do just that in the form of Halloran. Protecting Brian Halloran was going to be a major problem, though. He was bull-headed and glued himself to Callahan around the Irish bars of Boston. Yet the information he was giving us was priceless. He admitted, for example, that his buddy Callahan had been the one to propose the Wheeler murder to Whitey. He furnished info that Martorano wore a golf cap, sunglasses, and a fake beard in Oklahoma when he shot Wheeler between the eyes at Southern Hills Country Club— information that had never been revealed to the public. I needed to keep Halloran safe long enough to help me turn Callahan for corroboration and to testify before a grand jury, so I followed the proper channels in reaching out to O'Sullivan to get him into Witness Protection.

"I'll review the file," O'Sullivan said, so eager for me to leave his office he hadn't even shut the door or offered me a chair.

"We need to move fast."

"You have any idea how many requests like this I get?" he challenged.

"It's the first one you've gotten from me. This guy's giving us Martorano as the shooter on Bulger's direct instructions. Claims Martorano used Callahan's condo in Florida to hide out."

"You believe him?"

"I wouldn't be here if I didn't."

"I'll review the file," O'Sullivan repeated, reaching for his phone as a clear sign it was time for me to take my leave. "But I'm telling you right now Halloran's a known drunk and I don't trust drunks."

His body language, lack of surprise, and interest at what I was telling him left me no choice. Halloran's info was so sensitive that I walled it off from much of the Boston FBI office. This was the first time in my career that I actually couldn't trust the agents in my own office. I removed Halloran's informant files and cases from the squad bay and placed them in my office safe. I had become a "mole," funneling extremely sensitive information to HQ only to have supervisors in Washington funnel it back on the "Q.T." to Morris and Connolly. So, in ironic and ultimately tragic counterpoint, the prime beneficiary of my info was none other than Whitey Bulger.

I have never seen a major case handled with so much ineptitude. My reporting to O'Sullivan on the Wheeler murder for prosecutive action should have led him to set up a coordinated effort with Oklahoma prosecutors, while procedure dictated FBIHQ similarly coordinate the investigations of different FBI offices toward prosecution. O'Sullivan took no steps in this regard at all and ultimately decided against putting Brian Halloran in the Witness Protection Program, claiming I hadn't made a strong enough case.

The U.S. Attorney's Office had jurisdiction in such matters, so, livid, I went over O'Sullivan's head to Bill Weld, the U.S. attorney at the time and eventual governor of Massachusetts. I told Weld flat out that Halloran would be killed if we did not protect him. The Strike Force controlled the purse strings, so to speak, and we needed money to safeguard Halloran appropriately. Weld said he would look into it. The problem was O'Sullivan was saying and doing just enough to appear as if he wanted to prosecute Bulger and Flemmi, but claimed the evidence hadn't developed against them. He didn't think Halloran's claims held any validity and he argued that point to Weld.

"Fitzy said to me, 'You know people always say there's a danger for this snitch or that snitch,'" Weld conceded in court years later in his testimony during the Wolf hearings. "'They may be killed for cooperating. I'm telling you this guy [Halloran]—I would not want to be standing next to this guy.'"

Ultimately, Weld opted against overruling O'Sullivan's decision.

O'Sullivan, most likely at Morris and Connolly's request, was stalling—just long enough for Whitey to get to Halloran before I got what I needed from him: enough to get Callahan to squeal on his pals, too. Based on Halloran's assertions that John Connolly spoke to Bulger "all the time," I turned the focus of my investigation toward him. Proving that he was giving information to Bulger would allow me to kill two birds with one stone: nail Bulger and begin the process of rooting a myriad of corruption out of the Boston office. Because of a similar experience during my time in Miami, I had no compunction about investigating Connolly, a fellow agent, as the pipeline to the Irish wiseguys.

I recalled that shortly after my ABSCAM case wrapped up, Tom Kelly had reminded me about the story in Miami wherein Title III tapes were found that should've been in the Miami evidence room. These tapes were found in one of the supervisor's desk drawers, and when listened to proved to be explosive, since they indicated that the Miami police homicide detectives were being used as hit men against drug couriers in the Miami area.

Tom asked me to review the tapes and I did, becoming both alarmed and upset by the fact that drug cartels had infiltrated the Miami Police Department, and more critically the FBI. What was not known was that the drug cartel traffickers had infiltrated law enforcement in such a way that cops were not only killing people but were also selling drugs.

I learned through sources that one of the agents on my squad in Miami had an association with the cartel through a drug lord named Rodriguez. The source advised me that the agent had a six-figure balance at the local bank, the same bank where the drug lord kept most of his drug money.

When I started to nose around, the agent grew scared and confronted me.

"What the fuck you think you're doing? I'm clean. You think I'm on the take, you piece of shit?"

"If you're not, the investigation will prove it."

"I got the best fucking informants down here. You know what that means? It means you're shit in this office."

"Get back to your desk. Get back to work."

"I don't have to listen to you."

"Yeah, you do. Now get outta my office and back to what you're supposed to be doing."

"Go fuck yourself."

I got up in his face, hoping he'd take a swing at me, feeling like I was back in the boxing ring. "You wanna take your best shot, go ahead. Otherwise, get back to work."

The agent shrank back and stormed out of my office, rushing upstairs to tell his side of things to the Special Agent in Charge of the office.

I called Tom Kelly to alert him. I briefed him and succinctly related the information I had with regard to the Miami agent having possible involvement with the drug lord. Unbeknownst to Tom and me, the agent told a different story, whereupon the SAC sought our input in this matter. I briefed the SAC about the information I had and about the sensitivity involved, including the agent's possible association with the drug lord. The SAC simply told the ASAC to handle it and that if I had any problems I should return to him immediately. But I had a penchant for handling things on my own, man-to-man, face-to-face.

In retrospect, I should have heeded the advice of a seasoned agent about the consequences of high-profile cases and taking down powerful people.

"Watch out, Fitz," he warned me, "they will never let you forget this!"

Back in Boston, as if to make that agent a prophet, HQ personnel involved in the day-to-day handling interceded and in effect left Connolly to work Bulger, meaning it was business as usual even though a preponderance of evidence indicated it should be anything but. I was already following up an astounding number of leak cases when Agent Jim Knotts reported Connolly again for "robbing" sensitive informant information from his case files. I reported the matter in a memo to SAC Sarhatt who filed it without taking any action.

HQ listened to me, in effect, to keep me quiet, while Sarhatt and

O'Sullivan didn't listen to me at all. It didn't matter what I said or what evidentiary material I produced. The minds of all seemed already made up, and no one was about to spoil a potential takedown of the mafia.

Ultimately it was Brian Halloran who paid the heaviest price for this. His days might have been numbered, and the nights he spent in various safe houses might have been sleepless ones, but Brian Halloran had a lot to live for. His wife had just checked into Deaconess Hospital in Boston to give birth to the couple's second child. Just before dusk on May 11, 1982 Halloran was sitting in a Datsun with a friend, construction worker Michael Donahue, outside the Topside Lounge in Southie when a blue Chevy pulled alongside. Inside the car he spotted Whitey Bulger and another man wearing a mask.

According to testimony given years later by Bulger lieutenant Kevin Weeks, who claims he was serving as "lookout" at the time, Halloran got a look at Whitey and lurched from the car. He tried to flee as gunfire rang out, spraying the car and killing Donahue instantly. Halloran managed to get part way across the street before falling to a hail of bullets fired from a silenced Mac-10 submachine gun and Bulger's own .30 caliber carbine. A third shooter lunged from the backseat and rushed toward Halloran, firing several shots from a pistol into him from point blank range.

Seconds later, the Chevy screeched away from the scene as sirens wailed in the distance. When police arrived on the scene, they found Halloran's friend Michael Donahue dead (guilty of nothing more than being in the wrong place at the wrong time) and Halloran himself soon to be.

A Winter Hill Gang operative named Jimmy Flynn, also an FBI informant for John Connolly, was wrongly arrested for the murders. Whitey had framed him with the help of his police and Bureau sycophants. Flynn was finally tried and acquitted in 1986 and went on to appear in bit parts in films, including *Good Will Hunting*.

O'Sullivan's refusal to place Brian Halloran in Witness Protection, or even recognize him as an informant, had left my squad unable to offer Halloran the protection he desperately needed. He had been more willing to talk than ever, but the only thing we could promise him in return were bullets over Boston.

Actually, it turned out to be twelve.

John Connolly quickly went into cover-his-ass mode by filing a report claiming that Charlestown gangsters Halloran had long been at odds with, including Flynn, were responsible for his execution. I knew full well that Halloran was killed because Connolly had told Bulger he was talking, making him a direct accessory to murder, as the Wolf hearings revealed sixteen years later. But what about Jeremiah O'Sullivan, the Strike Force head, and Bill Weld, the then U.S. attorney? Hadn't they also failed to act on my recommendation to do everything possible to protect Brian Halloran?

They could try and mount a zero-sum game argument, Brian Halloran becoming a necessary sacrifice to assure the takedown of the Providence and Boston La Cosa Nostra families under Raymond Patriarca and Jerry Angiulo. I can't understand myself, much less explain, how the vision of so many became so warped and narrowed that they couldn't see the truth that was right before their eyes. In that respect, those far above John Connolly used him to do their dirty work, knowing full well what would happen if they didn't move to close Bulger as I repeatedly recommended. They had basically chosen Whitey, who was giving them nothing, over the preponderance of evidence I was giving them.

There was more. Instead of moving him closer to us, Halloran's murder pushed John Callahan away, at least temporarily. After all, we were relying on Halloran's testimony, naming him as an accessory to Roger Wheeler's murder, in an effort to make Callahan turn state's evidence. With Halloran out of the way, Callahan figured he'd gotten a reprieve. While he might have been on the numbers side of things, Callahan fancied himself a wiseguy and loved the lifestyle that had him entertaining the Winter Hill boys down for a time in his native Miami. Halloran's murder filled Callahan with a strange sense of vindication and freedom, as if he no longer had anything to fear in his world of punks, two-timers, stone killers, and muffs.

Meanwhile, Tulsa homicide detective Michael Huff, the lead investigator on the Wheeler murder, continued to work that killing. Huff was a methodical, by-the-book cop who followed the trail where it took him, which in this case was Connecticut (home of another fronton owned by World Jai Alai), Miami, and Boston. He found plenty of cooperation in Connecticut and Miami, but little in Boston since both Connolly and Morris and Strike Force head O'Sullivan stonewalled his efforts to dig deeper into the doings of the Winter Hill Gang at every turn. Huff tried me but in the wake of the Halloran killing, my squad was effectively disenfranchised from the work being done by Morris's Organized Crime squad and O'Sullivan's Strike Force.

In fact, our work was paralleling Huff's in the sense that we were trying to work Callahan into a formal suspect, thereby making it easier to turn him by offering him immunity from prosecution for his part in the Wheeler murder. The problem was that word got around the office that Detective Huff was nosing around Boston in search of his Tulsa killers. Since the Winter Hill Gang had already surfaced in his investigation, John Connolly would have been a natural for him to talk to. While I'm not sure they ever spoke, I'm reasonably sure Connolly let Bulger know, as he had done with Halloran, that the investigation was honing in on Callahan, who could pin Wheeler's murder on Whitey.

Again, the actions themselves were John Connolly's. But he must have figured he was doing the bidding of Jeremiah O'Sullivan, John Morris, and the Organized Crime staff at FBIHQ. Protect Bulger at all costs had become the code he lived by, but I doubt he conceived it alone. All of these people were in so deep at this point they must have felt the very real concern that Whitey could take them down at the same time. So their actions weren't just self-serving, they were also about self-protection. Imagine if I had been able to arrest Bulger for the Wheeler murder and he decided to turn on his former protectors by confessing how he had bamboozled them and used their auspices to fuel his own murderous rise through the Boston underworld.

Whitey may have been a psychopath, but he was far from stupid. He had found that the path to criminal power without fear of censure was paved with 209 informant forms and commendations to the agents beholden to him. As long as he appeared to be giving the FBI what it wanted, he could steal, extort, terrorize, and even murder without any fear of repercussions. And because the cadre that allowed this to be was in so deep with him, they had to let it continue in order to save their own asses.

Mike Huff and his associate detectives in Connecticut, meanwhile, kept at it, gradually accumulating evidence that would be enough to get an arrest warrant for John Callahan. They intended to fly down to Miami personally to serve it. Callahan must have gotten word of his pending arrest and quickly made overtures to Miami agents working with my squad to pick up the discussions that had been abruptly halted with Brian Halloran's murder. The problem was the Boston office must have picked up on that, too, likely from Huff and his Connecticut partners. As traditional cops with no real grasp of the depths to which the Boston office had sunk, they were strictly following protocol since their investigation involved another ongoing one.

Again the word came down from on high, in this case north in Boston, about what was soon to go down. In August 1982, Huff and his Connecticut counterparts headed to Miami. They landed and boarded a cab that drove right past a parking garage where John Callahan's body had been stuffed in the trunk of his Cadillac, shot in the back of the head. The twentieth victim of John Martorano.

This particular murder also profoundly affected me on a personal level, once my fiancée Jane witnessed the look on my face when I received the fateful call about Callahan's murder. As a nurse who worked reglarly in emergency situations, she'd seen more than her share of deaths from gunshot wounds and other forms of violence. Suddenly she began to obsess about my life and safety, anxious over what seemed like the very real possibility that I might be next on Bulger's hit list, and for good reason. Jane feared for our future, the family we had every intention of starting. She was my second chance at happiness, and the whole sordid mess in Boston was now jeopardizing that.

John Connolly, and the culture of corruption surrounding and protecting him, had struck again, this time much too close to home for comfort. Bulger was still free and still killing, the FBI now a willing and unambiguous accomplice in his rise to the pinnacle of the New England underworld.

PART THREE
BEYOND BULGER

"Fidelity, Bravery, Integrity."

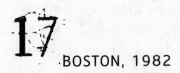

17
BOSTON, 1982

"I will support and defend the Constitution of the United States against all enemies, foreign and domestic; that I will bear true faith and allegiance to the same; that I take this obligation freely, without any mental reservation or purpose of evasion; and that I will well and faithfully discharge the duties of the office on which I am about to enter. So help me God."

I recited the FBI oath on a warm fall day at the age of twenty-five with the rest of my graduating class in the Old Post Office Building in 1965. It was a cavernous space and our voices echoed, reverberating in a din kind of like PA-speaker feedback. I remember hoping J. Edgar Hoover himself would be there, but he wasn't. I remember listening to similar words spoken during the introduction to those old radio shows. It should have been a happy moment, and I guess it was. But it was tinged by melancholy. Thoughts of my mother and memories of the Mount, how cold the concrete floor felt in winter. I don't know why I thought about that then, but I did.

But my melancholy swiftly vanished with my first posting in New Orleans in 1965. My supervisor, John Reynolds, commanded the #4 squad which was made up of about eighteen agents ranging from me, a shave-tailed twenty five year old, to Regis, a senior twenty plus veteran who was assigned to the JFK assassination case in New Orleans.

Reynolds used to yell across the glass partition, "Fitzpatrick, get your ass in here!"

Wry smiles flashed on the faces of my brother agents; we were all male agents back then in 1965, always a step away from a "whupping" by Reynolds, reputed to be the toughest supervisor in the FBI.

"I know you were a social worker in your other life," he said. Reynolds had thick bushy eyebrows and spoke in a voice permanently hoarse from cigarettes. He had a picture of his family framed on his desk but sometimes, when the discussion grew especially unpleasant, he'd turn the picture away so that his family wouldn't bear witness. "But, dammit, you're an agent now and these pabulum reports tell me you better get on the ball! You'll have to testify to this and the jury could care less about how you feel! Facts are facts and, dammit, from now on your reports will only contain facts. Do you read me, Fitzpatrick?"

The only thing I could mutter was, "Yes, sir."

"Then get the hell out of here!"

For all of the bluster, John Reynolds taught me how to write a report; an FBI report, one that would hold up in court under the best scrutiny. As a first office agent this was part of my indoctrination and probationary period. Hoover made sure all new agents went through such a probationary period, extending from training school to the first-year evaluation. Some agents were let go even before their first-year-evaluation rating, several more afterwards.

The fact that my initial reviews were positive led to my first bump up the ladder to an assignment as a lookout; specifically for two cop killers out of Oklahoma who had escaped from prison and were on the lam. The identification order claimed they liked to hang out around YMCAs, hitting the customers in violent smash-and-dash robberies. My assignment was to surveil a certain YMCA and watch for suspicious vehicles or persons.

Along about ten or eleven one night, lo and behold, two guys drove into the YMCA parking lot and took a position in a darkened corner diagonally across from me. After a few minutes, I sneaked up and grabbed the license plate number which, unbelievably, matched a car stolen by the Oklahoma escapees a few days earlier.

I crept toward the car and IDed two men in the front seat, apparently asleep and drunk. The driver had a gun in his left hand at the ready while the other guy's hand was hidden from sight. I staked out the car and called for backup. The case agent arrived and I briefed him on the facts at hand. A plan was drawn up to take the individuals down. The case agent, a hard-nosed FBI lifer named Ziggy, would make the arrest, while I covered him from the driver's side.

Being a brand new agent, I'm sure the seasoned agents were covering me, throwing me a bone as a gesture for alerting them to this potential grab. As Ziggy approached the car he wrapped on the window, startling both fugitives. When he yanked the passenger door open, the fugitive on that side made a sudden movement that ended when Ziggy stuck a gun in his face. The fugitive I was eyeballing slowly raised his hand, and I immediately wrapped on his window pointing my gun directly at his head.

"Gun!" I yelled, keeping with protocol.

The apprehension team responded in a flurry of movement that left the two fugitives squirming facedown on the ground.

Later, I was given the assignment and honor to fingerprint the fugitive cop killers. Still a little drunk and hostile, they fought my attempt to photograph and fingerprint them. The third time they resisted I gave one last warning. When they still refused to cooperate, I looked to a senior agent who nodded, the implication of his gesture clear. I pulled the third finger of one of the fugitives back until I heard a *pop!* as it broke. After howling and jumping up and down he settled in to be fingerprinted. The other fugitive offered no resistance at all.

We brought the first fugitive before the magistrate in New Orleans. The subject immediately protested that I had brutally broken his finger. The magistrate questioned me about it and I told him these cold-blooded killers wouldn't let me do my job. I cited that I had to establish identity in making sure that the subject was indeed the shooter since we recovered the gun that allegedly killed a police officer. The magistrate agreed that force was necessary and refused to concede that I had committed police brutality.

I'd graduated the Bureau's Training Academy certain that as long as I was an agent, I'd never lose sight of the FBI oath's words or its meaning. In my mind, that's what the whole Bulger mess was about. Agents were plainly violating that oath and sometimes much worse. But for me to have turned a blind eye to what was going on, to have not continued to pursue Bulger and his enablers at all costs, would have run counter to everything I tried to stand for as an agent. Some would call that stubborn, Irish stubborn, as they say. Some would call it simply tenacious. Bucking the system, while some would just call it stupid.

I call it simply right and it explains why I wasn't going to stop until the mess was cleaned up, no matter what. Until I was transferred to the Boston FBI office in 1981 I never had reason to question the integrity of a fellow agent or even the FBI as a whole. My fifteen-year tenure with the Bureau up until this time was marked by a steady climb, experiencing major roles in a series of high-profile and successful investigations. My assumption, based on that experience, was that all agents were like me. They had taken the oath, too, hadn't they?

Not John Connolly, apparently.

The culture of the Boston FBI office allowed him to set the tone and act as if he were in charge. This was best exemplified by a "point shaving" case involving the Boston College basketball team. A wiseguy by the name of Paul Mazzei was convicted for his involvement in a basketball scheme featured on the cover of *Sports Illustrated*. There were three groups involved: a Pittsburgh connection that involved a student named Tony Perla; a Boston College player named Rick Kuhn; and a New York connection with gangsters Henry Hill (from the movie *Wiseguy* who became an informant for the FBI in 1979 when I was in Miami) and James Burke, a Westie from Hell's Kitchen who ran away from Mount Loretto when I was there. The gangsters created "protection," and the players received $2,500 per game in exchange for ensuring that Boston College did not beat the point spread in games where the betting gangsters wagered against the team.

While this took place during the 1978–79 season, the trials came to a head early into my tenure as Boston ASAC. I was sitting in my office when my secretary buzzed to tell me that a high-ranking official from Boston College was on the phone. Perplexed, I took the call.

"What can I do for you, sir?" I asked politely.

Making small talk, the official said he was happy to chat with the FBI head in Boston and congratulated the office for a fine job cleaning up the town.

"So what I can do for you today?" I repeated.

"John Connolly said you might be able to do the school, and me, a favor."

"John Connolly?"

"Well, these kids are fine boys, but sometimes they get into trouble. Boys, you know."

"Pardon me, but are you talking about the Boston College basketball betting scandal?"

"These are good boys, Mr. Fitzpatrick."

"The case is currently being investigated by the FBI."

"Agent Connolly thought you might be able to help us out a bit."

"Agent Connolly is on one of the squads I manage, but he's not involved in the Boston College investigation."

"He said maybe there is something you can do."

"Bringing the boys into my office for a chat would be fine."

"I was hoping for something more."

I found it hard to believe that this official was hinting, on the suggestion of John Connolly, that I could make the case go away. I was both dumbfounded and livid at the thought. In spite of all my interactions with him and the clear displeasure I'd expressed over his job performance, Connolly still thought I was ripe for the taking. In Connolly's Boston and in Connolly's FBI, that was the way things were done.

I called John Morris, Connolly's supervisor, and ordered him in for an interview. I went up one side and down the other, leaving no doubt he and Connolly were in trouble before I got around to the Boston College official's thinly veiled request.

"Is this guy stupid or what?"

"No," Morris replied, somewhat indignantly, "the guy's an important man."

As if that's the way things were done in Boston, business as usual, as if I could be sucked into the culture of corruption. You go along to get along, right?

Not a chance.

I was called down to FBIHQ about this time for a special assignment designed to stop the leaks and, more important, the informant killings. HQ didn't let on but they were leery of the information about cases getting out. Continue working me as a "Serpico" was one idea, in that I'd be bypassing the traditional chain of command to make sure my reporting itself didn't fall victim to the same kind of leaking that plagued the office. So an even more secure system was set up whereby all of my communications with HQ would be through secret and clandestine contacts in person or by secure, coded teletype communications. Soon after the meeting FBIHQ sent out an "All Employees" warning to report all allegations of impropriety and criminal misconduct immediately. These requirements were usually a yearly edict to constantly remind all FBI personnel to report misconduct and breaches of FBI rules and regulation to FBIHQ. Failure to do so would be a serious matter, but equally important was an unwritten rule second only to the oath itself: Don't embarrass the Bureau.

You won't find that written anywhere, but it's imbedded in the minds of all agents. As much or perhaps even more than the military, the FBI is an insular organization that polices itself and expects everyone to toe the party line. Problems are dealt with from within the system and by the system. Of course, nothing like the problems in Boston had ever surfaced before, and I intended to solve them by sticking to established procedure and protocol in doing my job.

A job that was about to become even more difficult.

Larry Sarhatt's tenure as Special Agent in Charge came to an end right around the time of John Callahan's murder and my subsequent trips to headquarters in Washington. He'd had enough, although some said he was "pushed out" by HQ. In late November 1982, he was replaced by James Greenleaf, whom I'd met a few times back in HQ but didn't know that well. Greenleaf had been an assistant director at HQ in the Inspection and Planning Division, so his coming up to run the Boston office took plenty by surprise. After all, Boston was a coveted job, a top ten office amid a hotbed of activity. I knew that much from my tenure as chief of the Transfer Unit when I saw how many SACs coveted the top job there, to the point where some of them actively criticized Greenleaf's appointment as an "in thing" move.

I picked Greenleaf up at Logan Airport and we drove to Portland, Maine, where he hailed from, an opportunity for him to inspect the resident agency there. Our drive started out with small talk about our common acquaintances and experiences in Washington. Greenleaf was tall; an inch or two over six feet, blessed with an athletic build and a not unpleasant demeanor that should have made him the kind of public relations asset the Boston office was sorely in need of. I kept an open mind, even though chatter and rumor had Greenleaf involved with less than savory sorts in and out of the Bureau. I was warned in house by several agents to watch him because he was "a company guy." They provided me with several examples that put his character in question and spoke of possible involvement in ongoing criminal issues at HQ.

Greenleaf intimated that Sarhatt was forced out as Boston SAC because the feeling at HQ was that he wasn't running the office well enough, resulting in embarrassment and a tarnished image for the FBI in Boston. Could this have had something to do with the fact that Sarhatt agreed with me that Whitey Bulger should be closed as an informant? Dick Bates, my old SAC pal, thought so.

Before we got around to discussing Bulger or anything else of substance, Greenleaf asked me to stop at a liquor store where he purchased a six-pack of dark Heineken beer that he proceeded to drain during the course of our drive north. I thought this odd since drinking on duty was strictly prohibited by Bureau rules and regulations, but I gave my new boss a pass since he needed time to settle in. We talked about how the Boston office was set up, the different personalities and politics. At the time, all ten squads under me were making great strides in taking down all classifications of crime, since many of the operational and organizational changes I'd put into place were finally taking hold in the form of collars and convictions.

The difference between Sarhatt and Greenleaf, meanwhile, couldn't have been more pronounced. Sarhatt lived and breathed the Bureau; it dominated his life, all he ever talked about. Not so with Greenleaf. For him, taking over as SAC in Boston was just another rung to mount on his laddered career path.

"Jim, how exactly did you get Boston?" I asked him. "Everybody wants Boston."

He laughed and acknowledged it was a who-you-know proposition. This was apparent, since Greenleaf didn't have a lot of field or case experience and wasn't used to supervising squads or agents. His strengths were technical and procedural; he'd never really distinguished himself in the capacity of on-the-scene leadership that would be required of him in any SAC position. But he was savvy enough, politically anyway, to make a point of revealing HQ's perception that I was "combative" and "bellicose." Even though I didn't view his comment as confrontational necessarily, I did regard it as a thinly veiled threat that my dogged pursuit to close Whitey Bulger wasn't about to be tolerated any longer.

In that respect, maybe James Greenleaf was actually the perfect guy for the job—living proof of an unspoken message from HQ about Boston that I never quite read right. Could be it was about choosing sides, and his assignment clearly indicated HQ wasn't choosing mine, no matter what they said to the contrary. Clear now, but not nearly as so then.

These were heady, productive times for the Boston office, and Greenleaf's performance reports on me graciously reflected that. He continued to write me up as an exceptional ASAC, in spite of some clear areas of conflict that drove a wedge between us. Very early in his tenure, the new SAC instructed me to close a case at the Bath Shipyards in Maine, territory that fell under the Boston office's "resident agency" status. The case involved multimillion-dollar kickbacks and bribes by government officials. We identified a DOJ employee through informants showing he was involved in the bribery matter and we were close to presenting the case for prosecution when Greenleaf ordered me to close the investigation.

"I can't do that," I told him.

"I don't think you heard what I just told you."

"I heard you."

He hesitated before responding, clearly not used to be challenged. "Close the case, Fitz."

"Is that an order?"

"You bet it is."

"Then I respectfully decline to follow it."

Another heated pause, after which he asked, "What's it going to take to get you to close this case?"

I said that if the Director of the FBI advised me in writing to close the case I would close it. Amazingly, the next day I received a tele-type from Director William Webster instructing me to do exactly that. My oath was on the line and this order was unprecedented in my FBI career. To me it was tantamount to case fixing. But the order was approved by Washington, so I guess that took Greenleaf off the hook.

Greenleaf's next questionable decision was to replace John Morris as head of the Organized Crime squad with an agent named Jim Ring. On its own this was a fairly innocuous move, but Greenleaf also changed the office's chain-of-command structure whereby Ring would report directly to him, bypassing me entirely. Almost immediately Ring coddled up to John Connolly and, thus, Whitey Bulger. The implication of the move was as clear as the signal it provided: I was being taken out of the Bulger business. Nobody, from HQ on down, wanted to hear anymore that Bulger should be closed as an FBI TE.

Despite the success the office encountered under my steward-ship, there were so many leaks and infractions of policy under this new regime that the office became paralyzed by in-house investiga-tions. I had my suspicions that Greenleaf was behind at least some of the problems, but it was nothing I could prove or chose to pursue further. Since I was now officially working undercover, reports to HQ and the Director's Office were made confidentially in person and by written or verbal communication to HQ personnel outside of Boston. That should have assured the sanctity of the information I was providing. But I later learned through court testimony and federal appellate court briefs that Greenleaf had been fully briefed on my confidential status from the beginning in stark contrast to my stated mandate.

On one occasion the Department of Justice's U.S. attorney asked to speak with me privately. We met behind closed doors and he informed me he had knowledge that an agent was "on the take" and leaking info to LCN. This involved a $17,000 kickback from the wiseguys that was disclosed during an audit revealing missing informant money. Morris was not known at the time to have taken money himself from the wiseguys, but as the drug coordinator, this was his domain and his responsibility. Morris's response: telling his agents to watch their collective ass. I advised SAC Greenleaf and he took no action. In fact, I later learned that he, too, warned the agents of a possible investigation!

When I asked this particular U.S. attorney why he didn't just report this crime to SAC Greenleaf, he replied, "Because I don't trust him."

It's no wonder that the office became even more corrupt, instead of less. Agents know their job and are excellent investigators. Because the FBI is a militarylike organization, though, there remains a direct line of order, passing from one to another upward in a strict protocol. Every agent is reluctant to deliver the news that spells corruption, especially if it happens to involve the boss. Even my old pal and former SAC of Boston Dick Bates underestimated how bad things had gotten. He never spoke of the true gravity of the situation, thinking it would pass. Perhaps he had seen it all before and now in retirement he had no desire to watch the same show again.

Headquarters should have taken the drastic action required, both before SAC Greenleaf's arrival in Boston and after. As the former transfer agent at HQ, and one who previously handled every major case of this kind prior to coming to Boston, I knew that Morris and Connolly should have been transferred to another division to avoid any hint of impropriety and for preventative reasons. It was far more than a hint at this point. Informants' lives had already been lost and more certainly would be if something wasn't done.

What message was HQ sending by giving Greenleaf the Boston office? I thought a hefty part of it was about getting me to back off Bulger. Back then I took my undercover status as a sure sign of HQ's commitment to make things right in Boston. Now I see it more as a means to keep the information I was funneling under control.

Don't embarrass the Bureau.

Meanwhile, I turned my focus to the other major cases assigned to the Organized Crime squad I was running. There was no shortage of them. In fact, shortly after James Greenleaf's arrival, I had seven leak cases relating to corruption, graft, extortion, payoffs, and organized crime, several of them extremely high profile.

The LCN case fell under my domain and I was determined to bring down the Angiulo mob through traditional means and technical assistance, not relying at all on the bogus intelligence supplied by Bulger. I never took my eyes totally off Whitey, still determined to see justice done. But the atmosphere between rival agents in the office had become so venomous that my *original* mandate was just that. Agents knew I'd lost two informants who could have given me Bulger, and as the new guy in town, it was easy to side against me in favor of imbedded agents like Connolly and Morris. And it was becoming alarming to me which side SAC Greenleaf came down on.

But I had more important things on my plate than him. I was in the process of organizing the last remnants of the takedown of the Boston mafia. Gennaro Angiulo, the head of the Boston mafia, had run the Boston mob for a generation, having been installed as underboss by the head of the New England LCN, Raymond Patriarca out of Providence, Rhode Island. He was the son of Italian immigrants and served four years in the navy during World War II. The man loved boats and had actually just purchased a yacht he christened the *St. Gennaro* as we prepared to move on him.

On the day of September 19, 1983, I was about to serve his arrest warrant and I ordered some agents to dine at a small Italian restaurant called Francesca's in Boston's North End, a major ethnic section of the city. The agents were to nonchalantly order a meal and mix in among the other patrons. Angiulo dined there regularly and we had a tip that he'd be in the restaurant that evening.

After he arrived, the agents inside surreptitiously cautioned us that there was no unusual activity predisposing Angiulo's imminent arrest. So I entered the restaurant with "side-arm" agents and walked directly to Angiulo's table. The mafia chief's lieutenants sensed the potential calamity first. As Angiulo looked up to see the cause of the alarm, we looked squarely into each other's eyes. His scowl, a flinty-eyed sneer, fell over his face as he recognized me. My demeanor was a directed, businesslike look that showed determination and authority, but I still remember the red-and-white-checkerboard tablecloths.

"Angiulo," I said in a firm voice, "I'm Bob Fitzpatrick, ASAC with the FBI, and you are under arrest!"

I flipped my FBI creds on him and held out a gold badge with black casing identifying myself as the ASAC of the Boston FBI office and chief of Organized Crime in New England. He was shocked, to say the least. I made it a point to tell everyone at his table that only Angiulo was under arrest. For now, at least. I then informed Angiulo of the charges, a multitude of them, including conspiracy to murder. He looked shaken, with pasta stains mixed with the blood draining from his pale cheeks. Before he could react, I hustled him from the table and directed him toward the door, politely explaining that I would not cuff him until we were outside unless he caused an embarrassing scene in the restaurant. He nodded and put up no fuss whatsoever. Apparently mob guys don't want to be embarrassed in public anymore than the FBI does.

The plan was swiftly and skillfully executed. The only people eating in the restaurant that knew of the arrest were my agents secreted among the many diners. Angiulo's own lieutenants were left speechless and flabbergasted. Outside, we slapped on the bracelets and rushed Angiulo across the sidewalk. The familiar pat on the head prior to getting in the car caused him some consternation but it quickly passed.

I advised Angiulo of his constitutional rights and, as he listened, he looked like the proverbial deer in the headlights. His eyes, no longer enraged, were glassy. He still had a bit of spaghetti sauce on the side of his mouth. I thought I could hear his stomach grumbling instead of the usual mouthing off I'd become well acquainted with thanks to the secret wire that had led to his arrest.

"You got nothing on me," he managed feebly.

"Angiulo," I said, "don't be pissed. You know it's your yapping and your voice on the tapes. Maybe you should've kept your mouth shut."

This was an allusion to the years of clandestine, court-ordered wire recordings of his house where he'd discussed the "secrets" of his criminal enterprise. The loan-sharking, the extortions, the planning of murders. By grabbing Angiulo we brought his criminal enterprise to a grinding halt. All of his money, all of his property, including houses and cars, were confiscated. Almost overnight he went from being one of the most powerful men in Boston to a virtual ward of the state. I turned Angiulo over to the agents for processing, where he was dutifully fingerprinted, photographed, and brought before the magistrate in Boston's federal court where John Connolly showed up just to be photographed during Angiulo's "perp walk," in spite of the fact I'd deliberately kept him out of the Angiulo bust.

In 2009, a U.S. Navy honor guard would play taps at Jerry Angiulo's graveside after a funeral at St. Leonard's Church in Boston's North End, not far from the restaurant where we arrested him. And, in an ironic counterpoint, Angiulo died on the eightieth birthday of Whitey Bulger, whom the *Boston Globe* on September 4, 2009, referred to as "a longtime FBI informant who helped the bureau send Angiulo to prison."

Nothing could be further from the truth.

"You'll never close Bulger," John Morris had told me the night I interviewed Bulger at his Quincy condo.

Bulger was thought to be invaluable, a lynchpin in bringing down La Cosa Nostra, a tale propagated by Connolly and Morris and taken in, hook, line, and sinker by FBIHQ. Because of that he'd been protected at all costs, up to and including making the FBI a willing

accomplice in the murder of informants who could have given him
and his handlers up for prosecution. But now Angiulo was behind
bars, the Boston mob was in shambles, and not a single shred of
evidentiary material or testimony that had gotten it done had come
from the invaluable Whitey Bulger.

I prepared the communication to FBIHQ after calling the Director's Office to announce the mafia chief's arrest. This was a big deal
in the OC section and the kudos were generous and genuine. The FBI
chiefs in Washington were ecstatic. We had taken down the Boston
mafia "without incident"; no reprisals, no problems, and no embarrassment to the Bureau. Later, I celebrated with my fiancée Jane over
dinner at a North End restaurant and I never felt better. She had
brought a light back to my life I feared extinguished forever with the
breakup of my marriage, another casualty of the Bulger years.

I later learned that Jane was scared all through her dinner because she couldn't understand how I could come back to the North
End after arresting the mafia chief. We both laughed with a bit of
trepidation. She was the director of nursing at St. Elizabeth's Hospital in Boston at the time, living in a three-story tenement house we'd
bought in Brookline, which was convenient both to the hospital and
my office in the federal building.

"Cops marry nurses," I told her. "We both lead exciting lives and
meet all kinds of people under stressful situations."

"Never thought of that," she said.

I had accomplished a great portion of what I'd set out to do upon
coming to Boston, and was understandably gratified that in this OC
"leg" of my assignment I'd pulled off what would've been impossible
prior to my arrival. But Whitey Bulger was still running free on the
outside, while James Greenleaf was still in charge inside. Greenleaf
usually made himself scarce in the office, and in court testimony
would later repeat that he did not remember or recall, did not know,
or flatly denied certain things that were clearly evident. Not surprisingly, Greenleaf could always remember and recall the things he
wanted to take credit for. He was chided by agents and nicknamed
"Greenleave" by those befuddled by his absentee management style.
The Boston office, above all else, cried out for a hands-on approach

to leadership. Greenleaf, in stark contrast, seemed adverse to taking charge and offering the kind of direction that was so sorely needed.

Greenleaf, I began to suspect, was in league with the same higher-ups in Washington like Sean McWeeney, head of the Organized Crime section, who had ordered me to report directly to them. In this scenario, they would control the information and he would control me. The fact that my squad had taken down Angiulo in spite of Bulger, not because of him, left them with no cover and further complicated their plight. They were more frightened than ever that the truth of possible FBI complicity in the murder of informants, as well as the enabling and abetting of Whitey Bulger's rise to the top of the Boston underworld, would be revealed. Ultimately, that's exactly what would happen years later in federal court, much too late to undue the damage done by such an unholy alliance.

Don't embarrass the Bureau, the unwritten rule might have said, but that didn't stop the Bureau from embarrassing itself.

Greenleaf was the right man for the job, all right. I could only think that he'd been assigned to Boston to keep a lid on things, which required keeping a lid on me. As for Sean McWeeney, he continued to ignore the reporting he'd specifically requested I provide him. Several of these meetings were held in Washington with other members of the Organized Crime squad present, where I specifically detailed how leaks from the Boston office had led directly, at the very least, to the murders of Brian Halloran and John Callahan at the hands of Whitey Bulger. But Bulger remained open as an informant, again in spite of my protestations. And if that meant more informants had to die, then so be it.

18
BOSTON, 1983

It would be a year before my battle to close Bulger as an informant reached another crucial juncture. In the meantime, not only did one of my squads take down the mafia, but all of our priority Group I's, major undercover cases, were reaching culmination.

In White Collar Crime we knocked down a couple of wiseguys in the organized crime infiltration of the Boston stock market. I ran an undercover gig in a main case called "Fitzpatrick's Investments" that attracted wiseguys doing business in the penny stocks in play at the time. No one made the connection. In Public Corruption we grabbed public officials attempting to sell out the city. In one major undercover case called NECORR, New England Corruption, we were building a major case against Whitey's brother, Billy Bulger, still president of the Massachusetts State Senate at the time, and were on our way toward making a major undercover payoff to one of Bulger's cronies in the statehouse.

Some years later, Billy Bulger took the Fifth Amendment when questioned before the House Reform Committee about his involvement in the scandals and knowledge of his brother Whitey's underworld activities. Even after being granted immunity to compel his testimony, Billy's answers remained vague, often frustrating the committee members. Take his response to a specific question from Representative Dan Burton of Indiana in 2002 about what he and Whitey actually talked about in a call after Whitey's disappearance in 1995:

"I'm his brother. He sought to call me. Or he sought to call me and I told his friend where I'd be and I received the call and it seems to me, um, that is in no way inconsistent with my devotion to my own responsibilities, my public responsibilities as a, well, at that time, uh, president of the Senate. I believe that I have always taken those as my first, my first obligation."

In the drug area my squads were grabbing Irish and Italian cartel chiefs across a wide swath of drug involvement and smuggling. Marijuana cartel heads were arrested. All of a sudden, four years of planning an assault on crime in Boston was coming to fruition. Jerry Angiulo's arrest had only been the beginning. We were on a roll!

In still another case, we busted a notorious chapter of the Hells Angels motorcycle gang for trafficking in guns and drugs, especially methamphetamines. This chapter was at the forefront of setting up labs for making the stuff, archaic even by 1980s standards, and pushing their product throughout New England. The chapter's chief enforcer, a very dangerous, tattoo-covered thug, was holed up in a cheap motel room near Logan Airport in Boston.

That's where we cornered him. He was supposed to be "resting" following orders for another execution. We located his room and then got its layout in order to practice our incursion at a different location. This guy was a federal fugitive dimed by one of our Hells Angels informants. When we found a room similar to his we practiced entry so that the apprehension team, of which I was the lead agent, could grab the fugitive without incident. Each time the door was kicked open I was first to enter, and practiced taking the fugitive wherever he was in the targeted room.

This guy was one mean son of a bitch. He routinely severed the hands, legs, and heads of his victims to hide the evidence and foil identification through fingerprints and such. He was a cold-blooded killer steeled in the macabre art of "wasting" those marked by the

Hells Angels for execution. His girlfriend traveled with him as a sometimes accomplice, used to seduce the victim if necessary, and was known for concealing sharp instruments or razors for "protection." The Hells Angel was known to keep in his possession a Magnum, a .45 automatic, a sawed-off shotgun, and other firearms.

When it came time for the takedown, I laid a boot into the flimsy wood and sent the door to his room rocketing inward. My .357 Magnum service weapon drawn, I'd barely lurched into the motel room when the door bounced off the wall and ricocheted, smashing me in the face and knocking me back. Fortunately, the enforcer was passed out, zonked and snoring like a baby with his feet dangling off the end of the slight motel bed. It was the last time I ever kicked in a door. From that point on, I let the tactical specialists do their thing.

In another instance we got word back that a suspected snitch was going to be whacked by organized crime wiseguys. The plan was to garrote the guy with piano wire and put him in the trunk of a car. We had a moral dilemma in whether or not to warn him, since it would expose our informant and put his life in danger. But we figured out a way to alert the target without causing harm to our informant. Unfortunately for him, he didn't take the warning seriously, and to the best of my recollection, he was garrotted in spite of our efforts.

Dealing with Whitey Bulger, then, was not the only part of my job in Boston, and I wasn't going to let my frustrations affect the rest of what I'd been sent to the city to do. The leaks continued, even intensified. For instance, in the NECORR bribery and kickback case a state representative was investigated and accused of political corruption in violation of the Hobb's Act, a federal charge. But Billy Bulger, still president of the Massachusetts State Senate at the time, was the ultimate target. Our undercover operation hit several bumps in the road along the way before finally hitting pay dirt when our undercover (UC) agent had finally positioned himself to make a payoff to Vincent Piro, the Massachusetts State House assistant majority leader. Our hope was that Piro would lead us to the Speaker of the Massachusetts State House along with Billy Bulger.

I was in the control room with the prosecutor when the deal

went down. After our undercover agent paid Piro off, he reneged in an exculpation that sounded like script because that's exactly what it was. Piro had rehearsed the entire "give back" and completely changed his tune, clearly aware that his words were being recorded. We were flabbergasted. We knew our sting had been leaked, and the entire operation had been compromised by the insidious cancer that had infected so many Boston cases over the years. But Connolly wasn't to blame. I would later learn that the culprit this time was Connolly's supervisor, John Morris.

An investigation revealed that the UC agent had "inadvertently" told Connolly and Morris about the NECORR sting. And Morris told his old friend and mentor Dennis Condon who just happened to work for Vincent Piro's defense attorney. When I interviewed Condon about his role in blowing our case, he not only denied leaking or receiving info from agents but was livid that we would even suspect him. I believed Condon was lying and in my notes wanted to charge him with "1001," lying to federal agents, but the U.S. Attorney's Office took over the investigation and then dropped it. The case would eventually go to trial and Piro was acquitted.

Morris was involved in the investigation when the rep in question returned the UC payoff. The assistant U.S. attorney spoke with Morris and flat out asked him if he'd talked to Dennis Condon about the UC operation. Morris denied this vociferously and made a show of how insulted he was. A lousy act. I called the prosecutor and asked him to interview Morris again about the leak. Morris then admitted talking to Condon on the subject, but fabricated the details in an attempt to hide his complicity. A clear criminal action.

The fix was in, and the still-open case was given to a U.S. attorney who was a pal of Morris and Connolly. This attorney was the one who opposed using the consensual evidence that would certainly have resulted in the rep's conviction. He argued against the tape and was backed up by James Greenleaf among others.

These were tumultuous times with great unrest in the Boston office. It seemed that virtually everything we were doing was leaked to someone, causing great distrust. In my view, the turmoil was exacerbated by in the absence of true SAC leadership on the part of

Greenleaf, a faulty chain of command, and "end around" plays by Connolly and Morris. All the reservations and fears I had about Greenleaf from our initial meeting and drive to Maine had been confirmed. It had been folly to think him capable of taking the helm of a troubled office like Boston. But his friendship with Assistant Director John Otto, along with his willingness to hide the hole into which the office had plummeted, trumped all else. I had warned my supervisors that they were to report to me before others so that the information could be tracked and properly managed. If leaks happened, I wanted some tools to help determine the source, but it was like sticking my fingers in a crumbling dike.

One informant, for example, gave me strong intelligence on the North Community Co-Op Bank in the North End of Boston. The bank was involved in a huge Bulger money laundering operation that would, I later learned, become Whitey's personal piggy bank after he fled in early 1995. Bulger could and should have been prosecuted by O'Sullivan's office on the money laundering charge, but the case was thrown out in a veiled attempt to once again protect Whitey from prosecution.

During this period, agents of the Organized Crime squad, including Nicholas Gianturco and Michael Buckley, would receive gifts from Bulger as reported by Stephen Flemmi in court testimony, and later admitted to in court by several other agents. Flemmi told one jury that his and Bulger's payoffs to John Connolly alone amounted to $235,000 over time. While conceding Gianturco and Buckley had indeed received some gifts from Bulger, the other agents minimized the value of them. Testifying before the same jury at John Connolly's murder trial in 2008, Buckley went so far as to explain away his accepting a gift from a mob associate because the man's daughter had handed it to him. "I accepted it because she handed it to me and it was a gesture of kindness," Buckley recalled in his testimony as a witness for Connolly. "I didn't see any other reason behind it. There was no favor. There was no quid pro quo."

Maybe, but that wasn't always the case. Under a grant of immunity years later, John Morris admitted to taking $7,000 in bribes from Bulger and Flemmi. Did the fact that he also tipped them off to federal wiretaps and confessed to leaking the fact that Brian Halloran had become an informant count as quid pro quo in that case?

As ASAC, it wasn't that I didn't know what was going on. From the time Greenleaf replaced Larry Sarhatt in 1982, it was clear to me that our office had spiraled into a descent of treachery and criminality. SACs are supposed to set the tone, and in my opinion (and as I later said in court testimony and depositions), Greenleaf did just that, letting agents like Connolly run free without fear of repercussions. From 1982 to 1986, any report I made to HQ on Greenleaf's conduct was stifled and/or ignored and each time the bull's-eye painted on my own back got bigger.

But there was more. As referenced earlier, Dave Twomey was an assistant U.S. attorney who worked organized crime and drug cases under Jerry O'Sullivan on the Strike Force. I was the New England drug task force commander, so Twomey, as part of the Strike Force, had to liaise with me in taking down and prosecuting druggers and OC members.

Even as my OC and drug squads started making real progress in bringing down the cartels, which included Whitey Bulger's increasing involvement, Dave Twomey continued giving information to the very OC and cartel suspects we'd targeted. So I went to O'Sullivan to report this interference in our cases through the suspected leaking of highly sensitive material from the surveillance and "wires" that were going up, along with the names of other sources who were giving us information.

O'Sullivan was livid; not at Twomey, though, at me for insinuating such a thing was even possible. He demanded to know which Bureau informant had made the claim to my agents, Jim Crawford and Matt Cronin.

"You know I can't tell you that," I advised the Strike Force chief.

He scoffed and, some weeks later, proceeded to tell me that the informants, whose names I'd never provided, were "drunks" and thus should be considered unreliable at the time. Dave Twomey was neither relieved of his position nor reassigned, and no in-house investigation came to light. Generally, this information would have caused an OPR (Office of Professional Responsibility) inquiry and investigation. Yet business was allowed to continue as usual, and that in itself was not *un*usual.

But I wasn't about to let go of my pursuit of Twomey or anyone else. Here I was, ordered into a Serpico-like scenario where I was supposed to clean up the dirt in the Boston office, and all that dirt was now being swept under the rug. It was becoming increasingly clear that the people I was reporting to were potentially complicit in the very crimes on which I was reporting. Complicit because my reporting no longer allowed them to profess ignorance or claim plausible deniability later, even as another informant was about to die.

19
BOSTON, 1984

An unintended consequence of my squad's takedown of mob boss Jerry Angiulo was a sudden void in the drug distribution market. For years the Irish Winter Hill Gang, under both Howie Winter and Whitey Bulger, had pretty much ceded that revenue stream to the mafia under Raymond Patriarca out of Providence. That said, the myth perpetuated by those like John Morris, that one of the things that made Bulger "a good guy" was that he stayed clear of the drug business in general and within Southie in particular, was just that: a myth.

"There were U.S. Drug Enforcement Administration agents like Steve Boeri and Al Reilly, backed by DEA bosses like Paul Brown and John Coleman, who were especially galled that Bulger's defenders bogusly claimed he kept drugs out of South Boston," Kevin Cullen of the *Boston Globe* wrote years later. "The DEA men knew the only drug dealers Whitey killed were the ones who didn't pay him tribute."

Other than take that tribute from the dealers who moved their product through Southie, Bulger steered his people away from drugs only to avoid an all-out war with La Cosa Nostra. With Angiulo out of the way, though, he was more than happy to step in and fill the void, and why not? The FBI's providing him insulation from prosecution made him feel invincible and untouchable. If he could get away with murder, why not expand his reach into drug dealing? Whitey only needed to see the potential revenue that could further strengthen his hold on power in the Boston rackets, as well as the possibility of supplanting Patriarca as the most powerful gangster in all of New England. He was nothing if not ambitious.

Even if Bulger's move into drugs didn't lead directly to his downfall, it did yield another informant who could help me close him once and for all, an informant named John McIntyre. A veteran of the military, the gregarious McIntyre was a fisherman who built and repaired boats. But he was also heavily involved in the Irish gunrunning and drug deals out of Boston under the auspices of Joe Murray, another Irish gangster in competition with Bulger.

Murray traded in guns, drugs, and other contraband. He and Whitey might have been cut from the same cloth, so to speak, but they didn't see eye to eye at all. Murray wasn't part of the Winter Hill Gang, yet was still forced to pay tribute to Bulger for any drug dealing he did in Boston. Murray always suspected Bulger and Flemmi were informants, but to suggest such a thing would have been to assure his own death. So he remained silent and steamed over having to cut Bulger in on action Whitey otherwise had nothing to do with—a situation exacerbated by Jerry Angiulo's exit from the Boston crime scene since it left Murray competing within Whitey's expanding enterprise.

The one thing on which Murray and Whitey did see eye to eye was the IRA. Anything they could do for their Irish brothers in arms, they did, which mostly amounted to raising funds to purchase and smuggle guns back to the homeland. As a middleman for the deals, Bulger made his share of money, but he needed Murray's operation and boats for the procurement and shipment of the arms.

One of these boats was the now infamous *Valhalla*, and among its crew was John McIntyre, who was arrested for his small part in the operation in September 1984, setting the stage for his brutal murder just two months later. People in the know were always suspicious about how the *Valhalla* escaped capture off the Irish coast.

Looking back on things now, rumors that Bulger had been the one who snitched the IRA info to the Brits seem well founded indeed. After all, the eventual seizing of the *Valhalla* led to the takedown of Joe Murray, thus allowing Whitey to take over the few Irish gangs he didn't already control and further consolidate his power in the drug world and beyond. Now, instead of taking tribute from Murray, the network was Whitey's and Whitey's alone. He had effectively cut out the middleman, yet again.

Once McIntyre began to talk, I was notified immediately through Rod Kennedy, an FBI agent who liaised with the DEA, and I began to visualize Bulger caught in a fisherman's net. Kennedy represented me at a meeting in which McIntyre told of an upcoming drug shipment bound for Joe Murray, who, of course, paid tribute to Whitey in order to run his drugs in Bulger's South Boston territory. McIntyre was on board a ship called the *Ramsland* when it sailed into Boston Harbor in mid-November 1984, carrying thirty tons of marijuana. The cargo was seized, turning Bulger livid over his sizable lost share of the profits and looking for someone to blame.

Strangely, joining my squad on the dock that day when the *Ramsland* motored into port was none other than Martin Boudreau, former Strike Force attorney under Jeremiah O'Sullivan who'd recently gone into private practice as a mob lawyer. The fact that someone had leaked the coming seizure to him gnawed at me. How else, after all, could he have learned about it? But I had a major drug bust to oversee in tandem with the DEA, so that issue would have to wait.

Not only had McIntyre proven himself, he began to spill additional evidence he had of a link between Murray and Bulger, whom he'd never actually met at this point. And several three-letter agencies saw this as payback time. The DEA had been subjected to much the same "leaking" that I had witnessed and had seen a number of cooperative investigations go south thanks to FBI leaks or downright malfeasance.

The DEA knew where I stood on the matter so they reached out to me. McIntyre was just hoping to preserve his young family and simply wanted out. But he turned down the FBI and Customs' offer to enter the Witness Protection Program, while continuing to help them, and me, build a case against Bulger. We got an affidavit for a wire based on McIntyre's info, but it was never installed because of procrastination and stalling that seemed the very definition of bureaucratic incompetence or, worse, purposeful stalling on the part of those protecting Bulger. The DEA's involvement made this the greatest threat he'd faced yet since becoming an informant, and that was certain to reverberate all the way to Washington.

And then came the night that John McIntyre was lured to the house in South Boston to be tortured and killed by Whitey Bulger because he'd been given up by those he trusted to keep him safe. Given up to have his teeth pulled out, his body mutilated and then buried in another basement before being moved across from Florian Hall in Dorchester where he might never be found.

We know that now. At the time, though, all we knew was that John McIntyre had simply disappeared. All the intelligence he was providing was rendered moot since there was no one else around to corroborate it.

The existence of an informant willing and able to link Whitey to both guns and drug running, who could put Whitey on the docks as the weapons were being loaded onto the *Valhalla*, must have terrified his enablers no end. So, like Brian Halloran, John Callahan, and Richie Castucci before him, McIntyre had to be killed. The images of his brutal murder haunt me to this day. It's hard to revisit the terrible pain Whitey Bulger caused McIntyre to assert his own sadistic power, a bully to the end. For what? For being an informant? Well, what about Bulger and Flemmi being informants? Bulger broke the supreme Irish code of ratting out to his so-called enemies, while Connolly and Morris ratted out their fellow agents and informants. All of them much more deserving of the fate McIntyre ultimately suffered.

When I appeared on the *60 Minutes* TV program in the wake of McIntyre's body being recovered in early 2001, the now deceased Ed Bradley asked me, "As a former FBI agent, do you in, in any way hold other FBI agents, the Bureau itself, responsible for these murders?"

"Yes, I do," I answered simply, with no equivocation. "Yes!"

Bob Fitzpatrick as an altar boy at Mount Loretto, the orphanage on Staten Island where he grew up. *(Courtesy of Robert Fitzpatrick)*

Fitzpatrick pictured shortly after coming to Boston as Assistant Special Agent in Charge (ASAC) in 1981. *(Courtesy of Robert Fitzpatrick)*

The boat *Left Hand*, the undercover vessel used by Fitzpatrick in his ABSCAM sting operation in 1978. *(Courtesy of Robert Fitzpatrick)*

Fitzpatrick pictured with Boston Mayor Ray Flynn in 1982, just before they ran the Boston Marathon. *(Courtesy of Robert Fitzpatrick)*

A young Stephen Flemmi pictured in a mug shot from 1965. *(Courtesy of* The Boston Globe/*Landov)*

A young John Connolly pictured doing a "perp walk" in 1980. *(Courtesy of* The Boston Globe/*Ted Dully/Landov)*

An older John Connolly on trial for murder in Miami in 2009. *(Courtesy of* The Miami Herald/*MCT/Landov)*

Jeremiah O'Sullivan, U.S. Attorney and head of the Organized Crime Strike Force.
(Courtesy of The Boston Globe*/Barry Chin/Landov)*

Murdered informant John Callahan.
(Courtesy of The Boston Globe*/HD/Landov)*

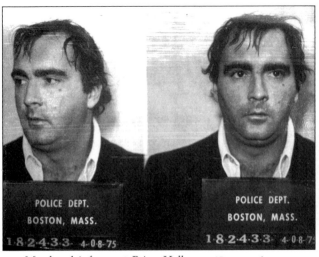

Murdered informant Brian Halloran. *(Courtesy of*
The Boston Globe*/HD/Landov)*

John Martarano testifying in the John Connolly murder trial, 2008. *(Courtesy of* The Miami Herald*/MCT/Landov)*

FBI officials flanking a Wanted poster of Whitey Bulger after Whitey's disappearance in 1995. *(Courtesy of* The Boston Globe*//Wendy Maeda/Landov)*

Murdered informant John McIntyre's body being unearthed in January 2000. McIntyre had "disappeared" in November 1984. *(Courtesy of* The Boston Globe/*George Rizer/Landov)*

Bob Fitzpatrick on the scene of the Dorchester gulley where John McIntyre's body was found. *(Photograph by Nancy Lane/*The Boston Globe*)*

A rare picture of Whitey Bulger. *(Courtesy of David Boeri)*

Whitey's brother, Billy Bulger. *(Courtesy of The Boston Globe/Tom Landers/Landov)*

Whitey Bulger upon his arrest in June 2011. *(Courtesy of David Boeri)*

It was the same answer I would have given in 1984, had anyone bothered to ask me.

There were plenty of hands to go around, all right, and plenty of blood to coat them all. But who had leaked John McIntyre's name to Bulger in the first place? Who exactly had cost this young man his life?

20
BOSTON, 1985

Remember Dave Twomey, the Strike Force attorney two of my agents had branded a leak? I did and I'd never let go of my resolve to see him brought to justice.

I got my chance in early 1985 when a DEA agent named Vinton reported he'd recently heard the very same thing through one of his own informants. Specifically that Twomey might well be funneling information to Martin Boudreau to aid in the defense of his mob clients whom the Strike Force was trying to put away. So at long last we arrested Twomey on charges of accepting bribes and obstruction of justice, among others. In December 1986 he was "convicted of four violations of federal law arising out of his sale of confidential law enforcement information to a drug smuggler whom he had investigated in the course of his official duties." (The decision was later upheld by the United States Court of Appeals for the First Circuit, which has appellate jurisdiction in Massachusetts.)

By all indications, though, Twomey wasn't the only one leaking. We knew the Boston office of the FBI itself had been plagued by leaks for years, and I was about to learn where at least some of them may have originated.

In June of 1985, Tom McGeorge, an agent who handled my Public Corruption squad, asked to see me in private.

"You're not gonna believe this, Fitz."

"What?" I asked him.

"I think I know who's been leaking. It's Greenleaf."

The way McGeorge said it, I don't think he could believe it himself. I was flabbergasted and nearly fell out of my seat. But the intelligence McGeorge related to me indicated that Greenleaf had, like Twomey, met with defense attorney Martin Boudreau, formerly of the Strike Force under Jerry O'Sullivan and now a known lawyer for the wiseguys. Greenleaf, according to McGeorge, told Boudreau that a "witness" to the drug cartel was prepared to dime Whitey Bulger and others. Was that witness John McIntyre? I'll never know. All we knew then was that McIntyre had disappeared and, in fact, had been labeled a fugitive. Whatever I and other agents suspected aside, we had no evidence of an underlying crime having resulted from that leak. McIntyre could have gone AWOL, after all. We looked for him for about a month, a touchy situation in itself since we couldn't give away his informant status either. McIntyre, like Halloran, was a key witness in getting the goods on Bulger so we could arrest him.

At this point I did recall Martin Boudreau's presence on the dock when the *Ramsland* sailed into port the year before. Someone had alerted him to the major drug bust we were about to make, and now it was becoming clear to me just who that leak may have been.

If McGeorge's assertions were correct, Greenleaf was furnishing federal grand jury information to a defense attorney in violation of federal statutes. Committing the very serious crime of revealing informant information that could not only jeopardize a case, but also get an informant killed.

I told McGeorge to make out a full report. In front of him I called the Strike Force chief and told him the story. In a cavalier manner O'Sullivan advised me that he "already knew about this."

"Why the hell didn't you tell me?" I asked him.

"Because it's none of your fucking business."

"What are you gonna do about it now?"

"Well, I guess I'll have to report it to OPR."

"You guess?"

"Yeah."

It wasn't that he couldn't believe leaking was taking place in his office; he knew it was. But he also knew that acknowledging that fact would undermine his credibility if revealed. And since the leaking filtered back to Bulger, and possibly Joe Murray, the results of a full investigation risked destroying the prized informant O'Sullivan had been protecting for years now.

I next called the Director's Office in Washington, D.C., and got the Director's standby John Glover. He was livid; more at me than Greenleaf, it seemed, and he ordered me not to write a report or tell Greenleaf anything.

The pit in my stomach was growing harder and I recalled one of my buddies saying, "If you take on the dragon you have to kill him!" I had laughed at the time, but I wasn't laughing now. After all, wasn't this my duty to report? Didn't I take an oath to do this very thing?

Never embarrass the Bureau . . .

But the whole arrangement grew even more incestuous and complex once Whitey Bulger began exerting more and more influence over the drug trade in his native Southie enclave and Boston environs beyond. Ultimately, the DEA professed to have little interest in working their cases in tandem with the FBI and, by connection, with O'Sullivan's Strike Force. No less a source than Stephen Flemmi himself would later admit that "Both in 1984 and 1989, the FBI made Mr. Bulger and I aware of a number of drug investigations."

As I told the *Boston Herald* in a story entitled "Ex-Agent Details Treachery in HUB FBI Office" that was published in April 2001, "'Innocent people were killed, murdered, and I hold certain agents responsible for that.'" The *Herald* reporters (Jonathan Wells, Jack Meyers, and Maggie Mulvihill) went further in linking everything together: "When the alleged leak occurred, Boudreau, a former federal Organized Strike Force prosecutor, was representing major drug traffickers. Also at the time, Bulger and Flemmi were collecting 'tribute' payments from traffickers doing business in the Boston area."

Of course, at that point all we were sure of was that McIntyre had vanished, complicating a case I was trying to make against Greenleaf since I couldn't use what I knew in a report HQ had ordered me not to file anyway. I'd become a real thorn in their side, and since they could no longer ignore what I was telling them, they told me to put no further reports in writing that could—you guessed it—embarrass the Bureau.

But Justice Department protocol told me something else. In fact, that protocol was reiterated to all office employees in a memo dated June 3, 1985, a few days before my reporting, that read in part, "I wish to remind you that it is your responsibility to inform the Counsel on Professional Responsibility of all such allegations which come to our attention and to advise him when inquiries into these allegations have been completed."

The memo was signed "Attorney General." It was circulated by Special Agent in Charge James Greenleaf.

As I told the *Boston Herald* for that same story in 2001, I filed my own memo directly under the subject heading "Alleged Disclosure of Information by SAC Greenleaf." My memo referred specifically back to our investigation of Strike Force lawyer Dave Twomey and the informant who told us about Twomey warning off the organized crime subjects of the Strike Force's investigations. The memo detailed how James Greenleaf had leaked the informant's name to former Strike Force attorney Martin Boudreau, who'd moved into private practice representing the kind of people he used to put away. This would not only allow Boudreau to impeach that confidential informant's character but also could have placed his very life in danger. Remember what had happened to Brian Halloran and John Callahan, not to mention Richie Castucci?

Even though I'd left out the most pointed allegation from my report, Greenleaf was pissed that I'd done my job by reporting him, afraid this time it would stick since I'd bypassed the traditional channels offering him cover. His ire knew no bounds. I had initially struggled with the filing of charges against him and was forbidden by FBIHQ itself to discuss that filing with the SAC either before or after. I never thought of myself as a "snitch" or that I was "diming" the SAC. In Washington, though, among those who had installed Greenleaf as SAC in Boston and continue to support him to this day, I was ostracized and deemed a pariah for telling the truth. Not only did the DOJ OPR not contact me, but the Director's Office continued to order me to keep everything I knew secret. The problem was I'd gone too far now to follow that order. I tried to report my suspicions about the SAC to the FBIHQ general counsel and the Director's Office of the FBI, keeping a copy of that report in the event they weren't acted upon, which, of course, they weren't. My report should have triggered an investigation—that's all. The allegation I leveled against Greenleaf was just that and nothing more. It was certainly explosive, but it was also procedure and should have been treated as such.

But it wasn't.

The FBI never asked for additional clarification of what I knew about John McIntyre's disappearance; if they had, they'd have evidence of corruption inside the Boston FBI at the highest level. In all my years working major cases, I had never seen the kind of abject corruption that I witnessed in Boston. Until John McIntyre's body was pulled from the ground on a cold day in January 2000, the truth behind his disappearance was never fully known. But the fact he had suffered the same fate, at the same hands, as Richie Castucci, Brian Halloran, and John Callahan was as unavoidable as it was obvious.

In that same 2001 article in the *Boston Herald*, Tom McGeorge was reported to have denied ever having that conversation with me during which he reported Greenleaf. McGeorge was running a private security firm in Florida at the time, and if he actually did deny our conversation to a reporter perhaps it was because he was afraid of getting involved. Interviewed by the same reporters, James Greenleaf offered no comment. Jeremiah O'Sullivan, meanwhile, flat out denied our subsequent conversation and my reporting.

"Absolutely and unequivocally this did not happen," O'Sullivan said at the time.

This is the same O'Sullivan who would later confess to lying and misrepresentation in his testimony before the House's Government

Reform Committee in 2002, including an admission that he knew Bulger and Flemmi were murderers. He died in February 2009, and at the time of his death a lawyer named Robert Popeo told the *Boston Globe* that, "For those in the highest levels, the admiration he earned for his conduct will stay with him forever. And there are those who don't know what it's like to be down in the pit and make these decisions. His legacy of fighting crime in Boston stands."

Popeo had once represented none other than Billy Bulger.

As for James Greenleaf, in 2006 he would testify in district court that investigations of Bulger and Flemmi "just didn't register" with him. This in spite of the fact that the appellate decision later found that "[Greenleaf] was not focused on the reports that Bulger and Flemmi had sources within law enforcement generally or within the FBI." The same court made note of the fact that "The FBI's recognition of the apparent link between the Winter Hill gang and three murders—Wheeler's, Halloran's and Callahan's—was reported in a November 1982 memo sent by the Chief of the FBI's Organized Crime Section, Sean McWeeney, to Associate Deputy Director Oliver Revell. The memo stated that 'there is evidence [the murders] were committed by an organized crime group in Boston, Massachusetts, the Winter Hill gang.' James Greenleaf, who became the SAC of the Boston Office on November 29, 1982, was among those copied on the memo, which was generated at FBI Headquarters in Washington."

I gave a deposition under oath for that same 2006 trial before a bevy of ten lawyers, including one representing James Greenleaf.

"At any time after McIntyre's disappearance did you come to believe that McIntyre's identity had been leaked?" the interrogatory attorney asked me.

"Yes," I answered unequivocally.

"And can you describe how you came to that belief?"

I proceeded to relate the details of my meeting with Tom McGeorge, stressing that McGeorge had specifically mentioned Greenleaf as leaking the informant's name to former Strike Force attorney Martin Boudreau and that I had immediately informed Jerry O'Sullivan of that.

No objections were offered by the attending attorneys.

"So you called the Director's Office," the attorney said, picking up the questioning. "And—"

"It was because it involved the SAC," I interrupted.

"And what did you tell the Director's Office?"

"That one of my supervisors just reported that the SAC of the Boston Division is a leak. We had a federal grand jury going on, and he had given away 6E, federal grand jury 6E information, which is a crime."

"And what, if anything, was done as a result of that report?"

"Nothing," I replied.

21
BOSTON, 1985

"It was the best of times, it was the worst of times."

The opening line from Charles Dickens's *A Tale of Two Cities* described things perfectly as 1985 descended upon Boston. It started out as a great year, one of the best of my life. My squad's takedown of the Boston La Cosa Nostra, which had begun with my arrest of the underboss Gennaro Angiulo in September 1983 had been parlayed into additional arrests as "made" guys turned against each other to avoid the same fate. Several of the public corruption cases came to fruition, and our financial squad and undercover cases netted several organized crime heavies in major cases involving infiltration into legitimate business and the illegal manipulation of stock on the OTC (over-the-counter) market.

Beyond that, my Miami experience in running ABSCAM had finally produced several trials and plea deals, and helped usher in a new age of accountability in Washington. That experience led directly to my investigations of illegal offshore financial corporations, a national con man indexing, a computerized crimes violations system that was way ahead of its time, undercover operations in PEN-DORF (a wiretap on Allen Dorfman, head of the AFL-CIO), BRILAB (our pursuit of bribery and labor racketeering in the unions), and multiple stings involving organized crime penetration of the New York Stock Exchange. The common denominator here was the Bureau's first ever "hands-on" Economic Crimes Unit to monitor drug laundering, international bank scams, and to establish a watchdog unit with Interpol to monitor organized crime infiltration into legitimate business.

And amid all my accomplishments, amidst the many problems we had resolved in the Boston office, I continued to be at odds with HQ and my own SAC, James Greenleaf. The Organized Crime section at HQ under Sean McWeeney appeared insulted that the ASAC in Boston had dared criticize the way FBI business was done. Mc-Weeney couldn't get past my dogged pursuit of Whitey Bulger, because his Organized Crime section felt their judgment was being challenged and that represented a direct threat to the FBI's quasi-military atmosphere. They also couldn't get past the fact Bulger and Flemmi had become part of the FBI's extended family.

Right around the time of McIntyre's murder, for example, Mc-Weeney learned that the DEA had launched a major drug operation called Operation Beans that was targeting Bulger and Flemmi, among other major New England drug figures. When he saw their names, he called Boston and got John Connolly on the phone.

"Aren't these our guys?" McWeeney asked Connolly, as reported in *Black Mass.*

So apparently Bulger and Flemmi were the FBI's "guys" while I, somehow, wasn't. The cadre at HQ had the data from all twenty-five organized crime national families. They were the experts and didn't want anyone telling them how to do their job in spite of the success I achieved doing just that in Boston. While busting organized crime remained every bit a top priority in Washington, my efforts and accomplishments were being demeaned by a groupthink mentality that led to a scenario of "us versus them," with me inexplicably linked with "them." There was no middle ground and no room for what Organized Crime or any other section deemed dissidents in the Bureau.

But my Bulger experience had branded me just that, and the Organized Crime section in Washington preferred to paint me as a "crazy" relegated to a distant corner, rather than to weigh my work in its totality. The Bureau's second in command, John Otto, who actually served as acting director between May and November of 1987, backed Greenleaf up at my expense. I believe that Otto served as both Greenleaf's cover and protective blanket, another cog in the machine. But that didn't stop him from jumping in when William Sessions was fired by President Bill Clinton after "findings by the Department of Justice that he engaged in legal and ethical misconduct."

"What the bureau cannot tolerate is people trashing it, and that is what Sessions has done," Otto told England's *The Independent* in July 1993. "He put himself and his own interests before the bureau, and that is taboo."

In a further bizarre twist, when Otto stepped down from his final post as associate deputy director of administration in April 1990, he was replaced by James Greenleaf.

The disconnect here was that I was lauded and given commendations for my accomplishments, while my warnings about the underlying cancer festering inside the Boston office were ignored. In an internal FBI Performance Appraisal Report issued on June 29, 1984, and still in my possession, my overall rating was called "Exceptional." Under "Program Management" the report went on to detail that "Achievements in the Organized Crime Program and White Collar Crime Program are a direct result of ASAC FITZPATRICK'S interest and enthusiasm for directing the programs. During the ratings period, many problems surfaced that required ASAC FITZPATRICK to address. These problems were overcome and many of the cases achieved successful resolution. Modifications were made to Boston's Organized Crime Program with the help of ASAC FITZPATRICK and Boston is now in a better position to address the narcotics and dangerous drug problem within its territory."

The evaluation was written by James Greenleaf.

The SAC's words, though, were backed up by neither his nor HQ's actions. The procedure-driven Organized Crime section in Washington under Sean McWeeney controlled my purse strings and thus thought they controlled me. And, yes, money normally affected all of the critical thinking and decision making, but I wasn't going to let it affect mine. I knew that Whitey Bulger and his right-hand man Stephen Flemmi were titular heads of the Irish OC families and that meant regardless of what anyone in Washington or Boston said, they would remain one of my top priorities. But the so-called experts subsumed all of my evaluations.

"You know, I have the advantage of overseeing all facets of Organized Crime and other crimes in Boston," I once told McWeeney.

"Okay," he replied, "what's your point?"

"That I could see the failure of putting our eggs in the Bulger and Flemmi basket right from the beginning."

I seem to recall him almost laughing at my insinuation. As my superior, he knew better; he knew *everything*. And he took his marching orders from John Otto who was Greenleaf's "guy" in Washington.

But then came August 1985, when I married my sweetheart, Jane. At our glorious wedding the unexpected showing of agents and friends sharing my earlier years was overwhelming. Here were Andy, Davey, and Bones, my old partners in crime from my first post in New Orleans, running on the beach in Charlestown, Rhode Island, after a raucous night out recounting our early exploits. We laughed at our younger agent days in Memphis and other offices where we were assigned. As first and second low-ranking office agents we got the "dreg" cases, the bottom of the barrel, dog-eared file cases that remained unsolved.

There was one in particular where a fugitive I was after in New Orleans at the outset of my career had a propensity for racetracks. The file was full of leads and pages recounting how other agents had tried to apprehend this guy by going to the racetracks firsthand. The Fair Grounds in New Orleans was a splendid racetrack of the antebellum age, with all the accoutrements: the fanfare, the banners flying, the horses decorated in beautiful spring colors as they pranced for the gate. We "shot a balloon" that day and went to the Fair Grounds in search of the fugitive.

Bones, being the comic agent, used every chance he got to declare, "There he is! Look, climbing up the flagpole. No, there he is on the back of horse number five!" When we got our tickets for the horse race to make the outing respectable, Bones yelled, "He's the guy behind the ticket window!" We all laughed and every fifteen minutes or so I would reexamine my photo of Harry, the fugitive, in the event that we might spot him among the huge crowd—not that any of us really thought we would.

A calm came over the crowd as the horses came to the gate. The announcer bellowed over the loudspeakers, "This is the third race at the Fair Grounds and the horses are nearing the gate." The other agents were doing their thing and nowhere to be seen. Finally, Bones came into my line of sight and, as I glanced at that photo once more, lo and behold, standing not far from him there was Harry!

I checked the photo again and again. "Bingo!" I thought, excited. "Damn, that's him!"

I sneaked behind the fugitive who was avidly screening the mounts at the gate, greeting him with, "Harry, how the hell are you?"

He turned around expecting to see a pal and, acknowledging my recognition, said, "Great!"

And then in the blink of an eye, he realized that this was an "aw shit" moment and tried to move away.

"Harry, I'm Bob Fitzpatrick, FBI, and you're under arrest!"

The look on his face said it all. Disappointment as he realized that this was no friend or acquaintance, this was the feds. As I approached Harry he held out his hands symbolically and I slapped on the handcuffs, strapping him around a flagpole.

Man, he was pissed!

"Take me outta here," Harry muttered.

Stalling for time, I told him I wasn't alone and had to find the other agents. The crowd milled around us oblivious to the man in handcuffs, intent only on the third race about to go off.

I said, "Look, there're other agents here and I'm afraid to take you in on my own."

He looked at me incredulously and repeated, "Just get me outta here. I promise I'll go quietly. No trouble."

Of course, what I didn't tell him was that I was stalling because I and the other agents had a bet on the race. The announcer barked, "They're off!" And off went the horses, kicking up dirt as they started around the track with our horse at the head of the pack.

Bones showed up just as excited as I was, especially when he spied the handcuffs fastened around Harry's wrists. "So, you won the race, eh, Fitz?"

Harry, getting more pissed by the second, just wanted to be arrested and taken away, while Bones and I were busy following our horses.

"Get me the hell outa here!" Harry bellowed this time, trying to be heard over the screaming crowd.

I finally relented. As I recuffed Harry and started to bring him around, the announcer gave the results of the race.

"Did you win, Harry?" I asked. "Because I did! Oh, that's right," I added, looking at his handcuffs, "you can't check your ticket."

The pissed-off look froze on his expression. We were ecstatic. Andy finally arrived and he laughed the loudest when we told him the story. And now all those years later here we were in Charlestown, Rhode Island, laughing out loud again. It was one of the greatest few days of my life, culminating in a marriage ceremony that was truly special, with all the most important people in my life gathered in the same place at the same time, including my brothers Larry and Gerard and my sister Diane.

Well, not everyone. My parents, obviously, were not in attendance. And neither was anyone from my years in the Mount. That period of my life was like a black hole that had swallowed my youth. But those same years had made me what I was, and the lessons of life in the Mount had been well learned, carried with me to this day.

At the reception, I looked over the group. Catching my eye were both Connolly and Morris, the two of them unusually sitting apart. Connolly in his flamingo tuxedo gabbing with table partners and seeming to lead the conversation, as was his custom. Morris was seated at a separate table in a dark suit, demur and quiet. Neither of them looked happy, making them stand out amid the revelry, and I was glad even for that small token of payback.

I thought about the reception dinner at the North End in Boston after the Angiulo takedown. My informant, Frankie, had thrown a party for the members of my squad and we had reveled in the excitement of being on top of the world. And on the night of my marriage to my beloved Jane I was on top of the world again, and no one, least of all John Connolly and John Morris, was going to bring me down.

Our honeymoon to Ireland continued the excitement. We traveled through our ancestral turf with Jane reading to me about the Troubles while I negotiated the troubles of the narrow Irish roads. We dropped into a different pub each day for "beer and soup," reminiscing about the Ireland of old. From there, we sailed through Limerick, Galway, Tipperary before venturing into Northern Ireland, the seat of the Troubles. We made it in fine, but getting out was a problem. The resistance and tension of the North was unmistakable. I thought back to my teaching days at the Academy, when I taught a course on hostage negotiation to the RUC, the Royal Ulster Constabulary. It was a unique experience because there were Irish Catholics in the class, a rarity in the mostly Protestant or British RUC. My course involved tactics and negotiation when dealing with hostage takers. The Protestants thought this was blarney, as the RUC had a much more severe approach toward the Catholic troubles.

Back in Boston, I had met the head of the Gardai, the police force of the Republic of Ireland, and knew a little something about how things were handled in Ireland, both North and South. Jane and I shared the history in what had become a major conflagration of fighting forces, the Irish Republican Army and the Ulster Defense Force and other groups. We laughed at how there were two prominent flags in my Boston FBI office: the U.S. flag and the tricolor flag of Ireland. It reminded me of the Irish mob back home and their internecine warfare and fights with the Italian mafia, a microcosm of the trouble abroad.

Jane and I had enough of the North. We trekked south toward the Irish border surprised to see a huge blockade with roadblocks of Brit lorries and armored cars. As we got closer the soldier smartly requested, "Registration and passports, please." I dutifully produced the documents and he inquired further, "Was your visit pleasure or business?"

I smiled at Jane and chuckled to no one in particular, "Pleasure, of course."

He then said without a trace of humor, "License!"

I tried to ask if there was a problem but he steadfastly parsed, "License!"

When I reached into my jacket for my license, I discerned that the soldier brought his rifle to a ready position. I stared at him because of his apparent defiant move and demanded, "Is there a problem?"

He examined the license and angrily noted, "So, you're from Boston and you're Irish."

Quizzically, I said, "Yeah?"

At that point, without giving my license and registration back, he ordered me to move to a different location in the blockade. I again inquired, "Is there a problem?"

He smugly gestured with his rifle in the ready position and said, "Move along."

I rolled unto the new blockade position, whereupon another soldier asked, "Pleasure or business?"

"Pleasure," I formally replied.

It became obvious to Jane that the soldier was all business and she became somewhat frightened, particularly as I pointed to a soldier camouflaged in a machine-gun nest directly in front of us.

"What's going on?" she whispered.

"Nothing," I said, feeling my own Irish temper rising, "they're just being smart-asses because we're Irish and we're from Boston."

The soldier overheard me and began to give me a ration of crap. I stared at him and demanded, "I want to speak to your supervisor!" The soldier came to attention as I saw his commanding officer approach the car, just as tense as his subordinates.

"Is there a problem?" I asked him now.

The officer asked for further identification and when I tried to ask him why, he abruptly and curtly demanded, "Do as I say."

I reached into my inside pocket, leery of their rising anxiety, and pulled out my FBI credentials and badge. "I'm FBI, United States law enforcement," I said in my sternest voice.

Both the officer and soldier were taken aback, even embarrassed, and did not know quite what to do from there. I knew from the teaching I did at the FBI Academy that the whole episode was recorded through hidden microphones on the soldiers' persons and thus wasn't surprised to see a higher-ranking officer approach the car. The officer greeted us with a huge and cheerful hello. He turned out to be a former student who recognized me from the Academy, of all places, where he'd been among the Royal Ulster Constabulary who took my course on hostage negotiation.

He apologized profusely, explaining that there had been a bank assault a short time earlier and the blockade represented a "high alert." After exchanging some light banter and reminiscences we were reminded to "be careful" along the way. I explained to Jane that a bank assault was actually a bank robbery and that we'd better scoot back to Southern Ireland. The irony, of course, was that Bulger's Winter Hill Gang, the very mugs I was pursuing, had been behind a huge portion of the import of illegal arms to the IRA rebels who had perpetuated the violence and were responsible for holding the entire nation in a grip of fear. The guns loaded in Boston aboard John McIntyre's *Valhalla* were just one example and not a good one, since they were ultimately confiscated. So you could say even all those miles from Boston, I couldn't escape the grisly shadow cast by Whitey Bulger.

22 BOSTON, 1985

When I returned to Boston after our honeymoon, one of my major investigations was in progress on Cape Cod. I was in charge of cartel drug cases and one of our informants had alerted us to a major drug buy. During the bust, one of my agents fired a shot at a suspect who ultimately surrendered with no further incident. But anytime an agent discharges a weapon, it's a serious matter that requires immediate follow-up and investigation.

Even though my plane had barely touched down, SAC Greenleaf, who was at a baseball game, ordered me to take charge of that investigation myself. I told him my doing so could represent a conflict of interest, since I was in charge of the entire case and the shooter was my agent. But Greenleaf persisted, so I agreed to head up the investigation. The agent, James Trout, a fellow military veteran and one of my SWAT team's most experienced agents, was caught in the crosshairs of a speeding car that was trying to run him over in a getaway situation. Trout immediately fired off several rounds to stop the car. The drugger was then apprehended and arrested without further incident, and we all thought the action commendable. After all, we'd just executed one of the biggest drug busts in New England history, and in the process recovered all of the drugs and money. With a suspect bearing down on him in a van, Agent Trout was well within his rights to fire; in fact, it would've been ludicrous to expect him not to, especially when the shot achieved precisely its desired effect of making the suspect surrender. After taking witness statements and interviewing all the principals involved, I filed my report to that effect, fully believing that that would be the end of things, since I'd done all the due diligence required and more. Everyone in the know objectively agreed the agent's response was appropriate, if not downright heroic.

Except for James Greenleaf, that is. The SAC was still angry over my memo about his alleged disclosure of information to mob attorney Martin Boudreau. He wasn't about to let go of the Cape Cod incident that had given him the opportunity despite the superlative job done by all the agents involved in the bust, including the shooter. I could only believe that retaliation against me was Greenleaf's hidden, perhaps only, agenda at this point.

One dark and melancholy day I was advised that charges were being leveled at me for "fictionalizing" reports following the major drug investigation I commanded on the Cape. These charges were based solely on Greenleaf's insistence that I had gone into my investigation of the "shots-fired" incident with my mind already made up. In retrospect, metaphorically anyway, those shots might just as well have been aimed at me. I would be charged with falsifying reports about the investigation Greenleaf had ordered me to conduct against my objections. I was accused of unreasonably exonerating the shooter, my agent, which was an utterly preposterous allegation to anyone familiar with field operations. But not James Greenleaf.

Ordered to take no action, and having already filed a report I'd been told not to file, I was left to swing in the wind and fend for myself. I was crushed in spirit and beginning to doubt my own sense of right and wrong. In spite of everything, I felt disloyal and dishonorable about reporting the SAC, dirty in a way no shower could relieve. I had taken an oath in the FBI to never lie, to never corrupt, and certainly be duty bound to report those who violated the rules and regulations. After all, as an agent of the FBI my job was to gather evidence and present it for prosecution no matter who the offender was.

I had been struggling with the idea of Fidelity, Bravery, and Integrity, the FBI motto, for a considerable time already and the hours spent away on my honeymoon only crystallized the issue further. Having served the government for over twenty-four years now, patriotism and honor were elements of loyalty I took for granted. As a young lad in the Mount, I dreamed about the FBI and idealized how my service might be. Taking my oath of service that day in the Old Post Office was the proudest moment of my life. And my early years progressing through the Bureau did nothing to make me feel any different or dispel my idealism. Even as a "grunt" in those initial stages I accepted decisions as honorable and necessary.

My Boston experience, though, left me questioning the way those kinds of decisions were now being carried out. I no longer took for granted the inherent drive that fidelity and mission were paramount. I no longer took for granted that bravery, going above and beyond, was the proper perspective in every instance. And I no longer took for granted that all agents were loyal and honest; I couldn't, not after Boston. I was becoming disillusioned but still loved the Bureau too much to recognize it, still believed I could triumph over wrong the same way my radio heroes had in *This Is Your FBI*.

In every other investigation in which I was involved, there was never any doubt about what to do or how to resolve these kinds of situations. My job in the Boston office was to command FBI efforts against organized crime, public corruption, and other violations of the law that harmed everyday people, the ones we were sworn to protect. Innocent people. However, when reporting the FBI's Boston SAC for what I perceived to be a violation, I was told in this case that was not my task. I was effectively shut out of the resulting investigation and could no longer find out what was being done. So in a bizarre and ironic counterpoint, I had become one of the innocents, harmed by the very system to which I had given my professional life. I considered Greenleaf to be a bully in much the same way as the counselors at Mount Loretto who specialized in brutality. Like them, he wielded his power as a weapon, hanging me, in a figurative sense, from the steam pipes.

Later, I became convinced that the investigation of Greenleaf was doomed from the start. The decision to do nothing by HQ caused me to question my own command decisions, and I no longer took for granted the inherent drive that fidelity to the FBI mission was paramount. I had witnessed firsthand truth being trampled in the pursuit of ego by those who were no better than the criminals to whom they owed the measure of their disgrace-marred careers.

The memo I wrote reporting James Greenleaf for allegedly disclosing information is in testimony and evidence at court. And in those moments I understood with a pained, jaundiced clarity why HQ had assigned James Greenleaf to Boston in the first place:

Because they knew everything I was saying about the office was true and Greenleaf was just the man to assure nothing was done about it. Roy McKinnon, the assistant director who assigned me to Boston, was long gone, and the Bureau's prized Organized Crime section had become inundated by bureaucracy since the appointment of William Webster. The last thing any chief, director, or bureaucrat for that matter wanted to do at this point was upset the applecart. Siding with me, and thus conceding the depths to which the Boston office had sunk, would've done that and far more. HQ would side with Greenleaf no matter what because as a matter of convenience it made sense, ignoring clear and evident facts that did not escape the attention of Judge Mark Wolf later in his 1999 landmark decision.

"As described earlier," Judge Wolf wrote, "in this period the Attorney General's Guidelines, which had been incorporated in the FBI's Manual, required that the SAC himself make certain decisions, including, after consultation with the United States Attorney, whether to authorize extraordinary criminal activity involving a 'serious risk of violence,' and reviewing all such criminal activity at least every 90 days. Greenleaf's approach, however, had the practical effect of delegating these responsibilities, among others, to an informant's handler and his supervisor."

In other words, to paraphrase the popular cliché, the fox was quite literally left in charge of the henhouse.

But what of Greenleaf's plight? HQ had placed him in an impossible situation to do their bidding, a fact later borne out in the courtroom of public opinion when his own admissions of laughable inaction and ignorance took the focus off Washington and cast the spotlight solely on him. So in that sense, ironically, Greenleaf was as much of a victim of the system as I was in many respects, his hands tied just as mine were. The difference, of course, was that his toeing the company line allowed him to continue rising through the ranks of the FBI and remain in public servce.

Acting upon my recommendations by doing the right thing would instead have forced the Bureau to embarrass itself. The age-old mantra you will never see written anywhere, but nonetheless is the creed agents live by, had become the means that would assure exactly the opposite. To hear them say it, I was the villain here, the whistle-blower who had lost sight of my duty when duty had been the one determining factor in all my actions. I could've backed off, could've played their game, and done the job the way they wanted it done instead of the way I'd been sent to Boston to do.

But I didn't; I couldn't. I opted to go to war instead, and it was a war I didn't believe I could win.

PART FOUR
AFTER BOSTON

"Their position was and continues to be adamant that they will not jointly work this case with the FBI."

On 8/5/80 Colonel O'Donovan, Massachusetts State Police, called and inquired as to whether I would be available to meet with him at 3:30 P.M. at the Brighton, Mass., Ramada Inn. Colonel O'Donovan referred to his conversation with you on 8/4/80 concerning a highly sensitive organized crime investigation being handled by the State Police.

—Internal memorandum from Boston ASAC
Weldon Kennedy to SAC Larry Sarhatt on
August 6, 1980 (later submitted in court)

BOSTON, 1985

That 1980 investigation encompassed the now infamous Lancaster Street Garage incident. Attendees at the meeting, held months before my arrival in Boston, included Newman Flanagan, the district attorney of Suffolk County; Bob Ryan of the Boston Police Department; and Joe Jordan, commissioner of the Boston Police Department. Colonel John O'Donovan, of course, was there, and so was Jeremiah O'Sullivan, head of the Organized Crime Strike Force.

The memorandum went on to say that "approximately one month ago, the Massachusetts State Police (MSP) developed considerable information concerning organized crime activities in the Lancaster Street Garage located on Lancaster Street in Boston, Massachusetts. It was determined through their investigative activities that virtually every organized crime figure in the metropolitan area of Boston, including both LCN and non-LCN (Winter Hill) organized crime figures frequented the premises and it was apparent that a considerable amount of illegal business was being conducted at the garage.

"Pursuant to these investigations," the report continues, "Colonel O'Donovan met with Jeremiah O'Sullivan, Strike Force, concerning the feasibility of obtaining authorization for an electronic surveillance of the garage. District Attorney Newman Flanagan was brought into the planning stages because of the obvious jurisdiction of state authorities. Conditions imposed by the State Police were that under absolutely no circumstances would they jointly work with the Boston Police Department or the Federal Bureau of Investigation on this matter. O'Sullivan attempted to convince them otherwise, but their position was and continues to be adamant that they will not jointly work this case with the FBI."

O'Donovan's reasoning for this was simple: He knew that the targets of his Lancaster Garage investigation, Whitey Bulger and Stephen Flemmi, were FBI informants. O'Sullivan knew it, too, and now so did DA Flanagan. MSP had evidence linking Bulger and Flemmi to several murders, including O'Donovan's own informant Richie Castucci. Castucci, he believed, had been ready to give up Bulger and Flemmi as far back as 1976 when he was murdered thanks to an FBI leak, and the crusty O'Donovan had been steaming about it ever since.

It was this meeting, and its aftermath, that made my coming to Boston as inevitable as it should've been unnecessary. Unnecessary, simply because there could be no doubt in anyone's mind, inside the FBI and out, that as early as the summer of 1980 Bulger and Flemmi were known to be murderers and should have been closed immediately as informants according to FBI rules and regulations. Since the Bureau opted not to do that, they needed cover. They needed someone to run interference for them between the various warring factions and sort through the morass. I was never meant to succeed and wasn't meant to fail either. No, what HQ hoped was that I could repeat what I'd done in the Miami office—that is, clean up the mess without attracting attention.

Don't embarrass the Bureau.

I had managed major cases without doing that in Miami and the plan was for me to do the same in Boston. The substance of my similar experience in Miami involved Title III tapes vanishing from an evidence room, only to turn up in one of the supervisor's desk drawers, and boy, were they explosive! The tapes, as I detailed earlier, indicated that Miami police homicide detectives were being used as hit men against drug couriers in the Miami area. Tom Kelly asked me to review the tapes and, after doing so, I was left with the unmistakable impression that drug cartels had infiltrated the Miami Police Department and, potentially, the FBI.

What was not known was that the drug cartel traffickers had infiltrated law enforcement in such a way that cops were not only killing competitors but were also selling drugs. As detailed earlier, I learned through sources that one of the agents on my squad had an association with the cartel and had taken money from a drug lord.

You will never read anything about that case because I handled it totally in-house. The agent in question had plenty of friends inside the office and boasted that he had the best informants of anyone, rendering him untouchable. Not to me, though. I took on that agent in the Miami office and initiated my own undercover investigation to ferret out "other" suspects who may have been involved. My squad and I met with several police authorities and ultimately we were successful in adjudicating the situation through indictments and court proceedings that avoided public scrutiny and didn't embarrass the Bureau in the least. Years later, because too many of my warnings and reporting on the depth of corruption in the Miami PD went unheeded, the department would be racked by a scandal known as the Miami River Murders. As multiple news sites, including the *Miami Herald,* reported, more than one hundred officers were arrested, fired, suspended, or reprimanded for corruption, coercion, drug dealing, and murder revealed during the investigation. Twenty were ultimately convicted and sent to prison. No surprise to me since my investigation years before had uncovered this corruption in its most infantile stages. I had helped clean up my house and left it to the Miami PD to clean up theirs.

In unspoken terms, that was what was expected of me in Boston. In presenting me as a candidate for Boston, Tom Kelly used Miami as proof of the trust in which I was held to solve problems, and Roy McKinnon agreed I was the perfect man for the job. But Boston presented a different set of problems. Things had gone too far and deteriorated too much to be dealt with aboveboard, as had been the case down in Florida. Weldon Kennedy, my predecessor as ASAC in Boston, wrote in his August 6, 1980, memo that "the FBI and more specifically John Morris and members of the C-3 squad have furnished information of a sensitive nature to organized crime elements in the Boston area."

I may have been the right man for the job, but I see now that HQ never intended to close Bulger as an informant; if they had, they would've done so before I arrived on the scene. It wasn't that they didn't know what was going on, as is often professed to this day; *everyone* knew. Colonel O'Donovan's dogged pursuit of Bulger and Flemmi, as by far the most heinous and dangerous gangsters in the city, confirmed that much at least, along with the fact that their informant status was a badly kept secret. Later years would see the blame cast on a single rogue agent, John Connolly, whose performance, while reprehensible, represented just one spoke in a much larger wheel that churned through the Justice Department without any of the truth sticking.

Jeremiah O'Sullivan worked for the DOJ, so DOJ knew. Connolly's supervisor, Morris, knew; SAC Sarhatt knew; the U.S. attorney knew; the district attorney knew; Boston police knew; and, of course, Massachusetts State Police knew. They all knew that Bulger and Flemmi had committed at least a dozen murders, including at least one informant (Richie Castucci) by that point, and yet Bulger and Flemmi weren't arrested. They survived and even prospered, and they did all this despite the fact that they were ineffective informants.

You'll never close Bulger.

John Morris's prediction to me after I told him my intentions following my one and only face-to-face with Whitey had become prophetic indeed. It was more than bravado talking. It was cold reason. My hands had been tied from the beginning, and as I neared my end in Boston, it all became clear, right down to James Greenleaf's appointment as SAC. Since I was no longer toeing the line in the wake of the Halloran and Callahan murders, Greenleaf's job, I believe, was to rein me in by whatever means were necessary.

In the aftermath of the Cape Cod incident, he took any number of punitive steps meant to embarrass and isolate me. First off, I was denied the opportunity to make an oral or written reply to the original charges levied against me over the shooting. Nor was I permitted to add testimony and additional mitigating factors. I was then told I could no longer participate in the Bureau's physical exercise program and was cut off from primary organized crime responsibilities even though I was handling major undercover operations at the time, including one against Billy Bulger, Whitey's pol brother. Greenleaf's intent was, it seemed, to cut me off from my squads as much as possible and render me a pariah in the office. This in spite of the accolades I had received for the many successful cases I'd made over the past four years, from arresting Angiulo to taking down the Hells Angels executioner, and many more.

Then, in mid-December of 1985, a report from Attorney Rogers from the Office of Professional Responsibility concluded that there was "no wrongdoing or criminal intent on the part of ASAC Fitzpatrick to deceive, cover up or omit details" in my reporting on the Cape Cod incident. This represented a Department of Justice edict, and by all rights and reason should've been the end of things. It turned out to be quite the opposite when Greenleaf introduced the notion and term "criminality" with regards to my reporting on the shooting.

Criminality? I couldn't make up a more ludicrous story. Even the Director himself, William Webster, wrote to the Bureau's general counsel, John Mintz, that he was "satisfied from your review and from my own cursory review of the record that this was not an instance of fictionalizing interviews." In the same letter Webster went so far as to recommend SAC Greenleaf be reprimanded but not censured, over the Cape Cod shooting incident. In spite of all this, I was never given the opportunity to air my accusations against Greenleaf. Nor to my knowledge was any investigation ever conducted regarding them. Greenleaf had HQ's ear in the form of Sean McWeeney and John Otto, and HQ was deaf to the truth behind what was going on in Boston that I could have provided. Taking my side against his, no matter the right and wrong involved, would have upset the Bureau, as would closing Bulger and Flemmi when they should have been closed. The hole the Bureau was digging just kept getting deeper.

The ensuing months passed in a blur that I only vaguely recall to this day. Despite the fact that I'd been cleared of the charges by the Director himself, the allegations continued to fester, rumors spreading of the actions Greenleaf intended to take against me with the apparent acquiescence of HQ in Washington. I was going to be transferred, demoted, suspended, or fired. It varied by the day, perhaps according to Greenleaf's whims and appetite for unjust retaliation. Agents who could and did try to offer the facts that would have exonerated me were bullied, intimidated, or ignored. Agent Paul Cavanaugh apologized profusely and offered to stand up for the truth. But word was out that to stand up for me was to stand against SAC Greenleaf, who was backed up by Washington.

Agent James Trout, the actual "shooter" in the Cape Cod incident, was convinced a cover-up was taking place, since all the reporting he provided was ignored. A seasoned field agent who'd been in dangerous undercover situations before, Trout felt that the additional HQ investigation was a gross waste of money for FBIHQ, given the fact that the shooting incident had resulted in neither a fatality or wounding with the suspect captured as a direct result of his actions. Paul Cavanaugh was convinced the Bureau was out to get both me and Trout. He claimed that the inspectors who interviewed him were deceitful and misleading, going as far as to insist to me that they "covered the FD-302 report so he could see only the bottom line."

I fought the spurious charges by filing a formal complaint with the United States Merit Systems Protection Board, the ultimate arbiter in such matters, in June 1986. In response to the question "Why do you think the agency was wrong in taking this action?," I wrote three answers: that I wasn't guilty; that I'd been denied due process by never having been given the opportunity to make an oral reply to the charges made against me; and that the charges had been brought against me in retaliation for being a whistle-blower. I had officially been removed as ASAC on March 6, 1986, and asked the board, in view of my exoneration by the Director himself, that I be reinstated to both my former position and pay grade, and that all Bureau records of any indications that the action ever occurred be purged. It only seemed fair.

The board agreed and, as a result, the Bureau offered me a compromise. Since it was clear I couldn't work under James Greenleaf anymore, they offered me the ASAC position in Omaha, Nebraska. But my wife Jane was pregnant and had built a great career for herself as director of nursing at St. Elizabeth's Hospital. All the moving around had already cost me one marriage and I didn't want it to cost me another. So I rejected the Bureau's offer and asked instead that I be reassigned to Providence as a "brick" agent, the same rank I'd held during the Martin Luther King investigation.

To its credit, the FBI acquiesced, but, since Providence was a satellite office of Boston, I continued to be approached by Boston agents complaining of continued corruption and leaking. My five-year war to bring down Bulger and clean up the office had taken its toll. The FBI had been part of my life for nearly forty years—first as a dream born of an old FBI radio show, then as a goal, and finally as a dream come true. Everything in my life from an extraordinarily early age had been about first becoming an agent and then being the best agent I could be. I had been involved in the Bombings in Mississippi investigation, the Martin Luther King assassination conspiracy in Memphis, and the ABSCAM corruption conspiracy in Miami, and come through all of them with flying colors. But none of them rivaled the conspiracy I confronted in Boston. To stand behind me would have been to concede the corruption that dominated the office. To stand behind Greenleaf was to cling futilely to a standard of honor that had been darkened by Paul Rico and Dennis Condon and then blackened by John Connolly and John Morris.

I could have stayed in Providence, but every man has a breaking point and I'd reached mine. So early in 1987 I tendered my resignation from the Bureau in bittersweet fashion, feeling I'd left too much undone.

Because here's the real rub. With all these crosshairs trained on me, a public corruption case against Billy Bulger floundered and finally collapsed under the weight of leaks.

And nobody seemed to care.

Whitey Bulger continued to consolidate his hold on power, murdering at will and whim.

And nobody seemed to care.

In late February 1986, as I was getting ready to pack my bags for Providence, Jerry Angiulo was found guilty for the RICO violations on which I arrested him. Not a single shred of evidence or information furnished by Bulger was ever entered at trial.

The end came for me, in ironic counterpoint, around the same time an FBI Special Agent testified that he ignored evidence that Boston city workers had built guardrails on private property around a South Boston liquor store "controlled" by James "Whitey" Bulger. Why had the agent ignored such an egregious example of public corruption?

Because John Connolly reminded him that Bulger was "an indispensable informant."

24
BOSTON AND PROVIDENCE, 1987

"Fitz, there's not a more honorable thing in this world you could do."

I wonder now what Father Kenny at the Mount would make of my departure from the Bureau. It wasn't dramatic or emotional really. I typed a series of letters to the appropriate parties to deal with retirement and pension issues, letters devoid of any inkling of the painful narrative that had taken me to this point. I had brought a cardboard box to pack my personal items, but hadn't been in Providence long enough to accumulate many, so the box still had plenty of space when I carried it to my car.

Another crucial part of the settlement agreement I'd reached with the Bureau was that my record and file be expunged so none of the false allegations stemming from the Cape Cod shooting incident could ever come back to haunt me in private life. I would later be told by a close source in the Bureau that Greenleaf had been formally reprimanded for pursuing charges against me stemming from the Cape Cod shooting incident. And by the time I turned in my retirement papers he'd already been transferred out of Boston and replaced as SAC by James Ahearn.

I shed no tears, cast no fond gazes back toward the Providence building which held my office. The pain was still there, reduced to a dull, persistent ache over how my efforts to do the job I'd been sent to Boston to do had been thwarted at every turn.

Ironically enough, a report issued by the President's Commission on Organized Crime that characterized Whitey as "a killer and crime boss" was issued shortly after I left the Boston office in 1986. Enough to consider closing Bulger as an informant, according to established DOJ and FBI guidelines. I suppose my former colleagues had missed reading it, or perhaps they figured they could run the commission members out of town, too.

But I took some solace in the notion of moving on, of turning my back at last on a phase of my life that held so many raw, angry memories. My many accomplishments seemed small consolation at that point. I thought in time that might change, that I'd learn to live with the betrayal experience and learn to put it behind me.

I was wrong.

Several years after my resignation from the Bureau, the federal government appointed Billy Brown, a former assistant U.S. attorney and current Boston lawyer, to counsel me during the many trials and depositions that resulted from the Bulger fiasco in court. It took Brownie a while to come around to the fact that I was actually telling the truth and not embellishing it at all. I can't really blame him, not when you consider the enormity of my accusations and the mere thought that an organization as storied as the FBI could possibly have let things spiral so out of control.

When it finally dawned on him that I was a man to be trusted and everything I was telling him was true, Brownie said, "You know, Fitz, in many ways, what happened in the Boston office is the same thing that happened in the religious scandal with priests abusing children in Boston. Just like Cardinal Law's hierarchy turned a deaf ear to what was going on, so did the FBI."

"Brownie," I told him, "it was different. Believe me. The complaints were so widespread and coming from the Staties, the Boston cops, the DEA, and even from inside our own office. It was useful for the FBI to pretend ignorance; I mean, after all, if you don't know, you can't be blamed for doing nothing."

As 1987 dawned, I looked ahead with a combination of excitement and trepidation. My wife Jane's support, in the face of her own career issues, was vital. Because of that, along with a desire to prove worthy of her faith, I got my PI (private investigator) license. I never saw myself following deadbeats and shooting pictures of men or women carrying on affairs to use in divorce proceedings. Fortunately, my considerable contacts in law enforcement allowed me to pursue higher-profile cases in the areas of corporate espionage, professional protection, security consulting, and fraud investigation. Some of these cases eerily mirrored my work in the Public Corruption arena with the FBI, like the Pete Rose baseball case I worked for Major League Baseball. Rose had been caught up in a gambling scandal and I wrote a report outlining how I'd found evidence that he had bet on himself in games. It was quite an investigation and grabbed the headlines for a time. I was finally leaving the past behind me.

But not for long.

In my new role as a private investigator, I got a call from a client who wanted information concerning Whitey's brother Billy, the still all-powerful president of the Massachusetts State Senate, and possible payoffs he may have gotten in the infamous 75 State Street scandal. Through sleuthing and contacts I managed to locate an account linked to something called St. Botolph Realty Trust that had made out two six-figure checks totaling nearly a half million dollars (as also reported in *Black Mass*) to Bulger for "a loan in anticipation of a legal fee."

I still wanted to see justice done and called John Morris, not knowing he was in trouble himself. Since John headed up the corruption case in the FBI, I gave him the information that I felt would have subjected Billy Bulger once and for all to a public corruption charge, or at least provide Morris with "probable cause" that a crime had been committed.

Morris and acting U.S. attorney Jeremiah O'Sullivan formed the team that would ultimately affirm or decline prosecution in the investigation. I felt certain that I had given them the smoking gun and eagerly waited to see the news in the *Globe*; I just wanted justice done and didn't care who received credit. But I was astounded to learn that O'Sullivan was declining prosecution on Billy, immediately recalling the same kind of inexplicable behavior that had characterized his treatment of Whitey in years past. I called Morris and was stunned to hear him stonewall me with nonresponsive answers to my questions. In retrospect, I'm glad it was a telephone conversation and we weren't in the same room together.

"What the fuck, John?"

"Look, I can't do anything. This was O'Sullivan's decision entirely. I had nothing to do with it."

"Nothing to do with it? You're the one I brought it to."

"Yeah, but it's O'Sullivan's jurisdiction and his call. I gotta follow his lead."

I was steaming. "This whole thing's gonna break sooner or later, John, and when it does it'll be on your head."

"What's that supposed to mean?"

"You really think you can get away with this shit forever?"

No less an authority than Alan Dershowitz later wrote that "Billy got a free pass from prosecution for extortion after he received a quarter of a million dollars from the developer of 75 State Street, when the acting U.S. attorney [Jeremiah O'Sullivan] on the case just happened to be the only Justice Department lawyer in on the Connolly-Whitey secret."

In July 1988, shortly after the Bureau and Department of Justice, through O'Sullivan, failed to act on the intelligence I'd given them, Dick Lehr from the *Boston Globe* called, saying that he wanted to talk to me about the Bulger affair. He knew I had been Morris's boss and that I'd overseen the Organized Crime and Public Corruption squads in the past. Lehr drove to my house in Rhode Island and we went for a walk on the beach. The day was muggy and overcast and, more important, the beach was empty. I was rather abrasive with Lehr because he had intimated that he had gotten my name from someone who said I knew the whole story.

Walking alongside him on the beach that day, I really didn't know what I was going to say at first. Then I figured I'd just stick with the most simple and basic: I'd tell the truth. So I spent the next several hours laying things out for Lehr, about how Whitey Bulger was a liability who'd never given the FBI any information of substance, especially regarding the Angiulo mob my squad had brought down. I told him the very notion of having an organized crime kingpin as an informant went against every tenet of smart law enforcement. Because, I explained to Lehr, you never own the top guy. He always owns you. Just like he owned John Connolly and John Morris and proceeded to corrupt virtually the entire Boston office. Washington had chosen sides as soon as they named James Greanleaf SAC in 1982. Bulger was their guy now, too.

There it was. After all the years of frustration and betrayal, I'd finally gone public about what I knew and had experienced, and for the first time I didn't feel I was abandoning or reneging on the oath I'd taken as an agent. The only way the FBI could be fixed was to first acknowledge it was broken. Nothing I'd tried up to that point had worked, and more lives continued to be ruined or lost. By remaining silent I was essentially condoning that behavior. It wasn't about getting even; if it had been, I'd have gone to the *Globe* the day I resigned and packed up my desk in Providence. I'd thought, hoped anyway, consenting to the interview might excise the demons of that period that had destroyed my dream. Instead, rehashing the whole sordid experience only made things worse, and I realized it didn't mark the end of my war, only the beginning.

It started to rain while we were on the beach, so Lehr and I went back to my house. I remained both tense and pissed, since I had just relived the darkest period of my life in chronicling why I'd left the Bureau. It all seemed so clear-cut when articulated in succinct fashion, though not to the FBI. Couldn't they see the corruption? Couldn't they see that they had been taken over by a thug, a sniveling rat? To the Irish a tout is a tout, and Bulger was a tout! I told Lehr I had worked multiple informants throughout my career in equally high-profile cases, so I knew what I was talking about. I had taught at the FBI Academy about these very informant problems and had been a profiler of people and events that spawned such debacles.

I told Lehr about what Morris had said, "You'll never close Bulger." I was Irish, but not Boston-Irish. I didn't know the inner city, but my childhood experiences in the Mount made me understand the culture and mores of Boston's Irish Southie. When I started encountering Bulger and Connolly, I was quick to find out what made them tick. And yet the same pro-Bulger proponents continued to prevail. I had spent the formative years of my youth watching my back at the Mount and, thanks to Bulger and his Bureau cronies, I spent what should have been the peak of my professional life doing the same thing.

"The FBI is being compromised. That's what pisses the shit out of me. I mean the FBI is being used," I told Lehr.

Just as we were used as kids in the Mount, held hostage by bullies and counselors, forced to fend for ourselves as we carved out a reasonable degree of security that often extended no further than our bunks. The Mount as metaphor for Boston was especially fitting, given that the entire city was being harmed by the drugs and violence pushed by Bulger and the corruption that fed his empire. You just couldn't escape it. If it wasn't Whitey operating in the city's seedy underbelly, it was his brother Billy ripping off the city and state from his office in the State House. *The Brothers Bulger,* Howie Carr's brilliant and powerful study of the era, is subtitled *How They Terrorized and Corrupted Boston for a Quarter Century* for a very good reason.

I went on to tell the *Globe*'s Dick Lehr that the root of the problem came down to what I had taught at the FBI Academy. The most basic seduction facing any FBI informant handler was "overidentification." In other words, letting the informant run the agent instead of vice versa. To put it another way, Connolly and Morris had "gone native" with Whitey Bulger just as Rico and Condon had years before with Joseph Barboza. What was clear to me, and I hoped to Lehr, was that Bulger and other informants like Barboza had dragged the FBI's name and reputation through the mud. And, for trying to get the Bureau straight again, my name had ended up shit-canned by the very people who should've joined my efforts instead of fighting them tooth and nail. If this were the Mount, I'd still be hanging from the steam pipes.

The rain was still falling when Dick Lehr left my home, his windshield wipers fighting to slap it away as he drove off. I wondered what he'd do with what I'd given him and what he'd been able to glean elsewhere. Would the FBI squash his story somehow? Would power be exerted over his superiors at the *Globe* and its owners? After what had happened to me, anything seemed possible.

Two months later, on September 19, 1988, the *Boston Globe* published the first installment of Lehr's explosive Spotlight Series. The articles, which ran for four days, tore the lid off the whole unspeakable mess by encapsulating Bulger's hold on the FBI and how that derailed the attempts of locals cops, Staties, and drug agents to put him away once and for all. The evidence and will to nail Bulger had always been there, forestalled by the Bureau at every juncture.

The *Globe* series marked the first public exposure and rebuke of the FBI's handling of the Bulger fiasco. Mention of Angiulo, who'd been taken down by my squad, formed another ironic counterpoint, since that was what Whitey had been enlisted to help with but he instead ended up accomplishing nothing that didn't serve his own ends. The *Globe* series went on to describe, in fairly amorphous terms, the DEA's attempt to get Bulger via federal wiretaps (thanks in large part to intelligence furnished by John McIntyre before he "disappeared"). To no avail, of course, since Connolly, Morris, and probably others made sure Whitey knew his car and condo were all bugged.

In fact, as the *Globe* article from September 20, 1988, alluded, those in the DEA involved in the 1984 Bulger investigation had determined they couldn't even share their intentions or information with the FBI. As anyone in law enforcement knows, this represents an egregious break from established procedure and protocol, and the DEA would only have opted for it had they determined no other viable option existed. It seemed to me they'd come to the same conclusion I had long before: that the FBI had absolutely no intention or desire to deal with Whitey Bulger as a problem or even recognize that he posed one.

If I'd had any questions about Lehr's intentions or veracity in our walk on the beach, his Spotlight Series written in tandem with Gerard O'Neill and Christine Chinlund pretty much vanquished them.

The series of articles chronicling the rise to power of Whitey and Billy Bulger finally dug deep enough below the surface to find the same mess I'd found eight years before when I arrived in Boston, and their reporting gave my own accusations a fair and thorough hearing.

"Part Three," for example, covered a portion of the FBI's complicity in helping to fuel Bulger's rise to power. (The series also expertly paralleled Whitey's pursuits with those of his powerful pol brother Billy, especially fitting since my investigation of at least one of the scandals involving Billy was derailed by my departure from Boston.) It was the beginning of the end for Whitey Bulger and his enablers, but, even then, the end would not come soon enough. The new Boston SAC, James Ahearn, would publicly defend the FBI position by flatly denying Bulger and Flemmi's informant status instead of the usual "no comment."

The Spotlight Series wasn't afraid to name names either, and did a commendable job of tying the disparate strands together, while suggesting some of the twisted connections that seemed too incredible to believe. It even revisited the 1979 Race Fix case that cemented Jeremiah O'Sullivan's complicity in the Bulger debacle and that remains to this day one of the clearest shots the Bureau had to get Whitey, although they failed to act.

The Race Fix case had sent several Winter Hill Gang members to federal prison. One of these, Anthony "Fat Tony" Ciulla, was unequivocal in his insistence that Whitey Bulger and his right-hand man Stephen Flemmi had taken a hefty cut of the profits. But the ever-crusty Jeremiah O'Sullivan, who saw his position as head of the Strike Force as a stepping-stone to a lucrative career as a high-profile defense attorney, which he went on to pursue in the 1990s, still refused to indict the two men who were the operation's kingpins.

"We had no evidence against them outside of Ciulla's word," he told the *Globe* reporters. "Very rarely do you indict on just the word of an informant."

25

BOSTON, 1995

"Did you hear about Bulger?" one of my old squad members asked over the phone in early 1995.

"What's he done now?"

"He's gone."

"Guess he got one last tip," was all I could think to say, a better prophet than I'd ever imagined, as it turned out.

I suppose I knew this day would come, the only conceivable resolution given the FBI clearly had no intention of ever prosecuting Whitey. I remember feeling strangely ambivalent at first, taking the news in stride. On the one hand, Bulger's disappearance dredged up all the painful memories about my failed attempts to close him. On the other, the fact that he had been allowed to slip away was final affirmation of the Bureau's utter incompetence and malfeasance in their dealings with him. This while providing no vindication for my efforts or claims at all, and only reviving my bitterness.

That wasn't all. The fact that Bulger was now on the lam presented a very real threat to me. He'd already made his intentions plain to John Morris, and the fact that he was now free to come after me, and my family, unsettled my wife Jane and our two young daughters, who were afraid to go to sleep, to school, or leave the house at all. Our friends offered us safe harbor, a place to hide from a man they knew wanted vengeance against me for pursuing him without end. Bulger had killed plenty for just talking about him, telling the truth, and I'd continued to do just that in my years after leaving the Bureau. The tension was palpable, increasing with each call from friends or associates to check on my well-being. I was never far removed from my gun and made sure the blinds were always drawn over the windows. Seeing the fear in the faces of my wife and daughters replaced my anxiety with anger over the fact that their lives were being disrupted by this psychopath who should have been jailed long before he had the opportunity to escape. I almost wish Bulger had come after me, so I could have settled things once and for all myself.

Bulger's disappearance became a de facto demarcation point whereby the debacle, as far as I was concerned, moved the action from the street almost entirely into the courtroom. John Connolly, who would soon face trial and imprisonment for his actions, had retired from the Bureau. John Morris would suffer a heart attack while in Quantico following a telephone call from Whitey apocryphally telling him "he was going down with the ship," a threat to effectively end his career as well. And not long after Whitey vanished, hearings before Judge Mark Wolf in Boston federal court would further expose much of the way the FBI had done business in Boston over the years.

The playbook had already begun to change with Connolly's retirement as 1990 drew to a close. It'd be easy to say he saw the writing on the wall, but the writing had been there for years, Connolly brash and arrogant enough to ignore it. Still, he saw an opportunity to get out while the getting was good. I heard a hell of retirement party was held for him; guess my invitation got lost in the mail. Whitey's, too. Connolly's loyal service to one Bulger, though, had earned him payback from another Bulger. Among the "perks" of his retirement package was a "lobbying job" for Boston Edison, a power company, at Billy Bulger's State House complete with a $112,000 annual salary.

"We take care of our own here," Billy had told me during our one meeting, as much a show of force as a warning.

And he had taken care of John Connolly splendidly. Connolly had paid his dues to the Bulger family and was now reaping the rewards. John Morris left Boston soon after, bound for Los Angeles to become Assistant Special Agent in Charge there, en route to his heart attack a few years later. I'd like to say I smiled over the irony of Morris assuming the same position in L.A. I'd held in Boston, but I didn't.

As for Whitey, years prior to his disappearance he hit the lottery on someone else's ticket. The jackpot number had been purchased at the Rotary Variety Store Bulger owned, and he was able to "cajole" the winner into splitting the proceeds fifty-fifty with him. That amounted to about $90,000 a year after taxes, enough to live pretty well on if it ever came to that.

But this time even Whitey must have seen the writing on the wall, especially with the security blanket he'd maintained, in the form of Connolly and Morris, gone. Not that he intended to lay low, not with the Boston rackets and a drug trade under his control. The new mafia boss, Frank "Cadillac" Salemme, may not have taken his orders directly from Bulger, but neither did he make any move that would have stoked the old tribal fires between Boston's Irish and Italian mobs. The only kind of peace Whitey knew was one that left him calling the shots, and Salemme was happy to cede whatever it took to keep that peace. Since he'd have far less insulation to cushion him the next time his escapades resulted in blowback, Whitey was more than happy to let Salemme take the heat while he laid low, at least in relative terms.

Then a new "sheriff" came to town, specifically an assistant in the U.S. Attorney's Office by the name of Fred Wyshak. The New York–born Wyshak had the advantage of a proven background, like mine, having successfully prosecuted the New Jersey mob in his last stopover. He didn't have to worry about John Connolly, John Morris, or James Greenleaf running interference for the murderous Bulger. Nor was he beholden to the legacy and rules of the FBI that had so hamstrung my efforts.

Brian Kelly, a thirty-year-old U.S. attorney who worked the case with Wyshak, couldn't believe the evidence before them, specifically that a pair of psychopaths, Bulger and Flemmi, had been able to run roughshod over one of the largest Bureau offices in the country. To Kelly and Wyshak himself, this was absolutely mind-boggling and further complicated by the fact that they couldn't find a single example over the past decade where information provided by the prized Bulger had led to an arrest, much less successful prosecution.

Fred Wyshak, who I met only briefly and with whom I had very little real interaction, didn't have to worry about embarrassing the Bureau. He had the entire United States government behind him and was smart enough to first target Howie Winter, recently released from a long stretch of prison. His Winter Hill Gang had been remade in Whitey Bulger's image. Operating out of Southie as a satellite of the Sommerville Winter Hill Gang, it was similar in a way to the North End as an organized crime satellite to Patriarca's OC Providence gang. It allowed Bulger to pull the wool over Winter's eyes because no one knew what was going on "down there" in Southie.

Howie Winter later remarked that Bulger built his power base that way, and Winter had no choice but to accept it: there was plenty of work to go around, some of which made him fodder for Wyshak on a drug beef. What's clear from this arrest was that Wyshak's focus was trained on Bulger. And when Winter refused to give Whitey up, clinging to an old code his Winter Hill rival had long abandoned, Wyshak resolved to find another way to get his true quarry.

That is, until the new assistant U.S. attorney fell victim to the culture of corruption that still pervaded the Boston office of the FBI, even with the recent departures of John Connolly and John Morris and less recent transfer of James Greenleaf. Wyshak wired up a Bulger money launderer named Tim Connolly (no relation to John) to get the dirt he needed, only to have Whitey suddenly clam up around Connolly. Stephen Flemmi would later testify that Whitey had been tipped off, the tradition seemingly having outlived its founders.

Still, Wyshak didn't give up. He set his sights on what he saw as the weak link of Bulger's operation—bookmaking—to make a federal racketeering case against him. With his FBI family and Jeremiah O'Sullivan no longer there to short circuit such efforts, Whitey found himself suddenly vulnerable. The man wearing the bull's-eye instead of the one painting it on others. Wyshak went after Bulger's army of bookies like a pit bull, ultimately accumulating enough evidence to secure racketeering indictments against Salemme, Flemmi, and Whitey himself in late 1994. Flemmi was taken into custody, Salemme fled to Florida where he, too, was arrested a few months later, but Whitey was nowhere to be found. Whether he was tipped off or not in one last show of deference by the Bureau, at least to some, remains in dispute. What isn't in dispute is that his gangster associate Kevin Weeks funneled enough money to Whitey early on to keep him on the lam through America's underbelly. Places he wouldn't have been caught dead in before, where his status as a legendary kingpin on the streets of Boston meant nothing.

The next contact anyone else had with Whitey was none other than John Morris in that phone call while Morris was serving as training director at the FBI Academy. There are differing versions of that conversation, but one thing is clear in all of them: Whitey warned Morris not to talk, not to give him up. Do that and Morris would be going down, too. Or worse. Bulger disappeared for good after that call and, other than a few rumored sightings, wasn't heard from again until his June 2011 capture in Santa Monica, California.

But his name surfaced plenty in the now infamous Wolf hearings that began three years after his disappearance. Infamous because the mob-related testimony and evidentiary material blew the lid off the FBI's casual use, and protection, of criminals as informants, and nearly blew up the case against Frank Salemme and the other defendants.

"The court has reviewed the defendant's Motion to Disclose Confidential Information and Suppress Electronic Surveillance conducted in this case," wrote the presiding judge, Mark Wolf, in one of his rulings after several days of closed sessions. "In this case, in which the defendants are charged, among other things with conducting a racketeering enterprise, the fact that a codefendant was during the relevant period a confidential informant for the FBI would, if true, constitute exculpatory information to which his code-fendants are entitled."

In other words, the State, and thus the FBI, had no choice but to reveal who their informants were and how exactly they had been used. What many had suspected for decades, starting with Colonel John O'Donovan of the Massachusetts State Police, the very root of the cancer that had infected the Boston office, was about to be laid bare for public inspection in open court. And that would mean, under no uncertain terms, many of the claims that had followed my interview with Whitey Bulger that night in his Quincy condo, and subsequent recommendations that he be closed as an informant, were going to be revealed. Specifically, that he had played the FBI for years without furnishing the exacting information that supposedly made him indispensable.

The bull had broken free of the barn and was running loose in the China shop, and now the FBI and Justice Department were about to be called in for a reckoning.

What followed through much of 1998 in Judge Wolf's courtroom was a virtual parade of the rogue's gallery responsible for the entire sham. Everyone from Dennis Condon, who had gotten the ball rolling, to John Morris, who had kept it going through the years, to forty-four more witnesses, who took the witness stand—everyone shed a different light on the business the Bureau had been doing in the dark. Among those not to testify at all or only briefly, this time anyway, was Jeremiah O'Sullivan, who'd recently suffered a heart attack. Since this had long been a classic mafiosa ploy to avoid court, O'Sullivan became the inside joke while nonetheless being spared the questioning that would have revealed either his incompetence or possible treachery in protecting Bulger at every turn.

Meanwhile, the rats fled the sinking ship and began to consume each other. Connolly turned on Morris, Morris turned on Connolly, and Connolly turned on everyone except himself. Even loyalist John Martorano, fresh from hearing testimony that Bulger and Flemmi had given him up to the feds, redefined his own code by ratting out those who'd first ratted him out. His philosophy said it was okay to rat on a rat. But he did two extra years in prison instead of cueing the feds to the truth about his brother and Pat Nee, and they received more lenient sentences as a result.

All I could think of was how so much of it could've been avoided if Larry Sarhatt and HQ had simply acted on my recommendation to close Bulger as an informant in 1981. The lives that could have been spared, the embarrassment that could have been avoided . . .

Don't embarrass the Bureau.

From my perspective, one especially revealing exchange on this subject took place once Stephen Flemmi took the stand to be examined by a frustrated, fuming U.S. attorney, Fred Wyshak.

"You had a good thing going," Wyshak said at one point. "You were committing crimes at will, putting money in your pockets, and, in your view, being protected from prosecution."

"You're forgetting one thing, Mr. Wyshak," Flemmi replied. "The LCN was taken down. That was the FBI's main goal. They were completely satisfied with that. We fulfilled our bargain."

"Do you think, Mr. Flemmi, that you and Mr. Bulger single-handedly took the LCN down?"

"I'll tell you something, Mr. Wyshak, we did a hell of a job."

"That's what you think?"

"I think we did. The FBI thought we did."

"And when the FBI did that, you and Mr. Bulger were top dogs in town, weren't you?"

Flemmi, dejected, said, "I'll assert the Fifth on that."

26

BOSTON, 1998

As I sat down with the Strike Force attorney in a preliminary interview on the morning the Wolf hearings began in 1998, I was apprehensive and wary. Why had the Department of Justice scheduled this interview so late and what could I tell them in this short time period? I had already provided Wyshak's team with other dates and times for an appointment, but they didn't seem responsive. The government's Strike Force attorney, James Herbert, greeted me cordially, skipping the usual pleasantries that preclude opening questioning. We opened with my tenure at the FBI Boston office and I named the characters involved. My apprehension in discussing Connolly and Morris and the whole corruption angle proved justified when Herbert flipped his pencil in the air, shaking his head and muttering something to the effect that he would never finish in time.

"Was it something I said?" I asked him.

"No," he abjectly responded, "it's just that we've run out of time."

"Are you pissed at me?" I asked, sensing his sudden tension.

He had a sullen look on his face underlying an even deeper hurt. Something serious was bothering him, but I was in no position to understand what. He apologized and then, obviously upset and writhing with indignation, left the room to head for his opening day in court. Connolly's pals had clearly bad-mouthed me to him, and I think Herbert had begun to see that, contrary to what he might have heard, I was telling the truth and that many others in the Bureau had lied to him.

My interview with James Herbert indicated that the prosecutors didn't have a grasp of how deep this went, even as the hearing was about to begin. Fred Wyshak had built a bookmaking case in masterful fashion. But the tentacles around the bookies inevitably reached out into murder and corruption inside the FBI. There was no way to separate one from the other. Bulger and Flemmi were literally joined at the hip to Connolly and Morris. I realize now that my answers must have scared the hell out of James Herbert and he couldn't wrap his arms around the breadth of what I was telling him.

The prosecutors, I believe, were caught totally off guard by that and the contents of Bulger's FBI files. No one outside the Bureau had ever seen them before and the portrait of corruption they painted was utterly devastating.

Remember, the purpose of the Wolf hearings was to resolve a very complex issue of law; specifically, whether Bulger (his disappearance was a point of fact, not law) and Flemmi were going to be allowed to testify in the Salemme trial based on their status as informants. And now the prosecutors saw me as a guy who might not be in their camp. I'd already sat down with the other side—Salemme's lawyer, Kenneth Fishman—as a matter of course, and Wyshak's team must have thought they had reason to believe I was willing and able to blow their case up.

When my day and a half in the witness box finally came, I had to recollect the years of past investigations while manager of the FBI Boston field office and cases where leaks emanated from the information collected. Ken Fishman, who also represented Flemmi, grilled me on the stand about the administration of the FBI office and about Bulger's status in relation to his handler Connolly. By the time I took the stand, there had already been much testimony related to Connolly's "control" of Bulger and Flemmi as informants and subsequent complaints that had been made against Connolly for leaking info to the OC wiseguys.

"Did you ever report agents for leaking FBI information to criminals and others not supposed to receive this information?" Kenneth Fishman asked at one point.

A nervous titter ran through the courtroom gallery. I waited for it to die down before leaning in toward the microphone.

"Yes," I replied.

Fishman then approached holding a document in his hand. He leaned in to ask me if I had ever bypassed my boss, SAC Greenleaf, to report such leaks directly to FBIHQ in Washington. In the dead quiet of the courtroom, I looked him square in the eye, feeling the gaze of Judge Wolf boring into me.

I felt nervous and my mouth was dry. I choked, "Yes," yet again.

Fishman stepped back, surveyed the eerily quiet courtroom and then asked me to elaborate the details of this reporting. My heart was pounding when I explained in a low voice that I reported the SAC of Boston for leaking information that revealed an informant's identity to a mob attorney. The gasps in the courtroom were palpable.

The prosecutor jumped to his feet, loudly objecting to my testimony. "The details of Mr. Fitzpatrick's report of a leak are immaterial!"

The judge and the attorneys went silent again. The judge called for a sidebar conference out of earshot and subsequently prevented my further testimony. "So, the unchallenged testimony is that in one instance Mr. Fitzpatrick went over the head of the SAC to headquarters and complained about a leak, and we're going to move on from here."

That was it. The subject never came up during the Wolf hearings again. How could it? After all, the McIntyre file had never even been delivered to Judge Wolf. I was devastated. As originally reported to me by Tom McGeorge of my Public Corruption squad, Greenleaf's alleged disclosure of information to mob and drug attorney Martin Boudreau, formerly of Jeremiah O'Sullivan's Strike Force, if proven, represented a severe criminal violation. This should have been exactly the kind of information Judge Wolf wanted to hear. Yet once again, regardless of the scope of the Wolf hearings and Judge Wolf's own good intentions, true justice was not served.

During subsequent trials and depositions, my memo accusing Greenleaf of disclosing information was submitted as evidence under the discovery rules of the federal court. This memo was furnished to the Director's Office of the FBI, and to the DOJ through the Strike Force office at Boston.

Connolly would later be convicted for, among other things, leaking federal grand jury information. Greenleaf, however, escaped any punishment, or any recrimination whatsoever in the findings ultimately reached by Judge Wolf.

With Wolf about to release his ruling, Whitey Bulger was added to the FBI's vaunted Ten Most Wanted list. The ruling itself ran 661 single-spaced pages, forming a chronological, blow-by-blow treatise on the entire blood-soaked era. While Wolf hadn't gotten everything right by a long shot (he continued to extol Bulger's and Flemmi's value as informants), he came down hard on the leaking that I had reported throughout my tenure in the Boston office.

"In an effort to protect Bulger and Flemmi, Morris and Connolly also identified for them at least a dozen other individuals who were either FBI informants or sources for other law enforcement agencies," the judge wrote, going on to say that, as a direct result of this, "Brian Halloran was killed." He failed to mention any of the others.

As for the bombshell I'd lobbed regarding the then "disappearance" of informant John McIntyre, Wolf simply brushed aside the allegations, writing that "important FBI documents concerning John McIntyre were improperly withheld by agents of the Boston FBI until it was too late to question relevant witnesses concerning them." His voluminous opinion went on to say John Connolly may have been informed "about McIntyre's cooperation and claims and, in view [of] the Halloran matter, [there is] reason to be concerned that Connolly may have told Bulger and Flemmi. These issues cannot, however, be resolved on the present record."

Diverting from the cop-out mentality that gave little weight to my testimony, Wolf aptly summed up the entire fiasco with a confirmation of "recurring irregularities with regard to the preparation, maintenance and production in the case of documents damaging to Bulger and Flemmi." This finding was supplemented by Wolf's conclusion that "Special Agent Paul Rico helped Stephen Flemmi escape the country before being prosecuted for a car bomb planted in defense attorney John Fitzgerald's car and that Rico subsequently arranged to have the charges dropped."

That the FBI had broken the rules was hardly news now; that a judge had issued a ruling, however incomplete, saying it had was something else again. The Bureau, long deemed beyond reproach, had gone down the wrong side of the road in spite of my best efforts to steer them right, and the price they would pay for that was just beginning.

Shortly after Judge Wolf issued his ruling, John Martorano struck a deal in which he admitted to killing twenty people, including Roger Wheeler and John Callahan, on orders from Bulger and Flemmi. The FBI's sins I had known about for years were finally exposed for all to see. It was redemption in some small sense, but it produced no satisfaction in me. The vagaries of Wolf's ruling left the recriminations against the Bureau as just that and no more.

"Prosecutors want to believe the system works," Wyshak later stated in a *Boston Magazine* article in 2008. "I can't say everybody who was responsible was brought to justice here, but the criminal justice system is served not only when people go to jail, but also when the wrongdoing is brought to light so that the public can see it."

27

But much of the truth remained cloaked in darkness. Take the next chapter in my own battle with the Bureau. My departure, while contentious, was sealed based upon a "no reprisals" agreement, arrived at after complex negotiations, that included the expunging of my file so I would not face continued reprisal in my private life.

At least, it was supposed to be.

Shortly before the Wolf hearings began, I was representing a guy named John Parigian, who'd been accused of money laundering in federal court. My investigation, though, revealed accusations that the government had broken into his house, stolen his computer, and then charged him based on what they'd illegally found. Parigian had made allegations of government tampering, claiming that his computer had crashed with the hard drive being irrevocably damaged as a result of their tampering. That meant the evidence the government claimed they pulled off it, based on a falsely obtained search warrant, had been lost before they could've legally inspected the computer's contents!

These allegations pissed off the government attorneys. What

pissed them off more was my working on behalf of their target in my capacity as a former FBI agent. The government's response: a threat to impeach me and my credibility based on the contents of my personnel file that was supposed to have been expunged in my settlement agreement with the FBI upon resigning back in 1987, over a decade before. The federal prosecutor made no secret he was out to demean my reputation, admitting in open courtroom discussion that "I recall that I asked the client's lawyer whether I really had to get Fitzpatrick's FBI file so that I could be prepared to impeach him and added, 'I hear it's a thick one!'" How could they use something that, for all intents and purposes, no longer existed?

Obviously my file had not been expunged; the FBI had broken their agreement with, and promise to, me.

Parigian had been a source of mine dating back to my days with the Bureau. He had given me information about Bulger and Flemmi's involvement in offshore money laundering. His lawyer agreed to hire me because of my previous cases as a PI and the fact that, in his mind, I was a stand-up guy. Now I found the government was trying to use the old lies and smear tactics to destroy my client's case in federal court.

I felt like I was stuck in some twisted version of the Bill Murray film *Groundhog Day*, where I just kept reliving the same old Bureau bullshit. This all dated back to my accusing SAC Greenleaf of allegedly disclosing the identities of FBI informants to a mob attorney, a fact that was hardly in dispute based on the confidential memos in my possession. I'd broken the cardinal rule of embarrassing the Bureau and now that I was standing up to them again, they were up to their old tricks, trying to destroy my newfound career.

My exposure of corruption in the Boston office continued to haunt me and my family. According to her physician, my wife Jane miscarried as a direct result of stress. And I began suffering symptoms akin to post-traumatic stress disorder, later confirmed by physicians at Massachusetts General Hospital to be linked directly to the punitive retaliatory measures taken by the FBI.

And now here was the government attorney threatening me with impeachment, in front of my client, for reporting the FBI SAC for criminality associated with the alleged disclosure of information. More than ten years after I left the FBI I was still being slammed for doing my job. I realized that what I had hoped to be able to put behind me had come front and center again. The FBI had committed an egregious violation of our settlement agreement, leaving me no choice but to again bring suit before the MSPB, a veteran's right in the Merit System Protection Bureau.

My case against the Bureau was about two things: showing serious corruption in the FBI for which a former FBI Director had publicly apologized, and insisting that the FBI remedy the effects of past corruption in addressing my problem. I put forth a prima facie argument of retribution and retaliation against me for trying to do my job faithfully in the face of corruption. The allegations were undisputed in court and were substantiated by my taking a polygraph, even as the stream of public revelations in the media and through other court testimony was emerging. I was able to show newly developed evidence in court that indicated undue pressure was applied by the FBI in the Cape Cod shooting incident, and I presented evidence of false and exaggerated statements that precipitated the action. I'd learn later that the FBI's legal counsel withheld information in my court case because, "We believed it was appropriate to take further action in hiding exculpatory information." Fidelity, bravery, and *what*?

Around the time of the Wolf hearings and ensuing court trials, improperly motivated charges were levied against me for something I'd already proven I didn't do. That threat of impeachment in the Boston business environment eventually chopped off a major part of my business, including a potentially lucrative job with a Fortune 500 company. Finally, just when the government agreed to accept a just and fair resolution, the FBI reneged! I was under the impression that the current FBI was striving to correct injustices of previous leadership. I believed it capable of righting the past wrongs in achieving a fair and just resolution.

I couldn't have been more wrong. The apparent vindictiveness knew no bounds, especially for those who are perceived to have embarrassed the Bureau.

Back at the Wolf hearings, my attorney, Brownie, told me that the government could no longer interview me now that the hearing had begun. The law forbade it, even though it was obvious James Herbert, and Wyshak's team, needed more information. Was it coincidence they'd waited until the last minute to interview me in the first place, essentially running out the clock? Was there something someone didn't want Wyshak to know? Salemme's attorneys had obtained my anticipated testimony and were in a better starting place as far as they were concerned. When questioning me about Morris, I had given them a book called *Lying* by Sissela Bok that Morris had given to me early into my Boston tenure. As I thumbed through it back then, I asked him, "Who's the liar, John, you or me?"

The Wolf hearings would later reveal, through Morris's own testimony under a grant of immunity, his pattern of lying and thievery in accepting bribe money from John Connolly and Whitey Bulger. I began to understand Strike Force attorney James Herbert's frustration. While I believe his efforts were sincere, I similarly believe no one on the prosecution's team had anticipated the depths of depravity they were about to encounter. I don't believe DOJ or FBI had been happy about my anticipated testimony, as it would reveal a lot more than they were prepared to confront.

But it marked only the beginning for me. The aftermath of the Wolf hearings initiated my involvement in numerous cases in federal court where I testified to the truth of Whitey Bulger's unholy alliance with the FBI. In one respect, it was the best way to fight the FBI's capricious and punitive retaliation against me. In another it was the best way to make sure the truth came out and the guilty were punished. These cases, for the most part, were brought by the relatives of those murdered by Bulger and Flemmi who, like me, were after one thing: justice. I wasn't the only one who'd paid dearly for the FBI's rampant corruption. The Wolf hearings and subsequent trials might have tried to place all the blame on John Morris and, especially, John Connolly for everything that had gone wrong. But those who'd seen lives destroyed or lost weren't buying it, and I was in a position to help them find the truth they so desperately sought in a U.S. district court in Boston.

During much of that same period, my own Merit Systems Protection Board case, stemming from the FBI's refusal to live up their settlement agreement to expunge my record, wound its way through the court system, fought every step of the way by the government's army of lawyers, both in and out of house. When I lost in district court, I appealed to the U.S. Court of Appeals. When I lost there in 2005, I appealed all the way to the U.S. Supreme Court. My filing contained the results of a polygraph test that I took and passed in relation to the Greenleaf dispute. To my knowledge, Greenleaf had never taken a polygraph. Neither had any of the other antagonists from that era, including those who arose out of additional complaints I'd filed on still more corruption I'd uncovered during my post in Providence. It all fell on deaf ears.

And the Supreme Court refused to hear my case on a technicality.

I felt used all over again. I felt like the FBI was holding "something" over me during the years of evidentiary hearings, testimony, depositions, and motions. More retaliation? I knew only one thing: If I told the truth I could live forever with that, and no one could take my integrity away. But none of the cases I brought against the Bureau in any court brought me any sense of satisfaction or, even more, vindication.

That would come another way.

PART FIVE

VINDICATION

"Do you swear to tell the truth, the whole truth, and nothing but the truth, so help you God?"

28
BOSTON, 2000

A team of Massachusetts state policemen pulled the body of John McIntyre out of a shallow grave in a Dorchester, Massachusetts, gulley on a cold, dark, and dismal morning in January of 2000. The gray sky hung over the town's brick housing projects nestled apart from the rows of tenement homes finished in peeling paint or cheap siding, while the skyline of nearby downtown Boston winked with the first light of day. Across the street, a worker replaced letters on the marquee of Florian Hall, a popular banquet facility, to greet the attendees of a Chamber of Commerce luncheon later that day.

The gulley had been dug out as part of the "Big Dig," a major highway project undertaken to reroute the traffic, currently buzzing above along the Southeast Expressway, underground—it would ultimately become the most expensive highway project in U.S. history. I stood on the lip of the gulley gazing downward at the scene, flanked on either side by local television news teams eager to scoop one another. McIntyre's remains, limited to bones and body parts, were forced from an unforgiving frozen ground by uniformed officers wearing surgical masks over their mouths as a precaution both against germs and the potential stench of decomposition.

No priest or cleric had presided over the funeral of John Mc-Intyre. No dark-dressed cortege stood in solemn silence, weeping in grief for a lost friend and loved one. There had been no wake, no eulogy, no visiting hours.

As I stood on the lip of the dirt pile, looking down at the assemblages of bagged and tagged pieces of what had once been a man, the war I'd waged against organized crime and my own associates in the FBI for that entire period hit me hard and fast. I would later learn how McIntyre's last rites had been given in the basement of a two-story tenement house in Irish-dominated South Boston, where he'd been lured on the pretext of a party. For sixteen years, McIntyre's disappearance remained unexplained and his body undiscovered until another informant's tip drew the Massachusetts State Police to this burial spot.

I'd been out of the Bureau for almost fifteen years by this point, but calls from both the media and some leftover contacts in law enforcement had brought me to the scene just past dawn, where I stood frozen in the frigid air. It was 1984 again, John McIntyre was still alive, and once more I thought I had what I needed to clean up a mess in the Boston office of the FBI many years in the making.

And here now, almost two decades to the day of my arrival in Boston, the bones being pulled from the ground told the same story I'd spent the last fifteen years of my life telling. While my personal efforts to seek vindication were being stymied at every turn, justice was about to be served. Attorney General Janet Reno appointed an assistant U.S. attorney from Connecticut, a bespectacled, ordinary-looking special prosecutor with an organized crime background named John Durham to finally do what I'd been prevented from doing: sort out the corrupt mess that defined the Boston office and clean it up. Sounds like a simple enough mandate, and for Durham it was. Like Fred Wyshak he didn't have to contend with superiors impeding his investigation, some of whom were corrupt themselves. He did have a substantial handicap, though. Durham knew most of the agents involved in the Boston organized crime debacle, which could influence him partially because he had worked with them on some of the same OC investigations.

Or, he could embarrass the Bureau all he wanted.

Durham turned his sights, initially anyway, on John Connolly. Connolly had always cultivated a high profile and now that would come back to haunt him by making him the most convenient target, especially since he'd left the Bureau and wouldn't have the insulation that comes with being an active agent. Connolly bombastically and combatively took shots at the FBI and the U.S. Attorney's Office, denigrating them in the media. Arrogance, I was reminded, was his calling card.

Authorities arrested Connolly shortly after Durham obtained an indictment on obstruction of justice and racketeering charges in December of 1999, just before the statute of limitations ran out. They arrested him as the holiday season was in full swing, Connolly led out dressed in pajamas with his usual neat and polished appearance in disarray.

His brashness and ego had made him an easy target. Believing himself immune to prosecution, ingratiating himself with the media, he had turned the Wolf hearings into his own personal sideshow both in and out of court by speaking out against his former colleagues and superiors. He lambasted John Morris by labeling him a liar and a fraud, while flatly rejecting the claims of another, Morris's successor as head of Boston's Organized Crime squad, Jim Ring. Everyone, from Connolly's perspective, was a liar except him. He alone stood above all the corruption either revealed or hinted at during the hearings, contesting that he was a pillar of integrity. Connolly had insulated himself in his blanket of delusion that he had single-handedly taken down the Boston mafia, thanks to his turning Whitey Bulger as an informant. Profiling Connolly, I called this delusion superego lacunae, or "holes in the conscience," opinion over fact.

Connolly had the ability to use defense mechanisms to see things as rosy as he desired. He was a hero, a legend in his own mind, and thus untouchable, and everyone else be damned. He brushed aside my claims about him; dismissing them out of hand while seeming insulted I'd even dare pose them. There were guys calling him "Cannoli" because he went over to the other side. He simply stopped listening to reason, along with whatever was left of his own conscience. I had dealt with a lot of aberrational subjects in my time and Connolly had dissolved into little more than one of them, having lived the lie so long that he now routinely accepted it as the truth.

But there was another side to the whole Connolly fiasco that has never gotten the attention it deserves, that being the real possibility that at this very time none other than Billy Bulger was putting Connolly's name forward to become police commissioner for the city of Boston. I'd heard the rumors but dismissed them out of hand until questioning of Bulger in 2002 before a U.S. House of Representatives committee revealed that was exactly the case. Billy tried to double-talk his way out of it, saying in part, "Maybe way back. Many years before, there was a neighbor of ours who was mayor, and I may have suggested John to Raymond Flynn. . . . I may have suggested him as a candidate, somebody that might be looked at."

Well, I ran the Boston Marathon with Boston mayor Ray Flynn during that period, and in my mind there was no way he'd ever even consider Connolly for such a positon. The point is that Connolly had always insulated and compartmentalized Billy from his brother, while protecting Whitey from arrest and prosecution at the same time. His taking me to meet Billy early into my Boston tenure was all about showcasing his power and making "we always take care of our own" a barely veiled promise. That's what Billy was doing now by pushing the then lobbyist Connolly for a "commish" job that would have put him in charge of fighting crime in Boston.

How ironic that around the very time Billy Bulger may have been pushing John Connolly for police commissioner, another gangster-turned-informant, one Kevin Weeks, led FBI and Massachusetts State Police officials to the site in Dorchester where he'd buried the body of John McIntyre and two more of Bulger's victims. Weeks had already admitted his involvement in five murders with Whitey and Stephen Flemmi while denying he ever killed anyone himself.

"It wasn't that I wouldn't shoot," he said, as reported in the *Boston*

Globe; he didn't have to, since Bulger and Flemmi "liked killing people."

Kevin Weeks was in the basement the night of John McIntyre's murder. I stood on the lip of the gulley that cold January day thinking about how these three victims (other bodies recovered included those of Bucky Barrett, another informant, and an ex-girlfriend of Flemmi's named Debra Davis, allegedly strangled by Bulger himself), whose lives had been reduced to the contents of black body bags, didn't have to die. They'd all been murdered after my claims about Whitey Bulger and repeated recommendations that he be closed as an informant.

John Durham, though, had only John Connolly in his crosshairs, and it should have been like shooting fish in a barrel. As it was, though, the lengthy trial resulted in more charges being dismissed than upheld, due in large part to the fact that much of the testimony presented against Connolly came from convicted hit man John Martorano, as well as Frank "Cadillac" Salemme himself. Both had already cut deals with the government and were even less credible than Connolly himself. In truth, Salemme would actually perjure himself to get Connolly. The former crime boss was an advocate of "what goes around comes around," and it was his turn to get even. Stephen Flemmi, too, from a witness chair not far removed from the jail cell where he was serving an abbreviated sentence thanks to a plea bargain, wasted no time in cutting Connolly down to size.

In May 2002, Connolly was convicted of racketeering, obstruction of justice, and lying to an FBI agent. The jury, though, failed to find him guilty of bribery or of receiving a two-carat diamond ring from Bulger. This in spite of the fact that Connolly had many times shown the ring off and made no secret of its origin as stolen property. Even agents on the OC squad heard the rumors of the infamous ring and winced each time Connolly ran it up the pole.

Connolly was ultimately sentenced to ten years in federal prison, stoically stewing there while prosecutors began to build a case against him in the 1982 murder of John Callahan in Miami. As that Florida trial was about to begin in 2008, I was interviewed by David

Boeri for an article he was writing for *Boston Magazine*. In "The Martyrdom of John Connolly" (September 2008), Boeri expertly handled much of what transpired subsequent to John Connolly's 2002 conviction with a scathing, eye-opening aplomb that stressed Durham's myopic vision of the problems he'd been brought in to deal with.

"Nobody in this country is above the law, an FBI agent or otherwise," Durham insisted in the wake of Connolly's conviction, seeming to indicate a plan, at least an intention, to pursue other guilty parties.

Nothing could be further from the truth. More than a decade later now, no additional arrests or prosecutions have taken place, in spite of the fact that I and a number of other law enforcement officials laid out all the evidence of corruption and leaking for Durham. We basically served up everything he needed on a silver platter, which he apparently ignored then and has continued to ignore since.

I indicated to Boeri for his article that the Department of Justice threw Connolly under the bus. Clearly no fan or close friend of the man either then or now, I continue to stand by that statement. Connolly was the fall guy, the most convenient to go after and nothing more. But his conviction on charges that only scratched the surface of what he was truly guilty of did little to address the scope and magnitude of the corruption I'd found in Boston. Durham never charged the top leadership, including James Greenleaf or Jeremiah O'Sullivan, with a single thing. Whitey, after all, was *John Connolly's guy*. Connolly had long proclaimed that to be so and had ridden Bulger's coattails to a decorated career and cushy retirement. But now he was finally paying the price for it. Of course, O'Sullivan had been a willing partner ever since the 1979 Race Fix case, in which he'd let Bulger and Flemmi skate even though he knew they were guilty. That should have made them beholden to him; instead the reverse turned out to be the case.

Durham's laserlike focus on Connolly, in my mind, made him appear little better than O'Sullivan and the Department of Justice that oversaw his Strike Force. Durham gave everyone else involved in or enabling Boston's culture of corruption a pass, just as O'Sullivan had given Bulger and Flemmi a pass.

"In short," David Boeri wrote me in an e-mail months before

publication of his article for *Boston Magazine,* "Durham protected the FBI, and the very team he relied upon—the State Police and DEA agents—who arrested, interrogated, and handled the major witnesses, rebelled against him and consider him a fraud. They believe he could have and should have prosecuted other FBI agents. But that he chose not to investigate further."

In hearings held in 2002 and 2003, though, the House Committee on Government Reform picked up the ball Durham had dropped. On November 20, 2003, the committee approved and adopted a report entitled "Everything Secret Degenerates: The FBI's Use of Murderers as Informants." "The 1979 Ciulla race-fixing prosecution memorandum provides extremely important information about how prosecutorial discretion was exercised to benefit FBI informants James 'Whitey' Bulger and Stephen Flemmi," the report said in part. "It demonstrates that former U.S. Attorney Jeremiah O'Sullivan's testimony before the Committee is subject to question. Perhaps more important, it shows that a 1997 FBI Office of Professional Responsibility conclusion that prosecutorial discretion had never been exercised by the federal government on behalf of James Bulger and Stephen Flemmi was not correct."

Also included in the committee's report was a scathing indictment of the work of Paul Rico and Dennis Condon. Rico and Condon were the ones who'd handled informant Joseph "the Animal" Barboza, going so far as to falsely imprison four innocent men in the 1965 murder of Teddy Deegan to keep Barboza from taking the heat.

"I must tell you this, that I was outraged—outraged—at the fact that if [the exculpatory documents] had ever been shown to me, we wouldn't be sitting here," testified the lead prosecutor in the Deegan case. "I certainly would never have allowed myself to prosecute this case having that knowledge. No way. . . . That information should have been in my hands. It should have been in the hands of the defense attorneys. It is outrageous, it's terrible, and that trial shouldn't have gone forward."

In October of 2003, the very same week that testimony was given, police authorities from both Miami and Tulsa arrested Paul Rico at his Florida home on charges associated with his involvement in the murder of Roger Wheeler, owner of World Jai Alai, back in Oklahoma in 1981. The information they needed had come from none other than Stephen Flemmi, who was more than happy to give up anyone he could to get his own sentence reduced. To some hard-nosed investigators this kind of dealing by subjects in custody to get sentences reduced was called "getting on the bus." Both strange and fitting, given that Rico had first tapped Flemmi as an informant, turning him over to John Connolly upon his retirement. Rico had managed to skirt the law for years, according to court records, and probably figured he'd gotten away with everything right up until that knock on his door, and he was arrested for involvement in the crimes he should've been fighting, according to federal court records.

The paradox in this irony was bitter and sweet at the same time, since so much of the culture that allowed the Boston office to spin out of control had been bred by Rico and his former partner Dennis Condon. Two of the four men they had wrongly jailed for the murder of Teddy Deegan, Henry Tameleo and Louis Greco, died in prison. (Their death sentences, along with that of Peter Limone, were commuted to life in prison following the U.S. Supreme Court's ruling in Furman v. Georgia, 1972.) Joseph Salvati and Limone, were finally freed not long before Rico's arrest. Rico might not pay for the four lives he had needlessly destroyed, but he would now pay for a fifth whose murder he'd reportedly engineered.

Rico died at the age of seventy-eight in 2004 prior to his trial, his appearance so wan and weak in those final months that even his most fervent enemies and accusers expressed sympathy for his plight. Justice had hardly been served, neither in Rico's case nor the Boston office itself, since only one of the perpetrators spawned by the era, John Connolly, had actually been jailed. The justice system had failed. Those at FBIHQ who'd continued to fight and belittle me and my efforts thought they could breathe easier.

They were wrong.

Because the floodgates had been opened and could not be shut. The failure of the criminal justice system sent those wronged by the actions of corrupt FBI personnel to civil court, backed up by the inescapable conclusions reached in the Wolf hearings, the Connolly trial, and the Rico arrest. The corruption I had fought for so long had at last found the proper forum; Joseph Salvati, for example, sued the Bureau for $680 million for wrongful conviction in 2003, and that was just the beginning.

In the ensuing years, more than a dozen civil cases were filed against the Bureau directly related to the actions I had been stymied from stopping or exposing. After fighting for years to make people listen, suddenly I had a willing and captive audience eager to depose me for what I knew that for so long nobody wanted to hear. Appearing on CBS's *60 Minutes* in 2001, I had extemporaneously held the Bureau guilty in answering a question about responsibility. Every plaintiff's attorney had a copy of that show. In one case, there were no less than thirteen lawyers in a conference room during my deposition, too many for all the chairs to accommodate.

In a separate venue with government lawyers alone, I got a taste of what shape their hostility would take later in open court.

"Don't answer that," my crusty lawyer, Bill Brown, instructed in response to a relatively simple question from a Department of Justice attorney.

"You can answer the question, Mr. Fitzpatrick," she extolled.

"No, he can't," came Brownie's retort.

The attorney kept her eyes squarely on me, avoiding Brownie altogether. "Answer the question, please. You have nothing to fear."

At which point, Brownie leaned over the table toward her. "Are you Mr. Fitzpatrick's lawyer?"

"No," she replied feebly.

"That's right. So stop giving my client legal advice. He won't be answering the question."

This episode made for a prime counterpoint to the way I'd been handled by the FBI following the shooting incident in Cape Cod. Back then, FBIHQ agents ordered me to attend a class at Quantico that I'd already taken. I was actually taken out of class one day and ordered to FBIHQ where I was grilled yet again without counsel or any legal recourse. I told my interrogators I wanted an attorney and was rebuffed repeatedly. It was like a scene from the classic novel

Darkness at Noon in which Communist interrogators continue to question and berate Nicholas Rubashov until he falsely confesses his guilt just to make it stop. And if they did this to me, it made perfect sense that they'd follow the same track with agents used to concoct the case against me, one of whom later admitted he was so scared that, as in *Darkness at Noon,* he made up a lie they wanted to hear rather than sticking to the truth. Make no mistake about it, though, I remained Rubashov in this twisted tragedy.

I wish I'd had Brownie on my side back then, since his intervention with government lawyers had been a prime example of his working to protect me. Wolf, in his hearings, had inadvertently made a finding that now included me as a defendant in most of the civil cases brought against the government. One defense attorney told me he had to name me as a defendant to assure my testimony at trial to win the civil case.

The battle lines had been drawn, and this time I had Brownie watching my back. There were enough cases and depositions to make all the Q and A's run together, with one exception that would provide me with an opportunity to achieve the justice I'd been seeking for twenty years. A case that was still etched into my memory from a cold, blustery January day in 2000 when I stood watching the remains of a long-buried body being lifted from the frozen ground.

The body of John McIntyre.

29

BOSTON, 2006

As I stood on that embankment in 2000, steaming over confirmation of what I'd suspected ever since John McIntyre disappeared in 1984, I never imagined I was looking at the means to achieve my long-sought vindication. The coroner's report on McIntyre's death and remains only strengthened my resolve, as it brought me back to a dark period that had sewn the first seeds of my departure from the Bureau.

McIntyre wasn't a made guy like Brian Halloran, or a wannabe like Richie Castucci or John Callahan. He wasn't even a businessman with something Whitey Bulger wanted, like Roger Wheeler. John McIntyre was just an ordinary guy from Southie who got himself jammed up with the cops and was looking for a way out. And Bulger didn't just kill him, as he'd had John Martorano do to John Callahan with a bullet to the back of the head. No, he tortured McIntyre to death. Clearly Whitey wanted something he was convinced McIntyre wasn't giving him. The IRA intelligence? Maybe—if, as I suspected at the time, it was Bulger who told Scotland Yard about the arms shipment that had started out on the *Valhalla*. Nothing scared Whitey, nothing in Boston anyway. The IRA was something else again. If he'd ratted the IRA shipment out, for whatever reason, the IRA would close Bulger in a way far more permanent than what I'd been seeking.

Yes, what Bulger, already a fugitive for five plus years in 2000, had done to John McIntyre made me want to get him even more. And if I couldn't get him, I wanted to get his enablers, the keepers of the corruption that had cost McIntyre and so many others their lives while the FBI turned a blind eye.

Between the Wolf hearings, the Connolly conviction, the Committee on Government Reform's report, and the arrest of Paul Rico, McIntyre's family figured there was a smoking gun that could prove the FBI was complicit in his brutal murder. So they filed a civil suit in district court, drawing a wheelchair-bound, old-school, no-nonsense judge named Reginald Lindsay in a case that became known on the docket as *The Estate of John McIntyre, Plaintiff v. The United States of America, Defendant.* And, in large part, I was to become the smoking gun they needed.

Bill Brown, my attorney, called me on an unseasonably chilly late spring day in 2006. "Get your ass up to Boston, Fitz. Big trial coming down."

"Okay," I responded. "What's up?"

Brown went on to tell me that Judge Lindsay was going to have a bench trial in the McIntyre case. "No jury," Brownie said. "Just a trial before the judge; in our case Judge Lindsay."

Up until this point I had been deposed numerous times involving about eleven cases, all seeking big bucks from Uncle Sam for "estate" suits in Boston's U.S. district court. That meant the McIntyre trial could make for a precedent-setting case with major consequences for the government, especially the FBI.

On another unseasonably cool, windy morning I boarded Amtrak in West Kingston, Rhode Island, for the hour-long trip to Boston. The sky was gray, like my thoughts, with a foreboding feel of cold rain. My thoughts were coldly calculated in remembering the McIntyre case and what it had meant to me. My trip that morning would become a ritualistic endeavor over the ensuing weeks of trial.

As the train chugged into the station I made out Brownie waiting with a huge satchel, his old brown boxlike carrier that could hold all the government documents necessary for the trial. It was like some wizardly thing out of a Harry Potter movie, the way he seemed able to pull infinite reams of material from it, inevitably knowing where every piece of paper had been filed. Brownie and I exchanged the pleasantries of reunion and he ushered me to a great restaurant where we talked about McIntyre and the impending trial for hours.

"You know they'll be coming at you," he said. "The government has an axe to grind and doesn't really want to pay out any money in these suits."

I nodded and Brown continued, "Fitz, you are a key witness in this case because of what you know and who you were. We both know you're not on anybody's side per se and only want to tell the truth."

My eyes glazed over as Brown opened his bottomless satchel, producing endless reams of depositions and discovery material relating to the case.

"This discovery stuff," he explained, "is your testimony over the past three years and will be used in the trial. I need you to get familiar again with the material so you'll be ready."

I shot a look back at Brown, "Brownie, when you tell the truth, you don't have to worry about what you'll say."

Brown, the experienced attorney and savvy courtroom expert, rolled his eyes with nuanced skepticism. "Fitz, just do as I tell you and we'll be all right."

We chatted about how all of the Bulger murders had a common theme. Most notably the fact that Bulger the rat didn't like rats, and he was especially vicious when dealing with other rats. Psychologically, I suppose this was a type of reaction formation or self-loathing often born of a long stretch in prison. Bulger, on the outside anyway, was a constant show of machismo, force, and bravado. But inside lurked a thug with low self-esteem buttressed only by the security he found in wielding power through intimidation and brutality. The very definition, in my mind, of weakness. A bully, plain and simple. A psychopath.

"Why did Bulger have to maul and torture McIntyre the way he did?" I asked Brownie, posing a question I'd never been able to answer for myself.

"Because that's the way he is," he replied simply.

Brownie told me Bulger was the worst criminal he'd ever dealt with, shocked at how he'd co-opted the FBI.

"This case is gonna be a tough one, Fitz," he advised in what sounded more like a warning.

When I was a kid in the Mount we used to queue up for confession every Saturday afternoon about four p.m., before dinner, which was at five. The usual priests were there: the "good" priest with a Hail Mary and Our Father for penance; the inquisitive one always asking for more detail; the "hard-of-hearing" priest who made all of us speak louder to the snide snickers of boys within earshot. This priest would come out of his "box" and grab those kids from other lines because his was empty.

I recall Father Kenny lecturing me about "scrupulosity" in confessing. Father cautioned me that I offered too much detail in confessing about situations that weren't as significant as I thought them to be. Wow, I thought, I was confessing too much, actually a good thing for the priests because it showed a good examination of conscience. But, on Saturday, with all the kids going to confession, it might be considered a waste of the priest's time. They wanted to eat on time, too.

I found out when the trial started that when asked a question in court I had a tendency toward scrupulosity. Brownie picked up on this and said, "Fitz, you know you can say 'I don't know.'"

I explained to him the problem was that I *did* know and only wanted to tell the truth. Like Father Kenny at the Mount, Brownie was only trying to cover my back.

He observed that a defendant like Greenleaf had already been singled out by at least one judge, Mark Wolf, remarking on his tendency "not to remember" or simply testifying "I don't know" even if he did. Brownie emphasized that the judges know who is telling the truth and that's exactly what I intended to do.

The courtroom in Boston boasts a formal setup that belies its new setting on the waterfront facing Boston Harbor. The judge sits atop a box higher than anyone else in a courtroom smaller than what movies and television normally depict. It was also unusually quiet, no background noise whatsoever with the heavy doors managing to keep even the clacking of footsteps in the hallways from being heard inside. Beginning on June 12, 2006, I sat in a box alongside the judge and followed his body language throughout the trial. Judge Lindsay would rub his semi-bald head whenever he became perplexed or anxious with testimony. Generally, he was an empathetic listener.

When McIntyre's mother heard testimony from Flemmi describing her son's death, her grief and sad whimpering could be heard throughout the courtroom. Recognizing her pain and anguish Judge Lindsay called out, "Mrs. McIntyre, do you need some time?"

She declined and with reverence he accommodated her distress as best he could. The courtroom was extremely quiet as the testimony continued about how Bulger and Flemmi tortured and murdered her son. I thought to myself about how each court had a unique personality set by the individual judge in tone and process. In spite of the obvious tension, Lindsay set a standard of fair and just decorum in his courtroom.

I was pretty much considered a hostile witness to both the plaintiff and the defendant over my six days of testimony. The former, as represented by John McIntyre's family, wanted to use me as a pawn to show how the malfeasance and incompetence running through the Boston office was a major contributing factor to the murder of their loved one. The latter, as represented by the government, wanted to impeach my credibility by proving I was part of the problem and not the solution. Based on the line of questioning both sides pursued, I must say neither seemed terribly interested in the truth.

But that's what they were going to get from me anyway.

In court there were three attorneys for the plaintiff and three more representing the Department of Justice. Most everything was stored and displayed on computers in addition to "hard paper" evidence like the kind tucked neatly into Brownie's well-worn satchel. There was a screen shared by all participants, including the judge. The formality and rigid procedure allowed for a high state of alertness. Testifying provides little room for error as testimony is about fact and direct knowledge with no guesswork intervening. Doing this over an extended period proved stressful and mind numbing, since the same questions were asked over and over again in different ways. The repetition was maddening at times, designed to trip me up at more turns than I could count. The judge intervened in unprecedented fashion, determined to get at something in which none of the other parties seemed nearly as interested in as they made their cases:

The truth.

30
BOSTON, 2006

Spring was stepping into summer the day I boarded the Amtrak train for Boston. Once at Boston's South Station, I hustled on this historic day to Fan Pier's U.S. District Court overlooking Boston Harbor for a momentous day in the beginning of testimony at John McIntyre's "estate" trial that would decide a legal battle between the government representing the FBI and the family of McIntyre mourning his murder.

Courtroom 2, a usually sparsely attended courtroom, was packed to the gills with all sorts of people. Attorneys both in and out of the case were there, as was the media representing print and TV reporters. The families of the victims, including the McIntyre family, were in attendance, along with former FBI and other law enforcement officials and a plethora of individuals wanting to see history in the making.

Just as I arrived the bailiff announced, "Hear ye, hear ye, all rise!" as the judge entered in his wheelchair from his chambers to take his high seat among the gallery. It was 9:17 a.m. and the bailiff wasted no time in calling "Robert Fitzpatrick" to the stand. My heart was pounding as I walked up the aisle, took my place in the "testimonial box" and recited "I do!" to telling the truth, the whole truth, and nothing but the truth. . . .

Those in attendance were probably unaware of how flushed and nervous I was in the courtroom. I recognized a few faces in the gallery, but before I knew it, the trial had begun. The plaintiff's attorney, Steven Gordon, began by reviewing my FBI background and experience to establish my credibility and expertise. It was midday before he got around to the subject at hand.

THE FIRST DAY, JUNE 12, 2006

"And as a result of that background and experience, did you undertake specific work at the FBI in that area?" Gordon asked me.

"At the Academy I was assigned to the behavioral science unit. My job was primarily an area developing programs: homicide, sex crimes, profiling, hostage negotiation, terrorism, mostly the psychological application of that program."

"And as part of that training, how many hours of specific training in that area would you say you have within the Academy?"

"Hours?" I asked him back. "It was years, three years. I traveled throughout the country and the world, traveled about half the year teaching classes, giving instruction, and visiting crime sites."

"And would part of this training and experience be an ability to work with particular informants to assess their credibility?" Gordon followed immediately.

"Yes, yes. I taught a course, the psychology of informants and the psychology of all kinds of crime regarding informants. What we were doing was giving attendees an opportunity to understand the psychology of informants, which is, well, among other things, that they go both ways."

"What do you mean by both ways?"

"Well, some informants tell the truth and some don't."

"Would you train other agents how to identify factors to determine whether an informant was being truthful?"

"Yes."

"And did you lecture or train with regard to informants having to do with organized crime?"

"Yes."

"And did that pose any special issues for you or for the FBI?"

"Yes. It's a higher echelon informant."

"Mr. Fitzpatrick," Gordon started next, leaning forward as if he was coming to an important point. He looked down at the pages before him. "If you go down to the third paragraph, 'While the FBI recognizes the LCN as not being the only organized criminal element, it is nonetheless dominant and therefore continues to receive the prime investigative emphasis within the overall FBI organized crime program.' Do you see that?"

"Yes, I do."

"In the prosecution of LCN, what role did informants play in the C-3 [Organized Crime] squad?"

"Well, most of the informants are at least members of the organized crime syndicate, gang, whatever, and as such they are inside and able to afford information that we would normally not get."

"And would you describe that use of informants as being critical to the infiltration of LCN?"

"Most definitely."

"And would you consider critical the use of informants in the prosecution of LCN?"

"Most definitely."

"And you indicated also as part of your testimony that informants at times can 'go both ways.' Do you remember that?"

"This is true."

"And that there's a need to control informants so that they don't go both ways, correct?"

"True."

"And there is a danger if informants turn against the FBI?"

"True."

"And why so?"

Gordon had finally gotten to the heart of the matter. I weighed my next words carefully, knowing they would set up much of my remaining testimony over the ensuing days.

"Well, because they're privy to a lot of information that they're not just targeting but probably getting some information about what the FBI is up to, and they could telegraph that information or use it themselves."

"And so informants as part of their handling at times are given information about what the FBI is doing?"

"About a target, about a person, sure."

"And, therefore, as part of your job responsibilities, you want to do the best you can to make sure that informant does not misuse that information?"

"True."

"And the way an informant could misuse that information is notifying a target of the investigation that they're actually being targeted?"

"True."

"And it can be misused that an informant can learn who is cooperating with the FBI?"

"This is true."

"You know there's a risk that informants can misuse that information by harming other people who are providing confidential information?"

"It's a great risk, yes."

"And as a consequence of the difficulties in controlling informants the attorney general issued certain guidelines, correct?"

"True."

"And the FBI wanted, as far as you understood by the guidelines," Gordon picked up, citing the FBI manual, "wanted to make sure that they were using 'suitable' informants?"

"Well, that the informants were suitable to the task, yes."

"And do you see where it instructs if an informant is unproductive, unsuitable, or is not providing pertinent information, he/she must be closed? Do you see that?"

"Yes, I do."

"And was that your understanding that once an informant became unsuitable that informant should be closed?"

"That's right."

"And it indicates that if there is a serious act of violence committed by one of these informants connected with or unconnected with his assignment, then Washington needs to be notified."

"That's correct."

"And do you see the line where it states it is proper for the FBI to use informants and confidential sources in appropriate investigations but special care must be taken to carefully evaluate and closely supervise their use. Do you see that?"

"Yes, I do."

"And what did you understand 'special care' to mean?"

"That they, the FBI, follow the guidelines."

"And that an agent, because of the dangers in using informants, must pay special care not to violate the guidelines, correct?"

"If you're working organized crime, you work organized crime to the extent that you're going to prosecute those cases in organized crime. The special care involved would be that you adhere to the guidelines. That, in other words, you do what you're supposed to do."

"And it goes on to state that you're required, a special agent is required to ensure that individual rights are not infringed and that the government itself does not become a violator of the law. What did you understand that phrase to mean?"

"Well, that you adhere to the law and you adhere to the guidelines and you do what is correct and true."

"And the introduction goes on to state that 'though informants and confidential sources are not employees of the FBI, their relationship to the FBI can impose a special responsibility upon the FBI.' What did you understand the term 'special responsibility' to mean?"

"Sensitivity. Also confidentiality, and probably the term used before, suitability."

"Now, when you indicated that in adhering to the guidelines confidentiality was an important factor. What did you mean by that?"

"As we discussed before, it ensures the safety of the informant. It protects the information which will be used in prosecution, and it also is incumbent upon the agent to adhere to the guidelines in this regard."

"So that the agent does not begin to provide information to the informant that he should not."

"Well, we call that going native," I said, picturing John Connolly. I tried to see him as the cocky, insolent FBI agent he had been, but the only image I could conjure was of the prisoner now living in a tiny cell.

"What does 'going native' mean?"

"An agent who would perhaps become friends with the informant and not be as objective as he should be, and would then perhaps directly or indirectly be sharing information that they shouldn't."

"And was 'going native' a known risk within the office?"

"It's part of what I taught at the Academy. I would set up situations where the agents would 'go native' and identify or overidentify, compensate or overcompensate with the informants and do things that they shouldn't do. Compromise the investigation, compromise themselves, compromise the informant, and so on."

"Was it your understanding that any time the FBI learns an approved informant or confidential source is no longer suitable to provide information or operational assistance, his relationship with the Bureau shall be promptly terminated?"

"True."

"So if an informant was found or believed to be untrustworthy, [he] should be closed?"

I immediately recalled my many attempts to close Bulger. They all flashed before me in that moment, along with how the FBI had done everything it could to make sure that never happened.

"He would," I said, "probably by the agent himself."

"And if there was information that came to you that an informant was engaged in criminal activity that was not authorized, what was your understanding as to what an agent was to do?"

"Generally speaking, he would report it, it would be written up, and probably sent to headquarters."

"And if there was information that an informant was engaged in extortion, would that be information that should be forwarded to Washington?"

"Extortion would be something that would definitely be regarded as closable."

Mr. Gordon spent most of the day introducing my experience and expertise in being able to run an office of the FBI, especially in the area of priority cases like LCN and mafia-related violations. He honed in on informant rules and regulations and the need to pay attention to these rules and regulations, so that the informants receive proper guidance and instruction. Gordon made a case that the Boston FBI's informants had run amok, even though warned by me of the danger involved in not adhering to FBI guidelines. Those guidelines had been ignored along with my protestations.

The day ended around issues that suggested the FBI should have closed Bulger, as I had advocated, or any informant who was breaking the rules or not adhering to the guidelines.

The atmosphere had been electric throughout the opening day. The gallery was pinned to their seats. A poignant moment came when Mrs. McIntyre began to cry again, causing the judge to intervene. Reginald Lindsay's compassion added a kind touch to the otherwise brutal depiction of her son's execution at the hands of Whitey Bulger.

The second day of trial played to another standing-room-only gallery, and when the bailiff called my name I rose to the challenge of trying to make sense of the muddle that defined the entire Bulger era for the court.

THE SECOND DAY, JUNE 13, 2006

"Could you explain to the Court what a Top Echelon informant is?" Steven Gordon began.

"Well, a TE, a Top Echelon informant, is usually associated with organized crime. And the informant is an informant who provides very sensitive—highly sensitive, highly confidential—information about the entity, LCN entity, about associates, and about any other strategy, plans on the part of these individuals."

"And in the ranking of informants as being the most sensitive, where would Top Echelon informants be?"

"To the best of my recollection the highest level."

"And the reason for that is that a Top Echelon informant is providing information about managerial decisions being made by LCN?"

"This is true."

"And the Top Echelon informant, the TE, would actually be sitting in or could be sitting in with the board of directors of organized crime?"

"True."

"And the TE would be in a position to gain the information that he learned at those meetings and provide that to agents of the FBI?"

"True."

"And Bulger was a Top Echelon informant?"

"Yes, he was."

Gordon stopped there and stared across the courtroom toward me in the examination box. I could feel Judge Lindsay leaning forward a bit, as if sensing a crucial point was coming. My anxiety was palpable, my heart beating so hard and fast I thought the judge might be about to ask me if I was all right as he had for John McIntyre's mother on numerous occasions.

"Mr. Fitzpatrick, was Mr. Bulger kept open as an informant?"

"To the best of my knowledge, yes."

"And when you went to Boston, Mr. Sarhatt sat down with you?"

"Right. Mr. McKinnon told me I was walking into a buzz saw."

"And did you ask him what the buzz saw was?"

"You don't ask the assistant director of the FBI what the buzz saw is."

"You just walk?"

"I just listened."

"And then when you got to the Boston office, did Mr. Sarhatt explain what the buzz saw was?"

"Yes, he did."

"And what did he tell you?"

"Well, ASAC Larry Sarhatt told me that there was a fight between the Massachusetts State Police and the FBI agents Morris and

Connolly, as I recall; and there were accusations flying back and forth to the extent that Morris and Connolly were undermining the state police investigation at Lancaster Street."

"And they were undermining the investigation by leaking information to informants?"

"That's what MSP said, yes."

"And at the time that you came to the Boston office, were you asked to conduct any investigation as to whether or not it was correct that Morris and Connolly were leaking information to the informants?"

"Well, at some period thereafter I was asked by Mr. Sarhatt to go out and interview the informant, to actually assess the informant Bulger."

"And why were you selected to assess Bulger?"

"Well, Larry knew I had a background in psychology, that I taught profiling at the FBI Academy, and I had a particular expertise in certain personality traits of the criminal and so forth. He wanted me to use that advantage. He wanted an objective assessment in terms of Mr. Bulger's suitability and his continuance as an FBI informant."

I believe it was during this period when the judge wanted to know how come no one else in the FBI could see the danger in keeping Bulger open as an informant. He cited the fact that the FBI offices in Miami and Oklahoma along with outside law enforcement offices all saw the problem with Bulger as an FBI informant; everyone, it seemed, did except the FBI leadership. In my mind I took this as a harbinger of what was to come regarding Judge Lindsay's reaction to the entire Bulger situation.

"And when you say 'suitability,' you mean along the lines set forth in the guidelines?" Gordon resumed.

"Suitability may not have been the word he used exactly, but it entailed what he wanted."

"And prior to that meeting with Mr. Bulger did you have any discussions with Mr. Connolly about Mr. Bulger as an informant?"

"No—not about Bulger. I had discussions with Mr. Morris," I corrected for the record.

"Okay. And what discussions did you have with Mr. Morris?"

"I recall in a briefing prior to going out to Bulger that there was a statement where Bulger and Flemmi were heads of the WHO, the Winter Hill Organization. And I remember chiding Morris, saying, well, how can you have, you know, the head of the Winter Hill Gang as an informant?" I said, coming to the heart of the matter. The attention in the courtroom became even more riveted upon me.

"And do you recall anything else that Mr. Morris said back to you?"

"Well, afterwards we had quite a discussion, and I told him I was going to close Mr. Bulger. And he kind of snickered. And I said, well, what's that about? And he said, 'You can't close him.' I said, 'What do you mean I can't close him?' And we had a bit of an argument, if you will. And I said, 'I can close him if I want.' To which he replied, 'No, you can't.' That it just wasn't going to happen. And that made me a little angry, to be honest with you."

Judge Lindsay could no longer restrain himself, taking the unusual step to intervene in his own proceedings. I noticed him scratching his bald pate, which looked shiny under the courtroom's bright lighting, a clear indication he was a bit flummoxed by what he'd just heard.

"May I ask a question?" he politely requested, not waiting for an answer before posing his question to me. "When you had the discussion with Mr. Morris about having leaders of a criminal enterprise as informants, what in your mind was the problem with that?"

I was, of course, more than happy to respond.

"Your Honor, if Bulger is the leader of the Winter Hill Organization, we would, in effect, be sponsoring the Winter Hill Organization. Because he would be privy to information, as we discussed, you know, during this trial and so forth. But my concern is that you cannot have the head of a group as an informant."

"And is that true even if you're using the head of the group to investigate another group?"

"Well, that makes it a little bit complex, and that certainly could have been part of the issue in trying to close Bulger. You could argue that point."

"I don't want to argue. I'm just asking."

The judge seemed to be trying to understand how the FBI could keep Bulger open as a TE when he was the titular head of the Irish OC gang. This flew in the face of FBI rules and regulations as stated in the FBI manual. Especially since my testimony revealed I also headed up investigations of "nontraditional" organized crime, which included the prosecution of Bulger for his crimes. I could see the frustration as the good judge rubbed his scalp again, struggling to sort out the contradictions of allowing Bulger to continue his association in the face of facts that would argue against it. I recounted my own frustration at having to deal with this problem ever since I had arrived at Boston. My protestations against Bulger always fell on deaf ears. Finally, I felt like the judge would be able to make sense of something that had eluded so many over the years and, for his part, Gordon just continued carrying the ball Judge Lindsay had handed him.

"To follow up on the point that the Court asked," he said, resuming his questioning of me, "one of the problems is that Bulger as an informant, as the head of one group, could be providing information to the FBI for his benefit to cause harm to that other group?"

"Well, he was allegedly providing information on the Angiulos and La Cosa Nostra."

"And the Angiulos and the Winter Hill Organization were competing actually in the same criminal areas, were they not?"

"I would not say the same, but they certainly had the same interest, criminality and grabbing the different operations around the city, yes."

"And if the Angiulos were in jail and couldn't operate their business criminal enterprise, Mr. Bulger would be better able to operate his?"

I tried not to smile. "That's right."

By the end of this day I felt that the truth had finally come out. How could anyone listening to the testimony not conclude that keeping Bulger as an FBI informant went against all the rules and regulations the FBI had set for itself? And as the third day of testimony dawned, I was beginning to feel more confident that, at last, the fight I'd waged for so long was not in vain.

**31** BOSTON, 2006

THE THIRD DAY, JUNE 14, 2006

"During the course of the interview with Bulger," Mr. Gordon began, "did you make any mental note at the time that your recommendation was to close Bulger?"

"Well, as far as notes, when I got back to my place, I did make notes. I jotted down a bunch of observations. About his personality, his character, so forth, about the whole incident; and made mention of Mr. Morris in my notes, you know, with his attitude and so forth. And that was part of my memo to Mr. Sarhatt."

"And did you write up a formal assessment?"

"Yes, I did."

"And approximately how many pages was that formal assessment to the best of your recollection?"

"I believe two pages."

"And who was it directed to?"

"SAC Boston from me. The title was Bulger, his symbol number, actually, and the facts."

"And your recommendation?"

"My recommendation was that he be closed."

"Would that memo go in Mr. Bulger's informant file?"

"It should have."

"Have you seen it at all since the time you wrote it?"

"Not that I recall."

"And if I represented that it was not in Mr. Bulger's informant file and has not been produced in this litigation, would that surprise you?"

"Yes."

"When you made the recommendation to close Bulger, did Connolly oppose that?"

"Oh, yes."

"And how was that opposition expressed?"

"Well, it wasn't expressed openly at first. It was more cloaked. Like Mr. Morris's snicker, if you will. There were those kinds of references. But when I called headquarters and I talked to Sean McWeeney, who was in charge of the Organized Crime section, I made it clear that I didn't think he should be continued.

"Mr. McWeeney started telling me how valuable Mr. Bulger was, in a nice way," I continued, "and really didn't deter me from expressing my view. Obviously, I expressed my view to Mr. Sarhatt and also to Mr. Morris, and Morris defended Bulger, just like everyone else, it seemed to me. Now, I must say that shortly thereafter we had an inspection, and that means that the inspectors from headquarters come in and inspect the whole division. This problem would have been an issue, particularly with Mr. Sarhatt. That would have been handled at an FBIHQ level, headquarters level. Now, I was not privy to that discussion or whatever they did, but after they left, Bulger was continued as an informant."

At this point, once more Judge Lindsay's exasperation was clear. His gaze was riveted upon me, as if we were the only two people in the courtroom.

"I just want to make sure I understand your testimony," he started, agitated, rubbing his bald scalp again. "When you say you talked to Sean McWeeney at headquarters, you're talking about somebody in Washington."

"Yes, Your Honor."

"He was the person who was in charge of the Organized Crime . . ."

"Section," I completed.

"—section. So is he the boss of the people in Boston?"

"Technically, Your Honor, he's the person that could rule on informants."

"And Mr. McWeeney told you that Mr. Bulger was very valuable?"

"Yes, Your Honor.

"Okay."

This was a pivotal point in my testimony, as I could see that the judge's frustration had been replaced by a keen understanding that FBIHQ was a willing and able accomplice in allowing Bulger to continue as an informant. Then Mr. Gordon took the baton and continued on the same line of questioning.

"And during that discussion Mr. McWeeney indicated to you that Bulger had provided valuable information with regard to Title III surveillance with regard to LCN?

"This is true."

"And that there was a need to continue getting this information from Mr. Bulger?"

"Mr. McWeeney discussed generally about how valuable both he and Stephen Flemmi were within the investigation."

"And the continued investigation of the LCN?"

"True."

"And that these informants were sufficiently valuable that they should remain open?"

"True."

"Despite your recommendation that they be closed?"

"True."

Judge Lindsay looked as if he'd taken as much as he could. He looked more angry than curious and I recall him actually shaking his head in disbelief.

"Who said that?" he asked me, not bothering to apologize for intervening. His hands were clenched before him, not rubbing his scalp this time.

"I'm sorry, Your Honor?"

"The question Mr. Gordon asked you about someone at head-quarters saying that Mr. Bulger should be kept open, who was that?"

"That would be Sean McWeeney. McWeeney was vouching about him as an informant and how valuable he was."

And here it was again that the judge was starting to grasp the role FBIHQ had played in keeping Bulger open as an informant, drastically raising the stakes since that meant this was no longer confined to a "local issue." The truth was finally emerging, if not winning out. By comparison, Mr. Gordon's resuming this line of questioning seemed anticlimactic. I remember looking up at the bench as he posed his next question and feeling the McIntyre family had won their case then and there.

"And were you also concerned with leaks that if the handler has information, such as Mr. Connolly, that that could potentially be passed on to the informant? Is that one of the concerns that you had?"

"Of course," I replied to Mr. Gordon, my eyes darting to Judge Lindsay to follow his reaction.

"Do you recall testifying in the Salemme case—Charles, 134, line 18 [before Judge Wolf]—that you were against using Bulger and Flemmi in certain areas of your investigation?"

"Well, around the Wheeler investigation, certainly."

"And your recollection is that some of the information may be getting out and we had leaks inside?"

"True."

"And the leaks inside had to do with the Wheeler investigation?"

"Yes."

"And I think you testified, 'In other words, we'd be giving out more information than we're getting.'"

"Yes."

"And you testified that what you meant by that is these people have access to information on a confidential basis. Do you remember that?"

"Yes."

"And the reason that they have that confidential information arises out of the informant/FBI relationship?"

"Association, yes."

"And that as part of the informant relationship between an agent and the informant, the agent has given the informant some confidential, classified information?"

"Yes."

I knew even before he spoke that Judge Lindsay was about to intervene once more, his question directed straight at me without equivocation.

"I have a question for you, Mr. Fitzpatrick. When you received information in Boston that Bulger was involved in the murder of Wheeler, did that lead to a further discussion of the suitability of Bulger as an informant?"

"Absolutely, Your Honor."

"What was that discussion?"

"Again, to the best of my recollection, this conversation here was with Sean McWeeney at headquarters; and I believe there were five or six other headquarters supervisors, which included the informant desk nationally, the Organized Crime unit and section. And the general discussion from my point of view was that we should target him, go after him; and we were, in fact, doing that."

"That he, Bulger, should be closed."

"That he should be closed, right," I said.

"And targeted."

"Yes, Your honor."

I finally felt a full measure of the vindication I had sought. After many years of grappling with the Bulger dilemma, I felt that this judge had actually honed in on the ultimate disaster of keeping Bulger open as an informant. In spite of my prior humiliation and shame, my testimony now left no doubt that the course of action I'd chosen then was justified. It was the principle of the matter to stand up for the truth and adhere to the oath I had taken as a young agent. I couldn't help thinking about all those who said they didn't remember, or didn't know. . . . How could that be? How could all of the others in the Boston office and Washington not understand the danger of leaving Bulger to commit more murders and more crimes? By all indications, Judge Lindsay felt the same way.

THE FOURTH DAY, JUNE 15, 2006

"Mr. Fitzpatrick," plaintiff's lawyer Steven Gordon began, "when we left off yesterday, we were talking about the information that Brian Halloran provided to the FBI in January of 1982. You were to manage that investigation for the Boston office. Is that correct?"

"That is correct."

"Now, with regard to that process, you learned, did you not, that there was a willingness by Mr. Halloran to actually wear a wire?"

"Yes."

"And, in fact, a request was made to Washington, D.C., FBI headquarters for authorization to have that wire?"

"I authored that document."

"And that the teletype went to Washington with a request that Halloran wear a wire in order to corroborate specific allegations by Halloran which implicates Callahan and others?"

"True."

"And it would be necessary for Halloran to engage in a discussion with Callahan, and a place was set for a public restaurant?"

"True."

"We also discussed the fact that Mr. Morris would be involved in surveillance of that meeting. Do you remember that?"

"Well, Mr. Morris was in charge of that LCN squad, and it was an LCN matter. So the surveillance would have to be Morris's squad."

"So Morris was informed of the fact that there would be a surveillance of Callahan meeting with Halloran?"

"Generally speaking, I made him aware that we were going to conduct an interview, and his job was to protect the safety and to see if anybody else had information about the meeting. There were several things he was tasked with doing. First of all, testing any leak in the investigation, and also the safety of the informant, but he wouldn't know every detail about what we were doing."

"May I interrupt you," said Judge Lindsay, his voice calmer this time, but back to rubbing his scalp. Seeming to dig lines in it this time. "Because I'm, to be perfectly frank, I'm a little confused. Mr. Gordon, help me. I'm going to see if I can get unconfused.

"Mr. Fitzpatrick," the judge continued, turning to me, "I understood you to have testified that you were in the Wheeler investigation trying to erect a wall, a Chinese wall, that separated the people involved in the handling of Bulger and Flemmi from the investigation of the Wheeler murder. Did I hear you say that?"

"Yes, Your honor," I told him.

"And are you saying now that Morris, who was Connolly's supervisor, was involved in this operation in which Halloran was going to have a conversation with Callahan about that murder?"

"Your Honor, Morris was the . . . was the squad leader, the supervisor of C-3. This case was really about the Wheeler murder, but also about the involvement of Bulger and Flemmi and others possibly in the killing. That involves LCN and other vehicles of organized crime. Morris, because of his supervisory position, would have to be involved because the people I needed to ensure the safey of my agents and my informant would have to know what to look for and be able to recognize potential danger from organized crime members. People who are not on the Organized Crime squad would not have that ability to recognize danger in the form of those who might come after this.

"Secondly, Morris was at the time a very reputable supervisory agent whom we trusted, we believed in. And there was no reason at that point to exclude him, because he would be the natural person to use. So there was no hint on our part that Morris was a turncoat or Morris was 'dirty.' That simply was unknown at the time."

What goes around, comes around, and the judge was understanding that Morris was used for assistance in 1981 and 1982 prior to our knowledge that he and Connolly had sold out the FBI. As I sat testifying I thought of the Morris book about lying and Connolly's rifling of files and how they were both protected by FBIHQ who thought them to be the best agents imaginable. But here today, in court, that picture was crumbling through a conflation of lies that was finally being exposed so that the truth could prevail.

"And was there a dispute in the office as to whether or not Halloran should go into the Witness Protection Program?" Mr. Gordon picked up.

"True, yes."

"And you recommended that he go into the Witness Protection Program, correct?"

"Right. I felt we had to take him off the streets and put him in the Witness Protection Program where he'd be out of harm's way, again, trying to box this thing in, if you will, and I expressed my concerns to Strike Force chief Jeremiah O'Sullivan and also to the United States Attorney Bill Weld."

"And at that time," said Mr. Gordon, "did you feel that you were getting all the information concerning the investigation of the Wheeler murder?"

"You never get all the information you want."

"Did you feel that at that time, that because of your desire to close Bulger, that people were keeping information from you within the office of the FBI?"

"My thinking was to get the information from Halloran, to get him in the Witness Protection Program, and to get the information we needed to go ahead and prosecute the subjects, Bulger and Flemmi."

"Do you recall going to a meeting in Washington to discuss this issue?"

"I do."

"Would you describe the nature of the meeting you had in Washington, D.C.?"

"Well, it's stated here in this memo to Larry. I met with Sean Mc-Weeney, Jeff Jamar, Randy Prillman all at headquarters. I don't remember Ronald Reese. I remember Anthony Amoroso being there, Joe Rush was the Miami agent. And we were discussing the planning of what we do next, how we proceed and so forth."

"And were the informants discussed, Bulger and Flemmi, at that time?"

"I believe they were."

"Do you remember discussions whether or not Bulger should be closed as an informant?"

"Yes. My position was that he be closed, but I was overrun. They decided to keep him open."

"When you say 'you were overrun,' what do you mean by that?"

"Well, that I have an opinion, they have an opinion, their opinion won out."

"And did you voice your objection to that?"

"I believe I did. I remember."

And here was an incredulous Judge Lindsay interjecting himself once more into his own proceedings.

"Let me see if I can understand this meeting a little better. You went to Washington, Mr. Fitzpatrick."

"Yes, Your Honor."

"To FBI headquarters, and you had a meeting with Sean McWeeney, Jeff Jamar, Randy Prillman, Ronald Reese, and some people from Miami as well."

"That's true, Your Honor."

"And in your discussion of the informants in Boston some of the people in Washington thought that Bulger should remain open."

"That's correct, Your Honor."

"Did that include Sean McWeeney, head of the Organized Crime squad at headquarters?"

"Yes, Your Honor."

"Was there anybody else who thought that Mr. Bulger should be kept open?"

"My recollection is everyone at headquarters thought he should stay open."

"Mr. Fitzpatrick," the judge continued, "you've talked this morning about Mr. Bulger having been suspected of involvement in the murder of Wheeler, of Halloran, of Callahan, and suspicion of being involved in drug trafficking."

"That's true, Your Honor.

"Now, I understand that we're only talking about suspicion. In the time that you were ASAC in Boston, if you have an informant who has as much suspicion as you've testified to this morning, did that cause any concern, even if the suspicions were never proven out?"

"It caused a great deal of concern to me."

"I mean, beyond you."

"It should have," I told him, the two of us again seemingly alone in the courtroom. "It should have called for an inspection by head-quarters. And, in fact, during this period, we were inspected, but the inspectors who have access to the files, who are supposed to inter-view people, didn't. I've served as an inspector myself and I can tell you that was never done."

Gazing up at Judge Lindsay, I felt certain in that moment he'd made his decision. I knew that he'd gotten the picture of truth and was re-solved that the FBI was responsible for McIntyre's death and others, as indicated by the line of questioning he pursued with me. Brownie mentioned that he thought my testimony would leave the judge no choice but to find the government and the FBI "guilty." But now it was time to turn the court's attention to the true subject at hand, the mur-der of John McIntyre at the hands of Whitey Bulger.

"Do you know an individual by the name of Rod Kennedy?" Mr. Gordon asked me.

"Yes, I do."

"And who is Mr. Kennedy?"

"Rod Kennedy was assigned to the C-2 squad, and he was one of the agents on that squad."

"And what were Mr. Kennedy's responsibilities?"

"Mr. Kennedy was primarily liaison with DEA, Drug Enforce-ment Administration."

"And with regard to this drug investigation, was this another one that you were to manage with regard to the investigation of Mr. Bulger and Mr. Flemmi?"

"He would have been privy to information, yes."

"Did it come to your attention that John McIntyre was cooperat-ing with law enforcement?"

"Yes."

"And when did that come to your attention?"

"I believe Rod informed me."

"And when Mr. Kennedy informed you of Mr. McIntyre's coop-eration, did Mr. Kennedy tell you what McIntyre was telling law enforcement?"

"That it was about the *Valhalla*, the IRA, the *Merita Ann*, and Joe Murray, his gang, the Irish gang and so forth."

"What about drug shipments?"

"Drug shipments were part of the investigation."

"And you use the phrase here 'attribution by Bulger' and so forth."

"Bulger was part of the information, yes."

"And this was information that was being provided by Mr. McIntyre?"

"Right."

"If you go to the last page of Exhibit Number 36, second page, do you see . . . could you read into the record the last sentence there?" Gordon requested.

I flipped the exhibit over to the proper page. "It says that 'McIntyre was released and stated that he would cooperate with the United States Customs and the FBI in the drug operations of Joseph Murray.'"

"Do you recall when you first learned that, and I'll represent to you that Mr. McIntyre was murdered on November 30, 1984, do you recall the first time you learned that Mr. McIntyre could not be located?"

"Not long afterwards."

"What happened with the drug investigation? Was Mr. Bulger indicted?"

"No, he was not."

"Was Mr. Flemmi indicted?"

"No, he was not."

"Did the investigation, in effect, shut down?"

"I can't say that. I don't know if it was shut down. It could have continued without me. I just don't know."

"Did you have any involvement after Mr. McIntyre's disappearance in November 1984?"

"Well, I submitted a memo in 1985 about McIntyre, but that was six months to a year later."

The memo I submitted was the one in which I accused the SAC of allegedly disclosing information on our informants to mob attorney Martin Boudreau. The rest of the next day's testimony only served to reveal how the FBI had abused their discretion in not following the established rules and regulations governing FBI informants in this matter. In all, I spent over six grueling days testifying, the longest ever in my career, and I was flat-out exhausted. My goal had been to tell the truth, the whole truth, and I did, leaving the rest in the able hands of Judge Lindsay.

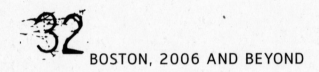

32 BOSTON, 2006 AND BEYOND

The truth had finally been told. Sitting in the witness box as McIntyre's lawyer Steven Gordon finished his line of questioning on the John McIntyre case left me feeling calm, relieved, but strangely unfulfilled. In reviewing all the facts of the story after so many years, I was struck even more that this young man didn't have to die. He was relying on the justice system to protect him and that system simply let him down. Another life senselessly lost because the FBI had not acted on my recommendation to sever ties with Whitey Bulger once and for all.

Now, though, justice had a chance to be done at long last, for both McIntyre and myself. My narrowly focused testimony in the Wolf hearings was hardly the right forum or opportunity for the world to learn the truth. District court in Boston under Judge Lindsay was something else again. If the Estate of John McIntyre prevailed, then the FBI in particular and the justice system as a whole would have no choice but to regard the conclusion I reached way back in 1981 with a new level of credence and validity. I would be vindicated, exonerated in a sense, as someone who had been telling the truth for twenty-five years—a truth that could no longer fall on deaf ears.

Two more days of testimony for me followed in the McIntyre trial. Day Five was mostly consumed by a seemingly endless line of questioning about "performance and evaluation" reports relating mostly to John Connolly. But it did feature one terrific exchange on the subject of James Greenleaf with the McIntyre family's attorney again doing the questioning:

"Okay," began Mr. Gordon, "I'd like to ask you a few questions regarding Mr. Greenleaf's style of management. When Mr. Green-leaf was the SAC in Boston, how did he manage the office? Did he have a hands-on approach?"

"No, he was totally different than Mr. Sarhatt. While Sarhatt perhaps did have a hands-on, I would say that Mr. Greenleaf did not. He was gone most of the time. He wasn't there a lot."

"Did you have trouble finding him if you needed to speak to him?"

"At times."

"And how did that come about? How long would it be that you would be trying to reach out to him and could not find him?"

"Sometimes I never found him."

"And did you actually have a nickname for Mr. Greenleaf?"

"His nickname was 'Greenleave.' "

" 'Greenleave'?"

"Right. He was never there."

This exchange became the precursor for Greenleaf's own frustratingly evasive and pointless testimony dominated by "I don't know" and "I don't remember." At one point, I remember Judge Lindsay just shaking his head at the absurdity of Greenleaf's Nuremburg claims, once saying just loud enough for the microphone to pick up, in obvious frustration, "Incredible."

And when Greenleaf did answer, his responses were ambiguous at best. As the appellate court would later note, on the fourteenth day of the trial Greenleaf would claim he "was not focused on reports that Bulger and Flemmi had sources within law enforcement generally or within the FBI." Adding more fuel to the fire he had set himself, he claimed to have no awareness of any "investigation being conducted in response to those reports." This in spite of the reports he was privy to from the Massachusetts State Police and DEA, just to name two, never mind my own reporting to HQ on the subject.

Peter Gelzinis picked things up from there in his column for the *Boston Herald* on Friday, June 23, 2006:

> Stephen Flemmi, the homicidal maniac who moonlighted for 25 years as an FBI informant, took to the witness stand recently and portrayed the Boston FBI office as a ship of fools.
>
> Yesterday, we met the captain.
>
> James Greenleaf was the special agent in charge of J. Edgar Hoover's Boston franchise from 1982 [to] 1986—the period known as Whitey and Stevie's golden years.
>
> Greenleaf was at the helm while the two "Top Echelon" gangsters were extracting teeth and tongues from doomed people, who were then dropped into holes.
>
> Jim Greenleaf said he was clueless about all of it. Never mind that he was boss, or that the informant files his agents wrote were crammed with references to Bulger and Flemmi wreaking havoc under the care and protection of a gangster agent named John Connolly.
>
> Captain Greenleaf said he never bothered to read the informant files and no underling bothered to mention what was in them. Asked about all the people in those files who turned up dead while he ran the Boston office, former SAC Jim Greenleaf turned into Sgt. Schultz. He knew nothing. . . .
>
> "I don't think I really focused on that issue," Greenleaf said, referring to other law enforcement agencies pursuing the FBI's two gangster stool pigeons. "I assumed a lot of other people were looking at them."
>
> Judge Reginald Lindsay, presiding over the no-jury trial, seemed baffled enough by the response to ask Greenleaf if he was "concerned" by the fact that a local DA, the state police and the DEA were all trying to get at Bulger and Flemmi, the gangsters hiding in plain view of the FBI.
>
> Looking like butter wouldn't melt in his mouth, Captain Jim Greenleaf looked at Lindsay and said, "That just didn't register with

me, judge." With that, this captain of fools sailed back into his retirement.

I felt then that McIntyre, and with him the truth, was going to prevail, and I was right. In September 2006, Judge Lindsay found for the plaintiffs, the Estate of John McIntyre, and against the United States of America and thus the FBI.

In a 110-page decision, Lindsay wrote that the FBI failed to properly supervise Connolly and failed to investigate numerous allegations that Bulger and Flemmi were involved in drug trafficking, murder, and other crimes over decades. Even though the FBI investigated Bulger and Flemmi for four murders, including Wheeler's, in the early 1980s, Lindsay wrote, "the truth is, however, that the FBI was not pounding the pavement looking for evidence that could 'stick.'"

"Instead," wrote Lindsay, "the FBI stuck its head in the sand when it came to the criminal activities of Bulger and Flemmi. The agents of the Boston office knew they had an obligation to report informants' criminal activity, so they carefully avoided knowledge of criminal acts by their informants."

The judge ordered the government to pay $3 million to McIntyre's mother for the conscious suffering he endured before his brutal slaying, $100,000 for the loss of her son's company, and $1,876 for funeral and burial costs. A princely sum on its own, but even more so when considering Lindsay had found the FBI guilty of clear wrongdoing, a virtual accomplice to John McIntyre's murder. Small consolation for the family that had lost a son to a night of torture and violence, and perhaps for me as well, after my lifelong dream had ended in pain and anguish a generation before. But I chose not to see it that way. For me, it had always been about the truth, and finally, the truth had won out in clear and unambiguous fashion.

And on October 16, 2008, the U.S. Court of Appeals for the First Circuit upheld Judge Lindsay's decision finding the Bureau responsible for McIntyre's death, saying in part, "because Connolly, acting within the scope of his FBI employment, disclosed information to Bulger and Flemmi sufficient for them to identify McIntyre as a government informant, and McIntyre's death was a foreseeable consequence of that disclosure."

Quoting Lindsay liberally, the Court of Appeals went on to state that "The McIntyre leak violated a bright-line law enforcement rule that informant identity never be revealed, and put at risk the life of an individual who was helping the FBI." The Court of Appeals went on to label the government's contention that it should not be held liable for a "rogue" agent's actions basically absurd. "Connolly's disclosure," the court found, "was within the boundaries of the FBI's long-standing method of handling Bulger and Flemmi through Connolly, and that it consequently is 'just' to treat the harm caused by the disclosure 'as one of the normal risks to be borne by the business in which the servant is employed.'"

In arriving at their findings, both courts were assisted in ways they did not then know by Brownie's co-counsel Doug Matthews. In the pretrial discovery that takes place in civil lawsuits, FBI lawyers had turned over some 170,000 pages of documents ranging from manuals of procedure, to intra-FBI memos, to raw 302s that were the original street agents' reports. The numbered pages of discovery· were assembled in an unindexed, pawed-over pile of thirty or forty 5,000-page file boxes in a dedicated research room in downtown Boston.

Figuring there might be something of value amid those reams, Doug sifted through the pages for most of the summer of 2006 before he found what he was looking for. It was a November 1982 memo hidden within an otherwise innocuous personnel file of an agent not even related to the case. The memo, sent from the Organized Crime section chief in Washington up the chain to an Associate Deputy Director, stated that there was "evidence" implicating the Winter Hill Gang, specifically Bulger and Flemmi, in the Wheeler, Callahan, and Halloran murders.

This proved crucial, not only because the memo affirmed everything I'd reported myself to HQ in 1982 but also because it stripped away the rationale that Bulger and Flemmi should be kept open until there was evidence to support my allegations. A direct contradiction *since the memo in question indicated such evidence already existed!* Doug made sure that McIntyre's legal team was made aware of the apparently concealed document. And its exposure during the trial clearly had a profound effect on Judge Lindsay's decision; he cited it multiple times, as would the First Circuit Appellate Court in its 2008 ruling.

The judgment ordered by Judge Lindsay was paid in full without further appeal.

Justice? I suppose but, assuming it was John Connolly who leaked McIntyre's name, how exactly had Connolly learned McIntyre was an informant? Connolly wasn't involved in the drug investigation centering on McIntyre's intelligence at all, meaning he couldn't possibly have leaked McIntyre's name unless someone had given it to him first.

"Aren't these our guys?" Sean McWeeney, head of the Organized Crime squad at HQ, had asked Connolly back in 1984 upon learning of the DEA's efforts to nail Bulger for drug dealing and distribution.

The murder of John McIntyre, the blame for which was cast on Connolly, in large part put a stop to those efforts. So where had Connolly come by the information? Theoretically, he could have gotten it from Greenleaf or, I suppose, John Morris, both of whom were aware of McIntyre's informant status. But whoever did the leaking, by connection, also remains in my view complicit in McIntyre's murder. (Remember, mob attorney Martin Boudreau had inexplicably shown up on the dock when we busted the *Ramsland* after it sailed into port thanks to intelligence provided by John McIntyre. And I'd already reported Greenleaf for alleged disclosure of information to the very same Martin Boudreau.)

And there was more to follow.

My story, which had fallen on deaf ears for so long, suddenly found a bevy of eager listeners who had been similarly wronged in tragic fashion by the culture of corruption that consumed the Boston office of the FBI. The case that drew the most attention in this regard was unquestionably that of John Connolly. Already in federal prison on racketeering charges, Connolly was finally going to face trial in

Miami on murder and conspiracy charges in the death of would-be informant John Callahan in the wake of Whitey Bulger's failed attempt to take over World Jai Alai and the murder of its owner Roger Wheeler in Oklahoma. The trial, coincidentally enough, would be decided within days of the Lindsay decision being upheld by the Court of Appeals.

Prior to that, a virtual rogue's gallery of faces from the past took the stand to shed light on the era that had seen the FBI co-opted from without and corrupted from within. "Whitey Bulger's Ex-Pals Line Up to Bury John Connolly," read the headline in the *Boston Herald* on September 14, 2008. There was Stephen "the Rifleman" Flemmi testifying that Connolly had told Whitey himself that "if they questioned [Callahan], he wouldn't hold up" and would "end up turning against him." And if there was any doubt whether Connolly knew what that meant, it was vanquished when Flemmi revisited the murders of bookie Richie Castucci in 1976 and Brian Halloran in 1982, both ordered killed by Bulger after tips furnished by Connolly.

"When you give us information on one person and they got killed," Flemmi testified, "when you give us information on a second person and they get killed, when you give us information on a third person and they got killed. I mean, he's an FBI agent. He's not stupid."

John Martorano added his own flavor to the pot, confirming much of Flemmi's testimony while providing the intricate details of John Callahan's murder at his hand from a bullet in the back of the head. As a sideshow, authorities like Tom Foley, former colonel of the Massachusetts State Police, were forced to defend the deals they cut with killers like Martorano.

"If John Connolly and the FBI had done their job, we wouldn't have been in that situation," he testified on Friday, September 19, 2008. "We were in a situation where we had no choice." He went on to add that "Because of the twisted relationship John Connolly had with Bulger and Flemmi, it put us in a position where he had to make a decision like that."

Foley had picked up the ball at MSP from my old pal Colonel John O'Donovan, inheriting the same mess that had led to my undoing with the Bureau. I followed the trial from my home in Rhode Island, convinced that the most unseemly thing about the whole tragic episode was not the deals the government had made with Flemmi and Martorano, but the fact that those deals had been necessary in the first place. Between them, Flemmi and Matorano killed dozens of people on direct orders from Whitey Bulger, a number of these occurring after I'd recommended Bulger be closed in 1981.

But he wasn't.

The men and women he killed subsequently didn't have to die.

But they did.

Thinking about those victims today still gives me chills. I get even more chills, though, when I think how the testimony of Flemmi and Martorano had indeed buried John Connolly while leaving so many other offenders unsoiled. Writing in the *Boston Globe*, Joan Vennochi skewered the Bureau's actions in a column titled "If Connolly Is So Guilty, Can the FBI Be So Innocent?," stressing the very absurdity that the culture of corruption began and ended with a single agent.

"Well, I knew they were protecting them because we were paying for the information," Kevin Weeks, the gangster-turned-informant who had led authorities to the body of John McIntyre in 2000, told reporter David Boeri on WBUR in August of 2011. "[Whitey] used to claim he had six FBI agents up there that he could call on anytime and they would willingly hop in the car with him with a machine gun. In other words, he's alluding to me that he'd call them anytime and they'd hop in the car and go on a hit with him."

"Were you ever curious who they were?" Boeri asked him.

"I figure I was better off not knowing."

John Connolly was convicted of second-degree murder on November 6, 2008, and was sentenced to forty years in prison the following January. James Greenleaf, the late Jeremiah O'Sullivan, Sean McWeeney, John Morris, and numerous others, meanwhile, have remained relatively unscathed, at least in criminal court. And right up until at least 1988, both O'Sullivan and James Ahearn, Greenleaf's replacement as Boston SAC, were claiming they had no idea Whitey Bulger had ever been an FBI informant.

"That is absolutely untrue," Ahearn insisted in response to a question from the *Boston Globe* about the FBI's relationship with Whitey Bulger. "We specifically deny that there has been special treatment of this individual."

But if all this remained a constant source of frustration for me, the results of another case in court left me with an added sense of vindication. In August of 2009 the First U.S. Circuit Court of Appeals (the same court that upheld Judge Lindsay's decision) upheld a lower-court judgment ordering the FBI to pay $102 million in a wrongful conviction suit filed by the families of Louis Greco, Henry Tameleo, Peter Limone, and Joseph Salvati.

They were the four scapegoats railroaded by FBI agents Paul Rico and Dennis Condon on manufactured evidence for killing Teddy Deegan in 1965, a murder actually committed by their FBI snitch, Joseph "the Animal" Barboza. Barboza, though, was deemed too valuable to the FBI's cause to be imprisoned, just as Bulger was deemed too valuable to be closed. Different names bred of the same culture of corruption that survived and thrived from one era to the next.

In this latter case, the district court was hardly random in coming up with that $102 million judgment; the figure was arrived at by essentially billing the government one million dollars for each of the years the falsely convicted four men spent in prison. Since both Tameleo and Greco died behind bars, they weren't in any position to enjoy the money. Salvatti and Limone, while still alive, lost their youth and the better part of their lives to an attitude and philosophy that spawned the Bulger era. And on April 30, 2010, the federal government, through U.S. Solicitor General Elena Kagan, elected not to appeal the decision by simply letting the deadline pass, meaning that $102 million judgment is sure to stand.

There was more.

"Judge Admits He Was Too Harsh on Mother of Whitey Bulger Victim," proclaimed a November 5, 2009, headline in the *Boston Herald*.

That victim was Debra Davis, strangled by her friend Whitey Bulger in 1981 after he grew jealous of her infatuation with Steve Flemmi. Her remains were found along with John McIntyre's and Bucky Barrett's in that makeshift grave back in the winter of 2000. I testified in that trial, filed on behalf of several Bulger murder victims, including Davis, Deborah Hussey, and an ex-bookie named Louis Litif who sought monetary damages on the grounds that the FBI was complicit in their deaths. Litif had been an informant for Connolly. Davis and Hussey were both young, attractive women linked sexually to Bulger. Their contention was that the FBI was responsible for the slayings because they knew Bulger and Flemmi were killers, but protected them anyway from prosecution because they were also informants. The Justice Department's response was that the FBI wasn't obligated to control Bulger and Flemmi.

There were several moments during my testimony before Judge William Young that caused a stir. The government attorneys, still smarting, took a couple of swipes at me, calling my integrity into question, raising the Cape Cod shooting incident yet again, and alluding to the cover-up Greenleaf had accused me of. They were intimating that I had gotten censured over it.

"They are lying," I told the judge.

Judge Young simply posed to me the same questions that the government attorneys had. "Let me ask you, then," he said. "Did you get in trouble over your actions regarding this incident?"

"No, Your Honor, absolutely not," I replied, to which the judge stated simply, "Fine," and resumed the trial.

My testimony, as in the McIntyre case, was centered on my efforts to close Bulger as an FBI informant being curtailed and waylaid at every juncture. In the end, an everfrustrated Judge Young agreed. At one point, he said, "I'm prepared to find there is a massive and widespread cover-up going on here."

In May 2009, Judge Young also awarded an $8.5 million judgment to the families of Brian Halloran and Michael Donahue since the FBI had turned a blind eye to their murders at the hands of Whitey Bulger in 1982. (The case was later overturned on appeal based on a procedural technicality—the family of Michael Donahue had waited too long to file.) A month later Judge Young awarded $6.25 million to the family of Richie Castucci. Young was assigned both cases after Judge Lindsay, who'd presided over the McIntyre trial, died in March of that year. But, as in the McIntyre trial, Lindsay had already issued his rulings, leaving it to Young only to determine how much the government should pay up.

There were other cases filed, including one by the widow of John Callahan, and many are still winding their way through a system of justice that has failed so many at every other juncture. But the Connolly, Salvati, and McIntyre decisions shed light at last on my claims that had for so long remained in the dark. In that sense, my life has come full circle: from a young boy listening to *This Is Your FBI*, to a twenty-year-plus career with the Bureau, to never letting go of my convictions after my departure, to finally seeing those convictions rewarded. I take great pride and comfort, even solace, in that sense of closure, but not pleasure. There's no pleasure, because none of the trials that have been or will be should ever have happened.

Fidelity, Bravery, Integrity . . .

If the FBI had just stuck to its motto, this never would've happened. If the agents had stuck to their oath, things would have been different.

The vindication achieved in these court findings restored at least a measure of my dream to me. And sometimes, once in a great while, I awaken to the reverie of soft murmurs of voices acting out the night's episode of *This Is Your FBI*. The words of my boyhood heroes sift down the hall into my bedroom, just as they did at the Mount, until they slowly dissipate, leaving a smile on my face as I drift back to sleep.

EPILOGUE

In the middle of the night of June 23, 2011, I received a call from a major TV group informing me Whitey Bulger was apprehended in Santa Monica, California, with his girlfriend Catherine Greig. Bulger, now eighty-one, was arrested following a tip from a woman in Iceland. The media jumped on that revelation, finding it incredible that it took a woman from Iceland to finally bring to a close a drama that had been going on since Bulger's disappearance in 1995. Over the years the FBI had battled the perception that it had not tried hard enough to find Bulger, despite listing him as the number two man on their Most Wanted list, just behind Osama Bin Laden. And in ironic counterpoint, he was captured just a few months following Bin Laden's execution at the hands of Navy SEALs in Pakistan. Both fugitives hiding in plain sight.

The comparison does not end there. Lenin once wrote that the purpose of terror is to terrify, and there is no more apt description of Whitey Bulger than that. The man who tortured and murdered John McIntyre, the man who strangled Debra Davis, may have also terrified the FBI for the information he could reveal about his sordid relationship with the Bureau and the fact that he provided virtually nothing in exchange for the protection afforded him. Between the time I recommended Bulger be closed as an informant in March 1981 and the time of his disappearance in 1984, at least eight people fell to his murderous hand, three of them informants willing and able to testify against him. Their names, which bear repeating, were Roger Wheeler, Debra Davis, Arthur "Bucky" Barrett, Deborah Husey, Michael Donahue, Brian Halloran, John Callahan, and John McIntyre.

And now he's been brought to justice, soon to stand trial before another in a long line of district court judges who have presided over cases in which the FBI's complicity in Bulger's murderous rise to criminal power first came to legal light. In the information-laden, explosive weeks after Bulger was captured I was contacted by a slew of media outlets, among them the *Boston Globe,* the *Boston Herald,* the *New York Times,* Fox, CBS, and NPR. All of them begging me to tell the truth no one wanted to hear during my tenure in Boston. I thought I'd achieved my vindication in the various trials that affirmed and corroborated so many of my claims that had fallen on deaf ears for so long.

I was wrong.

My true vindication has come now, in the court of public opinion, where the truth has finally come out. The *Boston Globe* ran an article entitled "Here's to Honest Cops Who Made a Difference," mentioning "Bob Fitzpatrick, a good FBI Agent who tried to save his agency from the rot that was Whitey Bulger." NPR/WBUR ran a story called "The FBI Agent Who Really Wanted 'Whitey'" that was broadcast across New England and proclaimed, "When Bob Fitzpatrick was brought into Boston as second in command of the FBI office in the early 1980s, it didn't take him long to figure out something wasn't right."

I echoed the perspective of a lawyer with South Boston roots named Ray Jennings III who reflected on hearing tales of Whitey Bulger from both his father and grandfather. In a July 11, 2011, *Boston Globe* article, he rightfully credited Lehr and O'Neill's *Black Mass* with finally exposing the truth behind the legend. Only one thing was missing.

"I hope we all have the opportunity to finally hear the ending," he told reporter Nancy Harris.

A short time after things settled down, I visited Mount Loretto, perhaps for the last time. I was surprised to see how it had all changed. As I turned the street corner, there was no fear anymore; the Gothic cathedral was there, the administrative house was there, the huge playing fields, but little else. Appropriately enough, it was a misty, rainy day, with gentle drops enhancing my melancholy thoughts. The bridge to the dining hall was gone, along with the cottages that held us together as young lads. The steam pipes were gone, no more hissing and clanking, and no more little boys hanging from them for dear life.

The "stone child" raised in that orphanage was still rooted in my soul. Here I learned to fight the good fight and never stopped fighting. Now that another chapter of the story is out, some former FBI agents commend me for falling on my sword while others still turn a blind eye to the FBI's complicity. New court appearances, more depositions, and additional trials await me, as well as other names from a past so long shrouded in darkness now finally assured of seeing the light.

This story has not ended, not even close.

I walked to the Mount cemetery, strewn with unmowed grass, and found Father Kenny's grave site. He had made monsignor before his death, according to the simple headstone, but he'll always be Father Kenny to me. I chatted silently with the good father and told him what had happened. He didn't chide me for being scrupulous in this confession, even when I paraphrased his own words back to him, "There's not a more honorable thing in this world to me than being an FBI agent."

I knew in my heart I'd always done the honorable thing and I believe Father Kenny knows that, too. Maybe that's what he meant all along. I try to hold on to him in my mind, as I feel memories of him and the Mount slipping away no matter how hard I try not to forget.

Sister Mary Assumpta is gone as well, along with her radio show, *This Is Your FBI*—a memory that, except for those occasional nights when I think I can still hear it, is fading, too.

APPENDIX CONTENTS

OFFICE OF THE DIRECTOR

UNITED STATES DEPARTMENT OF JUSTICE

FEDERAL BUREAU OF INVESTIGATION

WASHINGTON, D.C. 20535

April 23, 1968

PERSONAL

Mr. Robert Fitzpatrick
Federal Bureau of Investigation
Memphis, Tennessee

Dear Mr. Fitzpatrick:

The manner in which you carried out your assignments in the investigation of the Bombing Matters case involving Sam Holloway Bowers, Jr., and others was exemplary and I want to commend you.

Through your exceptional skill and resourcefulness in the developing and handling of two confidential sources of information, you contributed inestimably to the success achieved in this case. Your fine services are appreciated.

Sincerely yours,

J. Edgar Hoover

Appendix 2

DATE: 8/6/80

REPLY TO
ATTN OF: ASAC Weldon L. Kennedy

SUBJECT: MEETING ON 8/5/80
ASAC WELDON L. KENNEDY AND
COL. O'DONOVAN, MASS. STATE POLICE

TO: SAC Lawrence Sarhatt

       On 8/5/80 Col. O'Donovan, Mass. State Police, called and inquired as to whether I would be available to meet with him at 3:30 P. M. at the Brighton, Mass., Ramada Inn. Col. O'Donovan referred to his conversation with you on 8/4/80 concerning a highly sensitive organized crime investigation being handled by the State Police.

       O'Donovan told me that Jeremiah O'Sullivan, Chief of the Strike Force, would also be present at the meeting.

       Upon arrival at the meeting, present were Sgt. Long, Mass. State Police; Jeremiah O'Sullivan, Strike Force; Newman Flanagan, District Attorney, Suffolk County; Bob Ryan, Boston Police Department; Major Regan, Mass. State Police; and Col. O'Donovan, Mass. State Police. Approximately thirty minutes after the beginning of the meeting, Joe Jordan, Commissioner of the Boston Police Department, arrived.

       Col. O'Donovan and Newman Flanagan acted as informal co-chairmen of the meeting and the following is the substance of the meeting:

       Approximately one month ago, the Mass. State Police developed considerable information concerning organized crime activities in the Lancaster Street Garage located on Lancaster Street in Boston, Mass. It was determined through their investigative activities that virtually every organized crime figure in the metropolitan area of Boston, including both LCN and non-LCN (Winter Hill) OC figures frequented the premises and it was apparent that a considerable amount of illegal business was being conducted at the garage.

       Pursuant to these investigations, Col. O'Donovan met with Jeremiah O'Sullivan, Strike Force, concerning the feasibility of obtaining authorization for an electronic surveillance of the garage. District Attorney Newman Flanagan was brought into the planning stages because of

(1)

the obvious jurisdiction of state authorities. Conditions
imposed by the State Police were that under absolutely no
circumstances would they jointly work with the Boston Police
Department or the Federal Bureau of Investigation on this
matter. O'Sullivan attempted to convince them otherwise but
their position was and continues to be adamant that they will
not jointly work this case with the FBI.

O'Donovan explained that his reasons for this
position are that he strongly suspects that the FBI has one
or more highly placed informants who are quite possibly targets
of his investigation. In view of his strong feeling that to
involve the FBI in an investigation involving two of our
informants as targets was simply not feasible. More directly
stated, Col. O'Donovan said that although he did not wish to
imply nor was he making any accusation against the FBI or
any of its employees, that he simply could not bring himself
to trust such a sensitive operation to the FBI particularly
when Supervisor John Morris was involved as he believes that
the informants referred to were developed by Morris.

A microphone installation was completed on 7/24/80
and has been extremely productive to date. However, on Friday,
8/1/80, Supervisor Morris attended a party which was also
attended by Sgt. Bob Ryan of the Boston Police Department
Intelligence Unit. During the course of the evening, Morris
inquired of Sgt. Ryan as to whether or not they were conducting
investigation or if there was "something going" with regard to
the Lancaster Garage. Ryan informed Morris that he knew of no
activity but on the following day, Sgt. Ryan contacted Newman
Flanagan. Sgt. Ryan asked Newman Flanagan if he was aware of
any investigation or specifically whether or not there was a
"microphone" in operation at the Lancaster Garage.

Flanagan at that point explained that neither Sgt.
Ryan nor any person in the Boston Police Department had been
informed of the electronic surveillance which had been installed
on 7/24 and in fact Flanagan was in a difficult position because
although he was fully aware of the installation, he could not
tell the Boston Police Department in spite of the fact that
Sgt. Ryan had been pushing him for authority to install their
own coverage in the Lancaster Garage. The fact that Supervisor
Morris and Sgt. Ryan were apparently aware that there was some
investigation or activity at the garage became of extreme
concern to him and he, therefore, immediately contacted Col.
O'Donovan.

-2-

On Monday, 8/4/80, Col. O'Donovan contacted you concerning this matter as you are aware and requested that you determine whether or not potential targets of the State Police investigation were aware that there was some electronic coverage of their meetings.

To the best of Sgt. Ryan's recollection, Supervisor Morris asked him "Does the State Police have a microphone in the Lancaster Garage?" Sgt. Ryan got the opinion from the conversation that "the wise guys" know about the microphone.

Col. O'Donovan requested that this meeting be held in the strictest of confidence but expressed an extreme concern and requested that I speak to Supervisor Morris to determine answers to the following questions:

    (1) How does Morris know there is a microphone in the Lancaster Garage?

    (2) How did he know that the State Police were involved in the investigation?

    (3) How do other people know of the installation?

Following the meeting on 8/5, I conferred with Supervisor Morris regarding this matter.

Morris told me that approximately a month ago, a source of the Boston Office who frequents a restaurant by the name of Giro's located in the North End had heard a discussion to the effect that a lot of "new faces" had been seen in the vicinity of the Lancaster Garage and also in the North End. It was mentioned that they might be "statees" because the individuals involved in the discussion for the most part know the identities of Boston police officers and FBI personnel who are involved in organized crime investigations. However, the state authorities are not generally known as they have conducted little investigation in the North End.

Late last week, Morris advised that he had been informed that the "Skip Unit" (a special organized crime investigative unit of the Boston Police Department) had given a warning to all members of the unit to stay away from the Lancaster Garage.

-3-

Morris used 'stolen' info to "warn" Ryan knowing though Sgt Walsh that BPD were going into Lancaster.

Morris stated that these two facts when put together indicated to him that in fact some investigative effort was underway with regard to the Lancaster Garage and that it most probably involved the State Police and the Skip Unit since he is well aware that these two units have worked closely together in the past. When he ran into Sgt. Ryan, he decided that in view of the suspicion on the part of some of our sources that "something was up" with regard to the Lancaster Garage, that he should pass this information to whatever organization that was conducting the investigation. He asked Sgt. Ryan about the Lancaster Garage and Sgt. Ryan denied knowledge of any coverage. He, therefore, did not pursue the subject with Sgt. Ryan. Morris stated that he may have used the word microphone in the discussion but that this information was not received from our sources but was his own opinion of the type coverage that would be necessary in a location such as the Lancaster Garage.

I reiterated to Morris the instructions which you had given him on 8/4 to the effect that under no circumstances was anyone else in this office to be made aware of the State Police investigation or its targets and that if any further information was received from our sources, that it should be immediately provided to you or to me personally by Supervisor Morris.

OBSERVATIONS

As you are aware, the C-3 Squad has been extensively involved in several investigations during which allegations have been made that certain members of the State Police, namely, Major Regan and Lt. Masuret, if not criminally liable, are professionally liable for substantial misconduct with regard to their handling of informants. More specifically, in certain instances, there are indications that these two individuals furnished information of an extremely confidential nature to certain members of the criminal element in the Boston area.

It occurs to me that the stage has now been set with regard to this current investigation that if for any reason the investigation falters or is not successful with regard to the Lancaster Street Garage, that the State Police is now in a position to make allegations that the FBI and more specifically, John Morris and members of the C-3 Squad have

-4-

furnished information of a sensitive nature to organized crime
elements in the Boston area.

It was apparent during the discussions that although
unstated that everyone present in the room was aware of the
identities of two informants of this office and further that
at least on the part of the State Police, there is an extreme
suspicion on their part that our relationship with these two
sources is questionable.

Appendix 3

FEDERAL BUREAU OF INVESTIGATION

PERFORMANCE APPRAISAL REPORT

Cover Page

1. Payroll Name FITZPATRICK ROBERT	2. Office of Assignment 3090 BOSTON
3. Social Security Number	4. Merit Pay Indicator M3
5. Position Title and Grade 01 SUPERVISORY SPECIAL AGENT (ASAC) GM 15 78-FO-714	6. Overall Adjective Rating EXCEPTIONAL

7.   Rating of Critical Element(s)

S	E	E	E	S		
# 1	# 2	# 3	# 4	# 5	#	#

8.

Signature of Rating Official   June 29, 1984
SAC JAMES W. GREENLEAF   Date

9. I am aware that my overall performance, if below the Fully Successful level, may be the basis for the denial of my within-grade/step increase and could also preclude me from consideration for promotion, administrative advancement, and/or office of preference transfer.

This appraisal has been discussed with me and I ☐ do ☑ do not wish to respond. My signature only indicates that I have reviewed this appraisal, not that I am necessarily in agreement with the information herein or that I am relinquishing my right to grieve it.

Signature of Employee   June 29, 1984
ASAC ROBERT FITZPATRICK   Date

10. I have reviewed and approved this appraisal. ☑ See my comments attached.   620050-151

Signature of Reviewing Official   REC-132   8/13/84
J. Clyde Groover, Jr.   Date

11. I have reviewed the comments of my reviewing official with respect to my comments and/or any adjustments he/she made to this performance appraisal.
I ☐ do ☐ do not wish to respond to this appraisal as adjusted by my reviewing official.

Initials of Employee   Date

12. Type of Appraisal

A (X)Annual – Type   ☑ Regular
P   ☐ Presumptive
C   ☐ Conversion

S ( )Special – Type   ☐ Unacceptable
                        ☐ Requested by FBIHQ
                        ☐ Current Appraisal

MAY 1985
92

FD-593a (Rev. 8-2-82)

FEDERAL BUREAU OF INVESTIGATION
EVALUATION PAGE

1. Payroll Name of Employee	2. Social Security Number
FITZPATRICK, ROBERT	███████████

3. Specify general nature of assignment during most of the appraisal period.

Assistant Special Agent in Charge

4. Critical Element # __1__ as listed on the Plan.

SUPERVISION OF SUBORDINATES

5. Adjective Rating:　☐ Fully Successful　☒ Superior　☐ Other _____

ASAC FITZPATRICK has continued to personally supervise his subordinates
in a superior manner during the rating period. He held daily conferences
with those supervisors that report directly to him. Many of the Boston
specials came to fruition during the rating period requiring direct
supervision by ASAC FITZPATRICK. Each of the cases met or exceeded
goals established by ASAC FITZPATRICK as program manager as a result
of his guidance. The Boston Organized Crime Program and White Collar
Crime Program continue to achieve excellent results due to ASAC FITZPATRICK'S
close personal direction.

4. Critical Element # __2__ as listed on the Plan.

PROGRAM MANAGEMENT

5. Adjective Rating:　☐ Fully Successful　☐ Superior　☒ Other __EXCEPTIONAL__

Several of the Boston specials achieved success during the rating
period as a result of the initiative and creativity on the part of
ASAC FITZPATRICK. Achievements in the Organized Crime Program and
White Collar Crime Program are a direct result of ASAC FITZPATRICK'S
interest and enthusiasm for directing the programs. During the rating
period, many problems surfaced that required ASAC FITZPATRICK to address.
These problems were overcome and many of the cases achieved successful
resolution. Modifications were made to Boston's Organized Crime Program
with the help of ASAC FITZPATRICK and Boston is now in a better position
to address the narcotics and dangerous drug problem within its territory.

Initials of Employee

FD-593a (Rev. 8-2-82)

FEDERAL BUREAU OF INVESTIGATION
EVALUATION PAGE

1. Payroll Name of Employee	2. Social Security Number
FITZPATRICK, ROBERT.	

3. Specify general nature of assignment during most of the appraisal period.

Assistant Special Agent in Charge

4. Critical Element # ___3___ as listed on the Plan.

RESOURCE MANAGEMENT

5. Adjective Rating: ☐ Fully Successful   ☐ Superior   ☒ Other __EXCEPTIONAL__

ASAC FITZPATRICK has successfully managed both equipment and manpower
resources within the division. He has coordinated the transcription of
numerous tapes obtained during a White Collar Crime special. He has
adjusted resources accordingly to insure that Boston's White Collar Crime
Program and Organized Crime Program have been responsive to the needs
of the United States Attorney's Office as well as the Strike Force.
Success in these investigations to date is due to ASAC FITZPATRICK'S
ability to recognize in advance, problem areas and adjust resources to
meet the needs of the division. He has continually monitored administrative
information to insure that programs he is responsible for continue
to have appropriate personnel to meet the needs of the division, and
at the same time has always managed to locate resources to assist other
field offices who need Agent support.

4. Critical Element # ___4___ as listed on the Plan.

LIAISON

5. Adjective Rating: ☐ Fully Successful   ☐ Superior   ☒ Other __EXCEPTIONAL__

ASAC FITZPATRICK has maintained liaison with not only the United States
Attorney's Office, but also the local law enforcement community in a very
positive fashion. He has maintained contact with community leaders and
represented the FBI in an exceptional manner during numerous speeches.
He has made major speeches before law enforcement groups in our four-
state area. In each instance he has been recognized by the group for
his presentation. ASAC FITZPATRICK'S Media exposure has been somewhat
limited, but on those occasions that he has met with the press, he
has handled himself in an exceptional manner.

Initials of Employee

FD-593a (Rev. 6-2-82)

FEDERAL BUREAU OF INVESTIGATION
EVALUATION PAGE

1. Payroll Name of Employee	2. Social Security Number

FITZPATRICK,ROBERT

3. Specify general nature of assignment during most of the appraisal period.

Assistant Special Agent in Charge

4. Critical Element # ___5___ as listed on the Plan.

ASSOCIATE EXECUTIVE RESPONSIBILITY

5. Adjective Rating: ☐ Fully Successful ☒ Superior ☐ Other _____

During the rating period, ASAC FITZPATRICK, has in the absence of the
SAC, successfully managed the investigative and administrative
operations of the division. He has handled several delicate administrative
inquiries within the division in a professional manner providing total
independent supervision to the matters. He has established excellent
relations with DEA and has recommended the movement of resources to
assist DEA as appropriate. On at least one occasion, he responded to the
needs of DEA in the absence of the SAC, which resulted in a successful
investigation and closer ties with that agency. He continues to
carry out the policies of this office in my absence and his overall
dedication to the job has resulted in a successful year for the Boston
Division.

4. Critical Element # _____ as listed on the Plan.

5. Adjective Rating: ☐ Fully Successful ☐ Superior ☐ Other _____

Initials of Employee

Memorandum

To : ALL EMPLOYEES   Date   6/3/85

SAC JAMES W. GREENLEAF   (66-4173)

Subject : UNITED STATES DEPARTMENT OF JUSTICE
OFFICE OF PROFESSIONAL RESPONSIBILITY

         The following memorandum from the Attorney General
dated January 10, 1979, is set forth for your information:

         "To: Heads of All Offices, Boards, Bureaus, and
Divisions; All United States Attorneys.

         "Subject: Reporting Requirements of Departmental
Order Establishing the Office of Professional Responsibility.

         "The Department's Office of Professional Responsi-
bility was created to oversee investigations of criminal or
ethical misconduct by Department of Justice employees. As
head of that Office, the Counsel's function is to ensure
that Departmental employees continue to perform their duties
in accord with the professional standards expected of the
Nation's principal law enforcement agency. The Office is
responsible for reviewing allegations against Departmental
employees involving violations of law, Departmental regulations, or Departmental standards of conduct. To this end,
the Office of Professional Responsibility serves as a special
review and advisory body, reporting directly to the Attorney
General or, in appropriate cases, to the Deputy Attorney
General, the Associate Attorney General, or the Solicitor
General. See §0.39 et seq., Departmental Order No. 635-75,
40 Fed. Reg. 58,643 (1975). For this Office to perform its
function properly, it must be notified promptly whenever
someone makes an allegation of serious misconduct against
any employee of the Department.

         "Section 0.39a(f)(1) and (2) of the Department
Regulations require the Counsel to submit to the Attorney
General and the Deputy Attorney General 'an immediate

1-Each Employee
1-66-4173
1-66-161
EWL:rem

BS 66-4173

"'report' concerning any matter which appears to involve a
violation (1) of law, or (2) of Departmental regulations or
orders, or applicable standards of conduct which 'should be
brought to the attention of a higher official.' Section
0.39a(f)(3) requires the Counsel to submit a monthly report
summarizing the matters under the Counsel's review.

"I wish to remind you that it is your responsibility to inform the Counsel on Professional Responsibility
of all such allegations which come to your attention and
to advise him when inquiries into these allegations have
been completed. In addition, the internal inspection units
of the Department (or where there are no such specific units,
any units or offices discharging comparable duties) should
continue to submit monthly reports to the Counsel detailing
the status and results of their current investigations.

"Additionally, I want you to remind each of your
employees, in written form, of the Office's existence and
inform them that they may, at any time, bring allegations
directly to the attention of the Office as opposed to their
own internal inspection unit. You should continue to do
this periodically, not less than semi-annually.

"Attorney General"

Memorandum

To : SAC, BOSTON   Date 6/7/85

From : ASAC ROBERT FITZPATRICK (62-new)   CONFIDENTIAL

Subject : ALLEGED DISCLOSURE OF INFORMATION
BY SAC GREENLEAF

On 6/5/85 in the AM, in discussion with the SAC concerning the DAVE TOOMEY case (12-377), there was much discussion, but more specifically, some discussion centered around Supervisor JOHN BRADY and his former relationship with DAVE TOOMEY and the fact that information was now being received from one of the subjects in a drug case concerning FRANK LEPERE. Particularly, the SAC discussed the fact that SUPERVISOR BRADY has an association with former Strike Force attorney DAVE TOOMEY as a private attorney and SAC GREENLEAF intimated that this as an "OPR MATTER". My advice was to just confront SUPV. BRADY with some of the facts, however, the SAC reiterated that this was in fact an OPR matter. Following the meeting with the SAC, another meeting was held with SUPV. TOM MacGEORGE who is the supervisor of this case and questions arose regarding an alleged contact the SAC had with former Strike Force attorney and now present defense attorney MARTIN BOUDREAU.

There had been general discussion sometime ago in November or thereabouts - exact dates unknown - that JEREMIAH O'SULLIVAN and GREENLEAF had discussed GREENLEAF's alleged conversation with BOUDREAU regarding DAVE TOOMEY. Inasmuch as this information was nebulous and very general in nature with no specifics, OPR was not even a consideration in this matter particularly inasmuch as it was not known what specifics - if any - were discussed by GREENLEAF and BOUDREAU.

In contact with O'SULLIVAN and in an attempt to get clarification in allegations against SUPV. DAVE BRADY inasmuch as O'SULLIVAN is a part of the LEPERE interrogation, O'SULLIVAN provided the following information:

O'SULLIVAN volunteered that as a matter of record, GREENLEAF had discussed aspects of the TOOMEY investigation with MARTIN BOUDREAU. O'SULLIVAN stated that he felt any conversations SUPV. BRADY may have had where not to be explored as an OPR matter as SUPV. BRADY was considered to be not only a major witness in the LEPERE case but also a possible witness in the TOOMEY CASE. In view of this fact, O'SULLIVAN was emphatic about no other investigation "ruining the ongoing LEPERE/TOOMEY investigations". With regard to SAC GREENLEAF's contact with TOOMEY, O'SULLIVAN advised the information was "old information" and dated back to

ds

BS 62-new

the day after KIRVAN was arrested by DEA and allegedly furnished information regarding LEPERE and TOOMEY. It is not known what exact information was learned by GREENLEAF nor from whom he learned it; however, O'SULLIVAN advised the following:

He stated that GREENLEAF encountered MARTY BOUDREAU, a defense attorney from Boston, on a Saturday morning at a coffee shop in Hopkinton, Mass. He related that GREENLEAF told BOUDREAU "we've turned a witness (KIRVAN), we've got LEPERE, we took him off". There was an allegation made that KIRVAN had mentioned TOOMEY and also discussion that PETER VINTON, a DEA Agent, had grabbed KIRVAN on a warrant and also KIRVAN would not testify. There was much discussion, part of which was a discussion of a "leak" situation in the U. S. Attorney's office, whereupon KIRVAN said "There's a leak - it was DAVE TOOMEY". More specific information furnished BOUDREAU by GREENLEAF is not available; however, GREENLEAF told O'SULLIVAN what he did, according to O'SULLIVAN, saying "I think I've done something I should not have done".

It was explained to O'SULLIVAN that ASAC FITZPATRICK had been censured for allegedly "warning" an SAC in the past about sensitive information and because of this,he was not taking any chances but felt he could not alert the present SAC to what could be perceived to be an OPR matter. ASAC FITZPATRICK told O'SULLIVAN that according to his instructions, he had no alternative but to notify OPR and seek advice from them without notifying the SAC.

O'SULLIVAN advised that he would be notifying OPR, JUSTICE DEPARTMENT, to furnish pertinent facts.

On June 6, 1985, DAVE FLANDERS, OPR, was apprised of the above information and he advised ASAC FITZPATRICK that he should not relate this information to SAC.

- 2* -

UNITED STATES DISTRICT COURT

DISTRICT OF MASSACHUSETTS

* * * * * * * * * * * * * * *

THE ESTATE OF JOHN L. MCINTYRE,　　*

　　　Plaintiff　　　　　　　　　　　*

　　　vs.　　　　　　　　　　* No. 01-10408-RCL

UNITED STATES OF AMERICA, et al.,　*

　　　Defendants　　　　　　　　　　*

* * * * * * * * * * * * * * *

DEPOSITION OF ROBERT FITZPATRICK

Deposition taken at the offices of

Denner-O'Malley, 4 Longfellow Place,

35th Floor, Boston, Massachusetts, 02114,

on Tuesday, March 22, 2005, commencing

at 9:35 a.m.

Court Reporter: Dawn Griffin-Smith, CCR
N.H. Certified Court Reporter
No. 108 (RSA 331-B)

```
 1                          APPEARANCES

 2      Representing the Plaintiff McIntyre:
                          SHAHEEN & GORDON
 3                        By:  William E. Christie, Esq.
                          107 Storrs Avenue
 4                        Concord, NH  03302

 5

 6      Representing the Plaintiff Donahue:
                          SLOAN AND WALSH
 7                        By:  Edward T. Hinchey, Esq.
                          3 Center Plaza
 8                        Boston, MA  02108

 9

10      Representing the Plaintiff Hussey:
                          ANN M. DONOVAN
11                        By:  Ann M. Donovan, Esq.
                          1087 Beacon Street, Ste. 204
12                        Boston, MA  02459

13

14      Representing the Defendant Fitzpatrick:
                          OFFICES OF DOUGLAS MATTHEWS
15                        By:  Douglas Matthews, Esq.
                          35 Plymouth Boulevard
16                        Westport, MA  02790
                                    and
17                        OFFICES OF WILLIAM A. BROWN
                          By:  William A. Brown, Esq.
18                             Kate Miller Brown, Esq.
                          31 Milk Street, 5th Floor
19                        Boston, MA  02109

20

21      Representing the Defendant USA:
                          UNITED STATES DEPARTMENT OF
22                        JUSTICE
                          By:  Kathrine A. Carey, Esq.
23                        1331 Pennsylvania Ave,  N.W.
                          Washington, DC  20044
```

3

1   APPEARANCES (Cont.)

2   Representing the Defendant James Ring:
                       ROSE & ASSOCIATES
3   By: Alan D. Rose, Jr., Esq.
                       29 Commonwealth Avenue
4   Boston, MA 02116

5

6   Representing the Defendant Kennedy:
                       MERRICK, LOUISON & COSTELLO
7   By: Stephen C. Pfaff, Esq.
                       67 Batterymarch Street
8   Boston, MA 02110

9

10 Representing the Defendant Greenleaf:
                       ROACH & CARPENTER, PC
11   By: Christine Roach, Esq.
                       24 School Street
12   Boston, MA 02110

3

    Representing the Defendant Sarhatt:
                       MORRISON MAHONEY
                       By: Tory A. Weigand, Esq.
                       250 Summer Street
                       Boston, MA 02210

4

1   I N D E X

2

3   WITNESS:

4   **ROBERT FITZPATRICK**

5   EXAMINATION: Page

6   By Mr. Christie............................ 5

7   By Mr. Hinchey............................. 161

8   By Ms. Donovan............................. 192

9   By Ms. Carey............................... 204

10   By Mr. Weigand............................. 207

11   By Mr. Pfaff............................... 230

12

13   EXHIBITS FOR IDENTIFICATION:

14   Number   Page

15   1   4/1/81 Letter   67

16   2   4/9/82 Teletype (MCN051-0810-0831)   79

17   3   RAK013-0097   97

18   4   MCN023-3120 (9/2/99)   101

19   5   MCN055-2361 (5/21/82)   109

20   6   MCN055-2471 (5/27/82)   117

21   7   4/8/85 Letter   124

22   8   RAK002-0592   134

23

         ***Exhibits attached.

153

```
 1   A.  It was all reported.
 2   Q.  It was all reported to Headquarters?
 3   A.  All the things we've discussed this morning, yes.
 4   Q.  Did you ever receive directions from Headquarters
 5       about how to stop these leaks?
 6   A.  No.
 7   Q.  Do you recall at any time before McIntyre's
 8       disappearance any agent reporting to you that
 9       Bulger and Flemmi were aware of his cooperation?
10   A.  Well, first of all with regard to his
11       disappearance, I mean, I don't recall it that way.
12       He just wasn't around anymore.
13   Q.  Well, that's not my question.  My question was,
14       From the time he started cooperating to the time he
15       disappeared did any agent report to you that there
16       were reports --
17   A.  Not to my knowledge.
18   Q.  -- that Bulger and Flemmi were aware that McIntyre
19       was cooperating?
20   A.  Not to my knowledge.
21   Q.  If an agent was aware of that or had information to
22       that effect would you expect that agent to report
23       that to you?
```

154

1   A.   Oh, yes.

2   Q.   And why would you expect the agent to report that

3   to you?

4   A.   Because it's his job.

5   Q.   Because the informant's in danger; correct?

6   A.   Well, sure. That's his job. It's right on the

7   credits.

8   Q.   Right on the credits?

9   A.   Credentials. "Enforce the laws; furnish

10   information; give it to the government." We are

11   the government.

12   Q.   And if an agent failed to do that?

13   A.   That's a violation.

14   Q.   But no agent provided that information to you?

15   A.   I mean, not that I recall.

16   Q.   At some point McIntyre disappeared; correct?

17   A.   Yes.

18   Q.   And how did that come to your attention, the fact

19   of his disappearance?

20   A.   I don't recall. Remember, the case, as I told you,

21   was taken away. I would not be involved in that

22   anymore.

23   Q.   Do you know if any investigation was conducted into

155

1		his disappearance by the FBI?
2	A.	No, I don't.
3	Q.	You don't know one way or the other?
4	A.	No.
5	Q.	At any time after McIntyre's disappearance did you
6		come to believe that McIntyre's identity had been
7		leaked?
8	A.	Yes.
9	Q.	And can you describe how you came to that belief?
10	A.	One of my supervisors, my number one supervisor,
11		who is Tom McGeorge -- well -- and I believe you
12		have the information -- but there was a memo that
13		came down on June 4th, 1985. And the memo is a
14		constant reminder about all of the things you are
15		talking about: You must present this to the
16		government; you must tell them this; you are
17		required to go out and refresh the agents about all
18		this information that must be reported and so forth
19		and so on. That was sitting right on my desk.
20		On or about June 5th -- it's in a memo I
21		wrote -- Tom McGeorge came in and said -- oh, we
22		had a conference in the morning and we were
23		discussing Twomey and leaks, the leak situation.

KIRVN

156

1   And following the conference, McGeorge

2   came in and told me he found out who the leaker

3   was. And I said who is the leak? And he said, The

4   SAC. And I looked -- I was like flabbergasted. So

5   I walked over, closed the door, and I said,

6   McGeorge, you know, you better not be fooling

7   around about this. So he said, No, Bob. I have

8   information that Greenleaf told the defense

9   attorney about some of the informants -- it was

10   more than one informant that leaked. One name is

11   Cavan and McIntyre. I was literally incredulous.

12   I was scared to be honest with you, and I had never

13   had this happen before.

14   So what I did was I interviewed him,

15   obviously, asked him where he got his information

16   from; and he mentioned to me that Jerry O'Sullivan

17   knew about it. So in front of him I called Jerry

18   O'Sullivan and I said, Jerry, I got a guy in my

19   office here who says the SAC leaked information

20   about the drug investigations and so forth; and he

21   said, I already know that. And I said, What do you

22   know? And he said, Oh, that's old news. That

23   happened back in November or December or whatever

157

1   he said -- it's in the memo -- and so I said, Well,

2   why didn't you tell me? What are you doing about

3   it? And he just dummied up. I think he said, None

4   of your business. And I said, What are you going

5   to do about it? He says, Well, I'm going to call

6   OPR. So he's going to call Justice OPR.

7   So when I hung up I told McGeorge that I

8   have no alternative but to call OPR, and I did. I

9   call the Director's office at the Bureau.

10 Q. And when you say you called OPR --

11 A. I call the Director's office.

12 Q. You called the Director's office. And --

13 A. It was because it involved an SAC.

14 Q. And what did you tell the Director's office?

15 A. That one of my supervisors just reported that the

16   SAC of the Boston Division is a leak. He gave away

17   federal -- I mentioned that he furnished -- we had

18   a Federal Grand Jury going on, and he had given

19   away 6E, Federal Grand Jury 6E information, which

20   is a crime.

21 Q. And what, if anything, was done as a result of that

22   report?

23 A. Nothing.

NOTES

General sources include author's personal notes, recollections, daybook entries plus personal discussions with Colonel John O'Donovan, Dick Bates, Joe Yablonski, Jim Knotts, and Larry Sarhatt, as well as reports to FBI, DOJ, and federal courts.

PROLOGUE: *Murder of John McIntyre*

Page 13: *According to testimony:* Descriptions of McIntyre's murder drawn from court testimony and/or depositions and plea agreements by Stephen Flemmi, John Martorano, and Kevin Weeks; testimony from the 2006 McIntyre trial; sourcing from the *Boston Globe,* and *The Brothers Bulger* by Howie Carr (Grand Central, 2006, pages 265–66).

Page 13: *Torture of McIntyre:* Accusations supported by findings against FBI from decision by Judge Reginald Lindsay of the district court, upheld by the appellate court, finding the FBI complicit in McIntyre's murder and ordering a $3.1 million judgment. Judge Lindsay wrote in part: "For decades preceding the McIntyre murder, agents of the FBI protected Bulger and Flemmi as informants by shielding them from prosecution for crimes they had committed."

In upholding Judge Lindsay's decision, the U.S. Court of Appeals for the First Circuit went on to say that, "The McIntyre leak violated a bright-line law enforcement rule that informant identity never be revealed, and put at risk the life of an individual who was helping the FBI."

Part One: Coming to Boston

CHAPTER 1

Page 18: *ABSCAM and arrest of Senator Harrison Williams:* As detailed by *Time* magazine: http://www.time.com/time/magazine/article/0,9171,924247 ,00.html.

Page 19: *Harrison Williams's conviction:* Senator Harrison Williams was convicted of nine counts of bribery and conspiracy. He was fined $50,000 and sentenced to three years in prison. He died on November 20, 2001: http://www.nytimes.com/2001/11/20/nyregion/ex-senator-harrison-a -williams-jr-81-dies-went-to-prison-over-abscam-scandal.html.

CHAPTER 3

Page 26: *Word was the agents there had taken their mandate:* Internal FBI memo dated August 6, 1980, to Boston SAC Lawrence Sarhatt from ASAC Weldon L. Kennedy. (See Appendix, page 277)

Page 28: *Jerry Angiulo:* Jerry Angiulo's life and status as a mob boss was neatly summed up in his *Boston Herald* obituary in August 2009: http:// www.bostonherald.com/news/regional/view.bg?articleid=1194144.

Page 29: *Colonel O'Donovan:* Suspicions of Colonel O'Donovan of Massachusetts State Police raised in memo referenced immediately above.

CHAPTER 4

Page 40: *McDonald and Sims:* The status of Joe McDonald and James Sims as associates of Bulger and Flemmi and members of the Winter Hill Gang confirmed in *Black Mass* by Dick Lehr and Gerard O'Neill (New York: Harper Collins Perennial, 2001, pages 65, 68).

Page 40: Depiction of the meeting detailed here drawn from knowledge of former FBI agent Dick Bates and outgoing Boston office ASAC Joe Yablonski. Further affirmed later in testimony by John Morris in Wolf hearings after being granted immunity.

Page 41: *Connolly and Castucci:* Complicity of agent John Connolly in the murder of Richie Castucci supported by a superseding criminal indictment unsealed on October 11, 2000, accusing John Connolly of "leaking information to Bulger and Flemmi that led directly to the murders of three potential witnesses against the gang: Brian Halloran, John Callahan, and a third informant named Richard Castucci" (*Black Mass*, page 327). Also reported in a *Boston Herald* story that same week entitled "Blood on His Hands."

CHAPTER 5

Page 43: *The MSP didn't trust:* Colonel O'Donovan's suspicions, as relayed to author, were the subject of an internal FBI memo from ASAC Weldon L. Kennedy to Boston SAC Lawrence Sarhatt, August 6, 1980.

Page 44: *racehorse fix case:* Whitey Bulger and Stephen Flemmi's part in the 1979 Race Fix case detailed in the testimony of Jeremiah O'Sullivan before the House Government Reform Committee 2002 as reported in the Third Report by the Committee on Government Reform entitled "Everything Secret Degenerates: The FBI's Use of Murderers as Informants (pages 5–6): http://www.docstoc.com/docs/5997413/Everything-Secret-Degenerates-The-FBI's-Use-of-Murderers-as Informants.

This is further supplemented by John Morris's own testimony under grant of immunity during the 1998 Wolf hearings. As the *Boston Globe* has written: "Granted immunity from prosecution in exchange for his testimony during 1998 federal court hearings, Morris confirmed scathing allegations of FBI misconduct, admitting that he had alerted Flemmi and Bulger to an investigation targeting bookmakers in 1988 and had asked a federal prosecutor to keep them out of a 1979 indictment for fixing horse races": http://www.boston.com/news/packages/whitey/characters/morris.htm.

Pages 46–47: *One Boston agent, Jim Knotts, even insisted that John Connolly was fictionalizing information:* This and additional allegations lodged on these pages further supported by "The Official Bulger FBI Files: Some Tall Tales" by Dick Lehr and the *Globe* staff, *Boston Globe,* July 21, 1998: http://www.boston.com/news/local/massachusetts/articles/1998/07/21/the_official_bulger_fbi_files_some_tall_tales/?page=2.

CHAPTER 6

Page 51: *"to insure that [informants] are not provided any information":* from the *FBI Manual of Investigative Operations and Guidelines*, pages 137–38, 1978.

Page 52: *I was on special assignment:* Author's part in the Bombings in Mississippi investigation detailed in *Heritage: The FBI Oral History Project,* as supported by court documents, author's FBI personnel file, and testimony in federal court (SUPRA).

CHAPTER 7

Page 59: Author's account of his role in the Martin Luther King assassination detailed in *Heritage: The FBI Oral History Project*, as supported by court documents and author's FBI personnel file.

Depiction of author's interview with Bulger has been previously reported on *60 Minutes* and the National Geographic documentary *Bullets Over Boston.*

CHAPTER 8

Page 67: *My two-page report:* Author's two-page memo recommending Bulger be closed as informant allegedly lost, a fact testified to by author during the McIntyre trial and Wolf hearings as supported by trial transcripts. Its existence has never been the subject of any contention, except in findings against the FBI.

CHAPTER 9

Page 75: *Teddy Deegan was described:* Story of the murder of Teddy Deegan by Joseph Barboza, and covered up by FBI agents Paul Rico and Dennis Condon, was proven in court, a case in which the FBI was held liable for criminal wrongdoing and ordered to pay $101.7 million in damages to the plaintiffs ("Court Frees Limone After 33 Years in Prison," by Ralph Ramalli, *Boston Globe,* January, 6, 2001). The Obama Justice Department, and Elena Kagan as solicitor general opted against appeal. http://www.boston .com/news/nation/washington/articles/2010/05/01/us_wont_appeal_ver- dict_in_case_of_four_framed_by_fbi/.

The House Government Reform Committee also weighed in on this to a great degree in the Third Report by the Committee on Government Reform entitled "Everything Secret Degenerates: The FBI's Use of Murderers as Informants" (pages 5–6): http://www.docstoc.com/docs/5997413/Every thing-Secret-Degenerates-The-FBI's-Use-of-Murderers-as-Informants.

CHAPTER 10

Page 81: *"The successful prosecution of these subjects":* Associated Press, July 28, 2002: http://truthinjustice.org/blood-bargain.htm.

Page 81: *Barboza decided to get even:* Account of Joseph Barboza's changing his story supported by,

> Before long, however, he was threatening to recant his testimony unless given $9,000 for plastic surgery to change his appearance. If Barboza recanted, convictions "might be overturned and plunge the government into protracted and acrimonious litigation," federal prosecutors Edward F. Harrington and Walter T. Barnes warned their supervisor in Washington. In their Feb. 12, 1970, memo, they urged that Barboza be given the money. Six months later, Barboza did recant—but soon changed his mind and stood by his original story.

Associated Press, July 28, 2002: http://truthinjustice.org/blood-bargain .htm.

Page 82: *"What do you want from me? Tears?":* From government transcripts as reported in *The Brothers Bulger* (page 399).

Page 82: *Condon had opened:* Dennis Condon being the first agent to open Whitey Bulger as informant confirmed in *Black Mass* (pages 30–31) and *The Brothers Bulger* (pages 84–85).

CHAPTER 11

Page 84: *Bulger, though, resisted:* Connolly's initial recruitment of Bulger as informant detailed in *Black Mass* (pages 3–16).

Page 86: *"We knew what these guys were":* From U.S. District Court, District of Massachusetts, complaint filed by the Estate of John L. McIntyre, March 8, 2001, paragraph 367 of the complaint.

Page 87: *None of this was happening under the radar:* Internal FBI memo from ASAC Weldon L. Kennedy to Boston SAC Lawrence Sarhatt, August 6, 1980.

Part Two: Blowback

CHAPTER 13

Page 99: *An unethical, if not illegal, breach of policy:* Committee on Government Reform, House of Representatives, December 5 and 6, 2002, page 294 forward: http://www.gpo.gov/fdsys/pkg/CHRG-107hhrg10784604 .html/CHRG-107hhrg10784604.htm.

Pages 100–101: Allegations detailed here covered also in "The Official Bulger Files: Some Tall Tales" in the *Boston Globe* by Dick Lehr and the *Globe* staff, July 21, 1998: http://www.boston.com/news/local/massachu setts/articles/1998/07/2l/the_official_bulger_fbi_files_some_tall_tales/.

Page 102: *Strike Force attorney Dave Twomey:* U.S. Court of Appeals, Cases & Opinions: http://cases.justia.com/us-court-of-appeals/F2/806/1136/45629.

Page 103: *"No one disputes the proposition that destroying organized crime":* From "FBI Informant System Called a Failure" by Ralph Ranalli and the *Globe* staff, *Boston Globe*, November 21, 2003: http://www.truthinjustice.org/ corrupt-FBI.htm

Page 103: *The MSP and DEA became more and more frustrated:* Internal FBI memo from Boston ASAC Weldon L. Kennedy to Boston SAC Lawrence Sarhatt, August 6, 1980.

Page 104: *"The FBI," Stephen Flemmi would admit years later:* From *Boston Globe* article by Michaell Zuckoff and the *Globe* staff, July 23, 1998. The same article went on to add,

> Assistant U.S. Attorney Gary Crossen successfully won a court's permission to wiretap Bulger. But Bulger was never caught making incriminating statements or seen in any compromising positions; soon, the probe would end. Badly. On March 11, 1985, Bulger and his friend Kevin Weeks drove Bulger's bugged car into a garage on Old Colony Avenue in South Boston. DEA agent Steven Boeri was monitoring the bug—which had only been in place a few days—when Boeri realized that Bulger and Weeks had found the listening device.

Page 105: *Exchange between Jeremiah O'Sullivan and Chris Shays:* Committee on Government Reform, House of Representatives, December 5 and 6, 2002, page 294 forward. http://www.gpo.gov/fdsys/pkg/CHRG-107hhrgl0784604/ html/CHRG-107hhrgl0784604.htm.

Page 105: *"You got me":* From Jeremiah O'Sullivan in the Third Report by the Committee on Government Reform entitled "Everything Secret Degenerates: The FBI's Use of Murderers as Informants" (pages 5–6): http://www.docstoc.com/docs/5997413/Everything-Secret-Degenerates-The -FBI's-Use-of-Murderers-as-Informants.

CHAPTER 14

Page 107: Background on John Callahan and Roger Wheeler confirmed in both *The Brothers Bulger* (pages 208–14) and *Black Mass* (pages 139–54).

Page 109: *In May 1981:* Murder of Wheeler by Matorano confirmed in *Black Mass* (page 145) from Matorano's own admissions in a 1998 plea agreement in which he admitted to killing ten people for Bulger, including Roger Wheeler ("Ex-Mobster Reportedly Strikes Deal, by Shelley Murphy, *Boston Globe*, September 9, 1999: http://www.boston.com/news/packages/whitey/globe_stories/1999/0909_ex_mobster_reportedly_strikes_deal.htm).

CHAPTER 15

Page 114: *By early 1982, more and more circumstantial evidence: Black Mass,* page 152.

CHAPTER 16

Page 122: *Otherwise O'Sullivan feared the weight of the entire case:* O'Sullivan admitted to this in his testimony before the House Committee on Government Reform on December 5 and 6, 2002.

Page 122: *He'd already gone to bat for Bulger and Flemmi:* O'Sullivan admitted to this as well in same testimony referenced immediately above.

Page 124: *"Fitzy said to me, 'You know people always say'":* From the sworn testimony of William Weld at the Wolf hearings on May 26 and 27, 1998.

Page 125: *What was not known was that the drug cartel:* Allegations against the Miami Police Department and ultimate dispensation of the Miami River Murders supported by a series of articles appearing in the *Miami Herald* on December 27, 28, and 29, 1985. Quoting from the article that appeared on December 28:

> Three Miami police officers were charged Friday with the murders of three drug dealers in a botched cocaine rip-off, leaving the embattled

police department reeling under the latest allegations of official corruption. A fourth officer and a fifth man, who resigned from the department earlier this year, were charged Friday with racketeering and cocaine trafficking. The triple murder, according to court documents, was just one instance in a shocking pattern of casual drug deals.

Author reported these crimes as early as 1979 and 1980 to FBI headquarters and SAC Miami: http://nl.newsbank.com/nl-search/we/Archives ?p_multi=MH|&p_product=MH&p_theme=realcities2&p_action=search &p_maxdocs=200&s_site=miami&s_trackval=MH&s_search_type=key -word&s_dispstring=Miami%20river%20Cops%20AND%20date(1985) &p_field_date-0=YMD_date&p_params_date-0=date:B,E&p_text_date-0 =1985&p_field_advanced-0=&p_text_advanced-0=(Miami%20river %20Cops)&xcal_numdocs=20&p_perpage=10&p_sort=YMD_date:D &xcal_useweights=no.

Page 127: References to Jimmy Flynn found in *The Brothers Bulger* (pages 220–23).

Page 128: *I knew full well that Halloran was killed:* Judge Wolf's findings in his Memorandum and Order decision, page 84 would read in part: "Morris caused Connolly to tell Flemmi and Bulger that Brian Halloran was providing the FBI information that implicated them to the murder of Roger Wheeler. Halloran was murdered soon after. . . ."

Page 130: *Mike Huff and his associate detectives:* Passages highlighting Detective Huff and the Jai Alai murders also covered in *Black Mass* (pages 152–54) as well as the *Boston Globe, Boston Herald,* and Associated Press.

Part Three: Beyond Bulger

CHAPTER 17

Page 146: *"I'm Bob Fitzpatrick . . . you are under arrest":* Arrest of Jerry Angiulo on September 29, 1983, confirmed in his *Boston Globe* obituary (September 4, 2009). His arrest by me confirmed in FBI personnel files and case reports. All of this was testified to on numerous occasions in federal court.

Page 149: *Greenleaf, I began to suspect:* Allegations against McWeeney and other FBI officials supported by Judge Wolf's Memorandum and Order, September 15, 1999:

The Halloran murder presented a dilemma for the FBI. It precipitated a May 25, 1982, meeting at FBI Headquarters to grapple with Bulger and Flemmi's dual status as valuable FBI informants and also suspects in the investigations of the Wheeler and Halloran murders. Ex. 54; Fitzpatrick Apr. 16, 1998 Tr. at 94–102, Apr. 17, 1998 Tr. at 179. Representatives of the FBI offices in Boston, Oklahoma City, and Miami met with FBI Headquarters officials, including Sean McWeeney, Chief of the Organized Crime section, and Jeff Jamar, the Informant Coordinator.

http://www.thelaborers.net/court_cases/United_States_v_Salemme_Decision.htm.

Author testified to these facts in federal court and depositions on numerous occasions.

CHAPTER 18

Page 151: *"I'm his brother. He sought to call me":* Billy Bulger quote from Committee on Government Reform, House of Representatives, 2002. Also referenced in *The Brothers Bulger* (page 16).

Page 154: *During this period, agents of the Organized Crime squad:* As reported by Shelley Murphy, *Boston Globe,* October 21, 2008: http://www.boston.com/news/local/breaking_news/2008/10/by_shelley_murp_2.html.

The *Hartford Courant,* October 22, 2008, adds:

In addition to sharing meals, Gianturco said that he exchanged gifts with Bulger and Flemmi at Christmas. They gave him an attaché case and an Oriental figurine; Gianturco said they must have noticed that his wife collected the statuettes during one of their dinners. He wasn't asked what he gave in return.

http://www.courant.com/news/nation-world/hc-mobtriall022.artoct22,0,3665731.story.

Page 154: *"I accepted it because she handed it to me":* Buckley's testimony quoted in same *Boston Globe* article referenced above under Page 154.

Page 154: *Under a grant of immunity years later:* "The Martyrdom of John Connolly," by David Boeri, *Boston Magazine,* September 2008: http://www.bostonmagazine.com/articles/the_martyrdom_of_john_connolly/page2.

CHAPTER 19

Page 157: *"There were U.S. Drug":* "Here's to Honest Cops who Made a Difference," by Kevin Cullen, *Boston Globe,* July 3, 2011: http://articles.boston.com/2011-07-03/news/29733649_1_state-cops-fbi-agent-john-connolly.

Page 157: "FBI in Denial as Bulger Breaks Drug Pact in Southie" by Mitchell Zuckoff and *Globe* Staff in the *Boston Globe,* July 23, 1998: http://www.boston.com/news/local/massachusetts/articles/1998/07/23/fbi_in_denial_as_bulger_breaks_drug_pact_in_southie/?page=l.

Page 158: *Under the auspices of Joe Murray:* Joe Murray's criminal status covered at length in both *The Brothers Bulger* (pages 244–47) and *Black Mass* in which the authors refer to him as "the gangster who trafficked in drugs and stolen guns for the IRA and sometimes did business with Bulger" (page 240).

Pages 158–159: Numerous sources support this account including *The Brothers Bulger* (page 264).

Page 160: Stephen Flemmi pleaded guilty to John McIntyre's murder on October 14, 2003: http://www.ipsn.org/characters/bulger/doj_flemmi_press_release.htm.

Page 160: *And then came the night:* Flemmi's statements about the specifics of McIntyre's murder are contained in the transcripts from the 2006 McIntyre trial and quoted in part in *The Brothers Bulger* (pages 265–66). The entire exchange can be found at: http://www.thebrothersbulger.com/John%20McIntyre.htm.

Page 160: *When I appeared:* References to author's interview on *60 Minutes* supported by transcript and tape of segment.

CHAPTER 20

Page 164: *As I told the* Boston Herald: Referenced article from the *Boston Herald* appeared in April 11, 2001 edition.

Page 165: *"I wish to remind":* Referenced Department of Justice memo and FBI memo is in author's possession and was submitted as evidence in the course of numerous federal court cases in which author has testified. (See Appendix 4.)

Page 165: *I filed my own memo:* Entire memo reporting Greenleaf for alleged leaking can be found in the Appendix, pages 288–89.

Page 165: Author's suspicions were further borne out in the following excerpt from Judge's Wolf's 1999 decision: "In about April 1984, Stutman met with Greenleaf and explained that the DEA planned to conduct a major investigation, including electronic surveillance, of Bulger and Flemmi in which it wanted the FBI to participate because it was expected that the investigation would develop information concerning crimes that were within the jurisdiction of the FBI rather than the DEA. Stutman Apr. 14, 1998 Tr. at 10–18, 22, 82; Greenleaf Jan. 8, 1998 Tr. at 37–38, 66–69, 195–96. Stutman provided Greenleaf with detailed information about the investigation to date, including a description of the information that he felt should be of active interest to the FBI. Greenleaf Jan. 8, 1998 Tr. at 125, 195; Stutman Apr. 14, 1998 Tr. at 12. Stutman would have given Greenleaf any additional information that he requested. Stutman Apr. 14, 1998 Tr. at 90. Greenleaf did not, however, ask for more details or immediately respond to Stutman's request." http://www .thelaborers.net/court_cases/United_States_v_Salemme_Decision.htm.

Page 167: *including an admission that he knew Bulger and Flemmi were murderers:* From Committee on Government Reform, House of Representatives, December 5 and 6, 2002, page 294 forward: http://www.gpo.gov/ fdsys/pkg/CHRG-107hhrgl0784604/html/CHRG-107hhrgl0784604.htm.

Page 167: *"just didn't register":* From Greenleaf's testimony in the 2006 McIntyre trial, as also reported by columnist Peter Gelzinis in the *Boston Herald* on June 23, 2006. The quote is also referenced in the U.S. Court of Appeals for the First Circuit's affirming Judge Lindsay's decision in the McIntyre trial (page 33 of 44-page decision).

Pages 167: *"At any time":* Author has quoted deposition in his possession. (See Appendix 6.)

CHAPTER 21

Page 170: Allegations against Sean McWeeney supported by Judge Wolf in his 1998 decision as follows:

> In 1984, Sean McWeeney, the Chief of the Organized Crime Section at FBI Headquarters, told Connolly that the DEA was leading an investigation targeting Bulger and Flemmi. Connolly shared this information with his sources. § II.17.

http://www.thelaborers.net/court_cases/United_States_v_Salemme_Decision.htm.

Also supported in the U.S. Court of Appeals for the First Circuit's affirming Judge Lindsay's decision in the McIntyre trial (page 11 of 44-page decision).

Page 170: *"Aren't these our guys?":* As confirmed in *Black Mass* (page 186).

This was further articulated by Michael Zuckoff writing in the *Boston Globe* on July 23, 1998 ("FBI in Denial as Bulger Breaks Drug Pact in Southie"):

> In April, former Boston FBI agent Rod Kennedy testified that in 1984, a high-ranking Washington FBI official was told of DEA plans to bug Bulger and Flemmi. Troubled that another federal agency was targeting FBI informants, he called the Boston FBI office for an explanation. As it happened, Kennedy testified, the only person in the squad room was Connolly, who by answering the phone received advance knowledge of DEA bugging plans.

http://www.boston.com/news/localMassachusetts/articles/1998/07/23/fbi_in_denial_as_bulger_breaks_drug_pact_in_southie/?page=6.

Page 171: *In an internal FBI:* Quotes from internal FBI Performance Appraisal Report in author's possession and can be found in Appendix 3.

CHAPTER 22

Page 179: These charges and the determination that they were ultimately baseless are on record and file, along with a complaint author filed with the U.S. Merit Systems Protection Board to regain his status accordingly.

Page 181: *"As described":* Entire quote:

> As described earlier, in this period the Attorney General's Guidelines, which had been incorporated in the FBI's Manual, required that the SAC himself make certain decisions, including, after consultation with the United States Attorney, whether to authorize extraordinary criminal activity involving a "serious risk of violence," and reviewing all such criminal activity at least every 90 days." Ex. 274 (Under Seal), Manual § 137 F. (2) and (3) (1-12-81). Greenleaf's approach, however, had the practical effect of delegating these responsibilities, among others, to an informant's handler and his supervisor.

http://www.thelaborers.net/court_cases/United_States_v_Salemme_
Decision.htm.

Part Four: After Boston

CHAPTER 23

Page 185: *"On 8/5/80 Colonel O'Donovan":* Internal FBI memo from ASAC
Weldon L. Kennedy to Boston SAC Lawrence Sarhatt, August 6, 1980.
Contained in Appendix 2.

Page 186: *Castucci, he believed, had been ready to give up Bulger and Flemmi:*
As supported by the *Boston Globe*'s reporting on June 12, 2009, by Shelley
Murphy and the *Globe* staff:

> After years of legal maneuverings by Justice Department lawyers and a
> three-day nonjury trial, a federal judge ordered the government to pay
> $6.25 million to the widow and children of Richard J. Castucci, a Re-
> vere nightclub owner whose slaying was orchestrated by two of the
> FBI's most prized informants, James "Whitey" Bulger and Stephen
> "The Rifleman" Flemmi. Last year, a judge found that the FBI was to
> blame in the 1976 killing.

http://www.boston.com/news/local/massachusetts/articles/2009/06/12/
judge_awards_625_million_to_family_in_1976_mob_killing/.

Page 186: *The tapes, as I detailed earlier:* Allegations against Miami Police
Department and ultimate prosecution of the Miami River Murders supported by a series of articles appearing in the *Miami Herald* on December 27,
28, and 29, 1985. (See quote pages 305–306.)

Page 188: *Weldon Kennedy . . . wrote a memo:* Internal FBI memo from
Boston ASAC Weldon L. Kennedy to Boston SAC Lawrence Sarhatt, August 6, 1980. Contained in Appendix on page 277.

Page 189: *a report from Attorney Rogers:* Report of Attorney Rogers from
the Office of Professional Responsibility and response of William Webster were entered as evidence in legal complaints I filed against the FBI,
including at the Supreme Court, for releasing records they had agreed to
expunge.

Page 192: *"An indispensable informant":* From "Cases Disappear as FBI
Looks Away," by Shelley Murphy, *Boston Globe*, July 22, 1998: http://www

.boston.com/news/local/massachusetts/articles/1998/07/22/cases_disap
pear_as_fbi_looks_away/.

CHAPTER 24

Page 194: *"a killer and crime boss":* "Whitey Bulger's Life on the Run," by
Shelley Murphy, *Boston Globe,* January 4, 1998.

Page 195: *". . . something called St. Botolph Realty Trust . . .":* As also covered in *Black Mass,* pages 353–55.

Page 195: *75 State Street:* An investigation into corruption charges against
Billy Bulger was testified to by author in U.S. District Court and depositions, and summarized in a *Boston Phoenix* article by Seth Gitell:

> Bulger's law partner at the time, Thomas Finnerty, became involved in
> a real-estate deal with developer Harold Brown. Brown was putting
> together a project to construct a first-rate office building at 75 State
> Street. Then, as now, such projects didn't happen without the backing of
> political muscle. The pair allegedly made an agreement in which
> Brown would pay Finnerty $1.8 million through a combination of cash
> and equity in the building in exchange for Finnerty's assistance to
> move the project forward. Brown paid Finnerty $500,000 but made no
> more payments after that. Finnerty brought suit in Suffolk Superior
> Court, claiming that Brown had reneged on a legal agreement. Brown
> responded with complaints that Finnerty and Bulger were trying to
> extort him.

http://www.bostonphoenix.com/boston/news_features/top/features/
documents/02585299.htm.

Page 196: *"Billy got a free pass":* Quote from Alan Dershowitz in *Boston
Magazine,* May 15, 2006: http://www.bostonmagazine.com/articles/oh_
brothers/.

Page 196: *shortly after the Bureau:* Author's account confirmed in *Black
Mass* (pages 236–37).

Page 199: *Spotlight Series:* The series in the *Boston Globe* ran in four parts
between September 20 and 23, 1988.

Page 199: Globe *article from September 20, 1988:* The article said in part:

In the bitter aftermath, many who were planning the DEA's 1984 probe of Bulger were convinced they should not even tell the FBI, circumventing the policy that the FBI be notified of targeted figures. Despite the nearly universal feeling that no agent had or would intentionally warn Bulger about electronic surveillance, the fear of a leak persisted. But to avoid a feud, William F. Weld, then the US attorney in Massachusetts, and Robert M. Stutman, then the DEA special agent in charge, went to see James Greenleaf, then FBI special agent in charge of the Boston office. The FBI, according to federal sources, was offered a role in the Bulger investigation if it wanted one. Several days later, Greenleaf declined.

From "Law Enforcement Officials' Lament About an Elusive Foe: Where was Whitey?" by Chistine Chinlund, Dick Lehr, and Kevin Cullen, *Boston Globe*, September 20, 1988.

http://www.boston.com/news/packages/whitey/globe_stories/1988_the_bulger_mystique_part_3.htm.

Page 200: *"We had no evidence against them":* From the September 20 segment of the *Boston Globe*'s Spotlight Series.

CHAPTER 25
Page 202: *John Morris would suffer a heart attack:* Also referenced in *Black Mass* (page 275). Morris would testify to this in the Wolf hearings.

Page 202: *Among the "perks" of his retirement package:* Also referenced in *The Brothers Bulger* (page 9).

Page 203: *Then a new "sheriff" came to town:* Chronology involving Fred Wyshak covered and confirmed in *Black Mass* (pages 251–56).

Page 205: *"The court has reviewed the defendant's":* Quote from Judge Wolf's decision also appears in *Black Mass* (pages 283–84): http://www.thelaborers.net/court_cases/United_States_v_Salemme_Decision. htm.

Pages 207: *"You had a good thing going":* From transcripts of the Wolf hearings.

CHAPTER 26
Page 210: *"Did you ever report":* Testimony from transcripts of the Wolf hearings.

Page 211: *During subsequent trials:* Referenced memo can be found in Appendix 5.

Page 211: *"In an effort to protect Bulger and Flemmi":* From Wolf's Memorandum and Order: http://www.thelaborers.net/court_cases/United_States_v_Salemme_Decision.htm.

Page 211: *As for the bombshell I'd lobbed:* United States v. Flemmi, 195 F. Supp 2nd 243, 249–50): http://www.thelaborers.net/court_cases/United_States_v_Salemme_Decision.htm.

Page 211: *His voluminous opinion went on to say:* United States v. Flemmi, 195 F. Supp 2nd 243, 249–50: http://www.thelaborers.net/court_cases/United_States_v_Salemme_Decision. htm.

Page 211: *Wolf aptly summed up the entire fiasco:* F. U.S. v. Salemme, 91 F. Supp. 2nd 141, 181–82: http://www.thelaborers.net/court_cases/United_States_v_Salemme_Decision.htm.

Page 212: *Shortly after Judge Wolf issued his ruling, John Martorano struck a deal in which he admitted to killing twenty people:* From Matorano's own admissions in a 1998 plea agreement in which he admitted to killing ten people for Bulger, including Roger Wheeler ("Ex-Mobster Reportedly Strikes Deal," by Shelley Murphy, *Boston Globe*, September 9, 1999): http://www.boston.com/news/packages/whitey/globe_stories/1999/0909ex_mobster_reportedly_strikes_deal.htm.

Page 212: *"Prosecutors want to believe":* Wyshak quote from "The Avengers" by Dick Lehr, *Boston Magazine,* May 15, 2006: http://www.bostonmagazine.com/articles/the_avengers/.

CHAPTER 27

Page 215: *"I'd learn later that the FBI's legal counsel":* Corroborating document in author's possession.

Page 216: *The Wolf hearings would:* Allegation against Morris affirmed by Judge Wolf in his ruling: "In addition, the fact that Morris accepted $7000 from Bulger and Flemmi does not render . . ." (http://www.thelaborers.net/court_cases/United_States_v_Salemme_Decision.htm).

Page 217: *During much of that same period:* Author's assertions supported by court documents. Results of polygraph test in author's possession.

Part Five: Vindication

CHAPTER 28

Page 222: *a bespectacled, ordinary-looking special prosecutor:* Accounts of John Durham drawn from discussions with David Boeri for his article "The Martyrdom of John Connolly," *Boston Magazine,* September 2008. NPR has also covered these accounts in detail.

Page 224: *"Maybe way back. Many years before":* Billy Bulger's testimony before the Committee on Government Reform, House of Representatives, 2002. Also referenced in *The Brothers Bulger* (page 20).

Page 224: *"It wasn't that I wouldn't shoot":* From article by Shelley Murphy and *Globe* staff, *Boston Globe,* March 13, 2006.

Page 225: *In May 2002, Connolly was convicted:* As reported by Shelley Murphy, in the *Boston Globe,* May 29, 2002: http://www.ipsn.org/characters /connolly/connolly_convicted.htm.

Page 226: *"Nobody in this country is above the law":* Associated Press, January 2, 2008: http://www.msnbc.msn.com/id/22474868/.

Page 227: *"The 1979 Ciulla race-fixing prosecution memorandum":* From "Everything Secret Degenerates: The FBI's Use of Murderers as Informants": http://www.docstoc.com/docs/5997413/Everything-Secret-Degenerates -The-FBI's-Use-of-Murderers-as-Informants.

This was further affirmed by the U.S. Court of Appeals for the First Circuit in affirming Judge Lindsay's decision in the McIntyre trial: "Bulger and Flemmi were removed from a 1979 indictment charging a scheme to fix horse races, and listed only as unindicted co-conspirators, after a request by Connolly and his then-supervisor, John Morris, because of their value to the LCN investigation" 447 F. Supp. 2d at 80.

Pages 227: *"I must tell you this, that I was outraged":* From "Everything Secret Degenerates: The FBI's Use of Murderers as Informants": http://www .docstoc.com/docs/5997413/Everything-Secret-Degenerates-The-FBI's-Use -of-Murderers-as-Informants.

CHAPTER 30

Page 238: *"And as a result":* Drawn from trial transcript in the author's possession.

CHAPTER 31

Page 248: *"During the course of the interview":* Drawn from trial transcript in the author's possession.

CHAPTER 32

Page 261: *"Okay . . . I'd like to ask you":* Drawn from trial transcript in the author's possession.

Page 262: *"Stephen Flemmi, the homicidal maniac":* Peter Gelzinis's quoted column appeared in the *Boston Herald* on Friday, June 23, 2006.

Page 263: Lindsay quotes taken from his decision issued on September 5, 2006.

Page 263: *"because Connolly":* From the U.S. Court of Appeals for the First Circuit in ruling issued October 16, 2008 (document can be found in Appendix).

Page 264: *Figuring there might be something of value:* This version of events supported by materials furnished from attorney Doug Matthews himself and in author's possession.

Page 265: *"Aren't these our guys?":* As confirmed in *Black Mass* (page 186).

Page 266: *There was Stephen "the Rifleman" Flemmi testifying:* As also reported in the *Boston Herald* on September 14, 2008.

Page 266: *"When you give us information on one person and they got killed":* As also reported by Shelley Murphy in the *Boston Globe* on September 24, 2008.

Page 266: *"If John Connolly and the FBI had done their job":* Associated Press, September 19, 2008, and the *Miami Herald,* September 20, 2008. Author has the articles in his possession.

Page 267: *Writing in the* Boston Globe: Joan Vennochi's column in the *Boston Globe* can be found at: http://www.boston.com/news/local/massachusetts/articles/2000/01/25/if_connolly_is_so_guilty_can_the_fbi_be_so_innocent.

Page 267: *"Well, I know":* Transcript is in author's possession.

Page 268: *"That is absolutely untrue":* Shelley Murphy, writing in the *Boston Globe,* July 22, 1998.

Pages 268: *In August of 2009:* The entire decision from the U.S. Court of Appeals for the First Circuit upholding the ruling of the lower court can be found at: http://www.nlg-npap.org/html/documents/FirstCirrulinginLimonevUS.pdf.

Page 268: *And on April 30, 2010:* Solicitor General Elena Kagan and the Department of Justice's decision not to appeal the Salvati decision further can be found in the *Boston Globe,* May 1, 2010: http://www.boston.com/ news/nation/washington/articles/2010/05/01/us_wont_appeal_verdict_in_ case_of_four_framed_by_fbi/.

Page 268: *"Judge Admits":* Referenced article in the *Boston Herald,* "Judge Admits He Was Too Harsh on Mother of Whitey Bulger Victim," by Laurel J. Sweet, November 5, 2009: http://www.bostonherald.com/news/regional/ view.bg?articleid=1209873&srvc=next_article.

Page 269: *"They are lying":* Author's quoted testimony supported by trial transcripts.

Page 269: *"I'm prepared to find there is a massive":* As referenced in the *Boston Herald,* "Judge Admits He Was Too Harsh on Mother of Whitey Bulger Victim," by Laurel J. Sweet, November 5, 2009: http://www. bostonherald.com/ news/regional/view.bg?articleid=1209873&srvc=next_article.

Page 269: *In May 2009, Judge Young also awarded an $8.5 million:* From article by Shelley Murphy and the *Globe* Staff, *Boston Globe,* June 12, 2009: http://www.boston.com/news/local/massachusetts/articles/2009/06/12/judge _awards_625_million_to_family_in_1976_mob_killing/.

EPILOGUE

Page 272: *"Here's to Honest Cops Who Made a Difference":* Article by Kevin Cullen, *Boston Globe,* July 3, 2011: http://articles.boston.com/2011-07-03/ news/29733649_1_state-cops-fbi-agent-john-connolly.

Page 272: *"The FBI Agent who Really Wanted 'Whitey' ":* Article by Deborah Becker and Lisa Tobin, WBUR, July 7, 2011: http://www.wbur.org/2011/ 07/07/good-cop-2.

Page 273: *"I hope we all":* From "Setting the Stage for Whitey's Arrest," by Nancy Harris, *Boston Globe,* July 14, 2011: http://articles.boston.com/2011 -07-14/ae/29773902_1_bulger-winter-hill-gang-flemmi.

INDEX

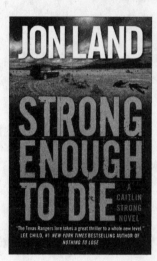
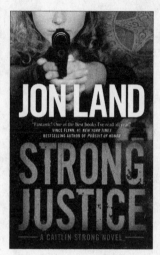
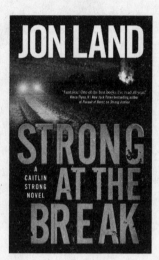